The

LOW-FAT
JEWISH
COOKBOOK

Other Books by Faye Levy

Faye Levy's International Jewish Cookbook

Faye Levy's International Vegetable Cookbook

Faye Levy's International Chicken Cookbook

Thirty Low-Fat Meals in 30 Minutes

Thirty Low-Fat Vegetarian Meals in 30 Minutes

Sensational Chocolate

Sensational Pasta

Fresh from France: Dessert Sensations

Fresh from France: Dinner Inspirations

Fresh from France: Vegetable Creations

Classic Cooking Techniques

La Cuisine du Poisson (in French, with Fernand Chambrette)

Faye Levy's Favorite Recipes (in Hebrew)

French Cooking Without Meat (in Hebrew)

French Desserts (in Hebrew)

French Cakes, Pastries and Cookies (in Hebrew)

The La Varenne Tour Book

The

LOW-FAT
JEWISH
COOKBOOK

*225 Traditional and Contemporary Gourmet Kosher
Recipes for Holidays and Every Day*

FAYE LEVY

C l a r k s o n   P o t t e r   /   P u b l i s h e r s
N e w   Y o r k

Published by Clarkson Potter/Publisher, New York, New York.
Member of the Crown Publishing Group.

Random House, Inc. New York, Toronto, London, Sydney, Auckland

www.randomhouse.com

CLARKSON N. POTTER is a trademark and POTTER and colophon
are registered trademarks of Random House, Inc.

Printed in the United States of America

Design by Susan DeStaebler

Library of Congress Cataloging-in-Publication Data
Levy, Faye.
Low-Fat Jewish Cookbook : 225 traditional and contemporary gourmet
Kosher recipes for holidays and every day / by Faye Levy.
Includes index.
1. Low-fat diet—Recipes. 2. Cookery, Jewish. I. Title.
RM237.L48 1997
641.5'638—dc20 96-29192

ISBN 0-517-70364-5

10 9 8 7 6 5

For my mother, Pauline Kahn Luria
And my mother-in-law, Rachel Levy

And in loving memory of my father, Louis Kahn
And my father-in-law, Zechariah Levy

Contents

Introduction

KOSHER EATING PRINCIPLES have been the guiding light of the Jewish diet since the beginning of Jewish history. Kashrut, or keeping kosher, is basically a framework for menu planning and for choosing what foods may be eaten. Behind many of the rules lie themes of compassion for animals and reverence for life.

In recent years, more and more people have been buying kosher foods and have embarked on this time-honored way to cook and eat. Some are rediscovering their Jewish roots or learning about their spouse's Jewish culture; others are attracted to the pure, clean, spiritual image of kosher cooking.

As a result of this revival of kosher cooking, there is a proliferation of kosher products in the markets. Kosher cooking has become "gourmet." It's easy to find kosher extra-virgin olive oil, pasta, dry wines, and other ingredients beloved by fine cooks. Now kosher cheeses, fish, and meat are more widely available in American cities. The broad range of kosher ingredients, along with today's superior selection of fresh produce and herbs, makes it much easier to prepare creative, delicious kosher menus than it was in the past.

From my upbringing in an Orthodox home, I learned that kosher food can be nutritious and taste delicious as well. My mother has been health conscious for as long as I can remember. Even in the fifties and sixties, she never used schmaltz (chicken fat) in her cooking, and she was careful not to use too much of other fats, either.

I find that kosher cooking fits in perfectly with healthy, low-fat cooking. Many of the high-fat combinations found in other cuisines, like steak in a buttery sauce, are simply not allowed. Although you can enjoy a steak or a butter sauce at separate times, the fact that they are not served at the same meal is helpful in restricting fat, especially the saturated kind, of which nutritionists recommend we reduce our consumption as much as possible.

The common image of kosher dishes is based mainly on prominent holiday foods—potato latkes for Hanukkah, honey cake for Rosh Hashanah, matzo balls for Passover, and gefilte fish and chopped liver for Shabbat and other holidays. Yet kosher cooking is for 365 days a year, and the number of delicious kosher dishes is endless.

We in America are most familiar with the Ashkenazic, or Central and Eastern European, Jewish culinary style. But there is much more to Jewish cuisine. The other major branch—Sephardic, or Mediterranean and Middle Eastern, Jewish cooking—deserves to be better known in the United States; in Israel, it is contributing to a renaissance in kosher cooking. Sephardic specialties, from stuffed vegetables to spicy stews to hearty soups, are flavorful and easy to prepare. In addition, they are ideal for a healthful diet, as they are part of the highly recommended Mediterranean way of dining focusing on smaller amounts of meat and copious amounts of produce.

My husband and I grew up in kosher homes—he in the Sephardic tradition and I in the Ashkenazic. As children and during the twenty-six years of our marriage, we have enjoyed many delicious holiday meals with our families. I have also had the pleasure of learning treasured dishes from friends and neighbors in the course of the years I lived in Israel and France.

Naturally, specialties of many cuisines can be kosher. For example, a classic vegetable or dessert soufflé needs no adaptation to be kosher, but because it contains milk, it should be served in a meatless meal. French-style boeuf bourguignon can be kosher, as long as the beef is purchased from a kosher butcher, is sprinkled with coarse salt to be "koshered" before cooking, is sautéed in oil rather than butter, and, of course, provided no bacon is included in the dish. These cooking adjustments also make the dish more healthful. The same is true for dishes of Asian, North American, Indian, and virtually every other ethnic origin.

The students in my kosher cooking classes and the readers of my kosher food column for the *Jerusalem Post* look for sophisticated menus as enticing as those in the epicurean magazines. In this book, I have presented a tempting selection of kosher recipes that every food lover will enjoy. I have adapted them to low-fat cooking, so that no more than 30 percent of the calories in any recipe come from fat.

I hope these nourishing dishes will contribute spice to your holidays, family celebrations, and everyday meals. *Le Chaim!* To life—a healthy and happy one!

1

Today's Kosher Kitchen

ONCE A PERSON LEARNS the rules of kashrut, or keeping kosher, he or she can easily adapt specialties from around the world to kosher cooking.

Keeping kosher has two major aspects:

1. Choosing kosher foods and avoiding nonkosher ones, notably pork and shellfish.
2. Eating dairy foods and meat products in separate meals.

Keeping kosher is a cornerstone of observing Judaism. Orthodox Jews believe that keeping kosher is a divine command. The laws of kashrut are outlined in the Torah, and over the years they have been interpreted and spelled out by the rabbis.

More and more people are interested in kashrut, as part of a general trend toward exploring our roots and respecting our people's customs. Some Jews, even if they do not follow all the rules of Orthodox Judaism, choose to keep kosher at home so that any Jew would feel comfortable eating at their table, knowing the food is kosher.

When I was growing up, there were almost no kosher cake mixes, packaged soups, or pizza. For kosher bread, we had to go to a kosher bakery. We could buy kosher chicken only from a kosher butcher. Today cooking kosher is easier than ever.

In recent years, the number of kosher products has increased dramatically. Many supermarkets have kosher food sections. It's easy to find cake, brownie, and cookie mixes, both for everyday kosher cooking and for Passover; kosher soup powders, concentrates, and frozen soups; frozen kosher pizza, knishes, bourekas (filo triangles), and other pastries; and even frozen already shaped challah, ready to pop in your oven. Kosher chickens are sold at well-stocked supermarkets, and so are kosher deli meats, breads, kosher wine, and kosher cheese. Recently, I found kosher fat-free tortillas, both corn and flour, at the supermarket.

The supermarkets carry more kosher foods in areas of the country where there is greater demand for them. However, the greatest selection of kosher foods can be found in kosher markets, and the array of foods differs from one market to another. For example, in my neighborhood there are Ashkenazic, Israeli, and Iranian kosher markets, each with its own character. At the Ashkenazic or traditional-style kosher stores, I find everything I need to serve the well-known Jewish specialties: gefilte fish, noodles, prepared noodle kugels, prepared potato pancakes, lox, smoked fish, bagels, and challah. At the Iranian markets, I find basmati rice, wheat grains in various sizes, a great variety of dried beans, and Iranian-style flatbreads. The Israeli-type kosher markets feature products from Israel that many Israelis miss—Israeli cheeses and other dairy products, pita bread, chocolate, cookies, soup mixes, as well as prepared Sephardic dishes like bourekas, Yemenite breads, and kubeh (Iraqi fried pastries). Naturally, there is a variety of products that all the stores have in common, especially challah for Shabbat, matzo, and kosher cheeses.

Kosher Foods
{ C e r t i f i c a t i o n }

The most widely used symbol to denote kosher is Ⓤ, the certification of the Union of Orthodox Rabbis. K is another widespread kosher symbol. Sometimes D or P is added, meaning certified kosher for dairy meals or for pareve meals.

The rabbis of some communities have established their own certification symbols for local products; these symbols may be the initials of the rabbis' organization or a certain rabbi's signature.

Keeping kosher is part of observing the precepts of Judaism and is integrated with these precepts. For example, cooking food on the Sabbath is forbidden; therefore, anything cooked on the Sabbath is not kosher, whether at home or at a restaurant. Handling money on the Sabbath also is not allowed; thus restaurants that are open on the Sabbath do not receive kosher certificates unless they have an authorized arrangement of payment before the Sabbath.

{ M e a t   a n d   P o u l t r y }

Pork is the best-known example of nonkosher meat. The Bible specifies that kosher animals have split hooves and chew their cud. This makes beef, veal, lamb, and goat's meat kosher, but not rabbit. All familiar poultry—chicken, turkey, Cornish hen, duck, and goose—can be kosher.

Kosher meat and poultry must be slaughtered in a kosher manner by a specially trained, certified kosher butcher. Therefore, hunted meats and birds shot with a rifle are not kosher. Venison can be kosher if it is properly slaughtered.

Cuts of meat from the hind part of animals are not kosher unless the sciatic nerve is removed. Few butchers do this, so these cuts of meat are not sold at kosher butchers in the United States. In Israel, this nerve is removed, and therefore you can sometimes find beef tenderloin and other hindquarter cuts.

Blood is not kosher, hence meat and poultry are *koshered*, or salted with kosher salt (coarse salt), before they are cooked to draw the blood out. Packaged kosher chickens and some meats have already been salted. If you buy meat that has not been salted from a kosher butcher, you can do it yourself (see page 7). Because blood is not kosher, meat in the kosher kitchen is cooked until well done.

Some people feel that poultry and meat acquire better tastes from having been salted. However, if you are new to kosher meat and find it too salty, the next time you prepare it, soak it in cold water for 30 minutes before cooking. You can also soak the meat if you are watching your sodium intake. During cooking, you will rarely need to add salt to kosher meat or poultry.

Meat and poultry must be purchased from a kosher butcher or be sold in a package with a kosher label.

{ F i s h }

To be kosher, fish must have scales and fins. Most popular fish, such as salmon, sea bass, trout, halibut, cod, haddock, sole, and tuna, are kosher. The law excludes all shellfish, mollusks, squid, and scaleless fish such as monkfish.

There are no special rules for preparing or cooking fish. In fact, fish does not have to be cooked. Sushi can be kosher. Several glatt kosher restaurants advertise that they make sushi.

Some brands of surimi (artificial crabmeat, or "sealegs") are kosher and have been used to make mock shrimp, which is sometimes sold as "kosher" shrimp. These products must be clearly labeled as kosher, however, because many types of surimi contain shellfish extracts and thus are not kosher.

{ E g g s }

Eggs that have blood spots are not kosher and must be discarded. Therefore, when you add eggs to a batter, each egg must first be broken into a separate dish so you can inspect it.

{ Dairy Products }

Kosher cheese must be made without rennet, an animal product often used in making such hard cheeses as Swiss cheese and Parmesan. Kosher versions of these and other grating cheeses can be found in kosher stores and some supermarkets. In addition, cheeses made without animal rennet are sold at vegetarian and natural foods stores.

Soft dairy products such as yogurt and sour cream, as well as ice cream, sometimes contain gelatin. If gelatin is used, it must be kosher gelatin; nonkosher gelatin is made from animal bones and would make the dairy product nonkosher.

{ Vegetables }

All fresh vegetables are kosher. In the kosher kitchen, greens, cauliflower, and broccoli must be rinsed thoroughly, not just for hygiene. The cook must be sure no bugs are inside because bugs are not kosher.

In the case of canned vegetables, check the label. Some are cooked with meats and might be nonkosher.

{ Wine }

A lot of us grew up with sweet wine for kiddush, the blessing over wine before Shabbat and holiday meals, but kosher wine is not necessarily sweet. There is a growing variety of dry kosher wines from the United States, Israel, and France. Ask at your local wine store.

{ Breads, Cakes, and Pastries }

Some baked goods contain nonkosher fats, cheeses, or gelatin. To be sure breads, cakes, and pastries are kosher, buy packaged ones with a kosher label or buy fresh baked goods at a kosher bakery.

For preparing mousses and fillings, buy kosher gelatin, which is vegetable based.

Kosher Menu Planning and Cooking

Kosher meals are either *milchig* (containing dairy products) or *fleishig* (containing meat). Foods that contain neither meat nor dairy products are *pareve* (or neutral) and can be served at either type of meal. Pareve foods include eggs, fish, vegetables, fruits, grains, and vegetable oil. Margarine can be pareve, but must be labeled as such.

To make meal planning easy, each recipe in this book is labeled meat, dairy, or pareve. In composing a menu, use all meat, all dairy, or all pareve dishes; or combine meat with pareve or dairy with pareve but not meat with dairy. In some cases, a dish might be labeled pareve *or* meat, depending on whether you use vegetable *or* chicken broth as the cooking liquid. Other dishes, notably cakes, are labeled pareve *or* dairy, depending on whether you use pareve margarine *or* one made with dairy products.

A kosher kitchen has two sets of dishes, flatware, pots, and other cooking utensils—one for cooking meat and one for preparing dairy foods (and two more sets for preparing Passover meals; see chapter 7). Separate sponges and dish racks are used for meat and dairy, and separate towels for drying dishes. The soap used to wash the dishes should be kosher.

Orthodox Ashkenazic Jews wait at least six hours after eating meat before eating dairy foods, but only half an hour after eating dairy to eat meat. In some Sephardic communities, the waiting times are different from the Ashkenazic.

Once you are used to kosher cooking, you will instinctively adapt recipes to make them kosher. Knowing the principles of kosher cooking can lead to the creation of new, interesting recipes. Over the years, many cooks have developed two versions of family favorites, such as vegetable soups or mashed potatoes—one for dairy and one for meat meals. Each has its unique flavor. If you're making a mushroom soup, for example, you can cook the mushrooms in vegetable broth for dairy or pareve meals or meat broth for meat meals. If you're using vegetable broth, you can finish the soup with milk or sour cream.

The same formula works for sauces. You can make velouté soup from a roux of butter and flour, and use vegetable broth and milk as the liquid; or you can prepare the roux from oil or margarine and flour, and stir in chicken or meat broth.

How to Kosher Meats and Poultry

Before meat and poultry are fit to be cooked and eaten, they must be "koshered," or salted and soaked in water, to rid them of as much blood as possible. Most kosher butchers sell meat and poultry that has already been koshered, to save customers time and effort. Packaged kosher poultry also has been salted and soaked.

If you buy meat or poultry that has not been salted, this is how you do it at home: Rinse the meat well, soak it in cold tap water to cover for 30 minutes, then rinse it again. Put the meat on a board set at an incline so the meat juices can drip into the sink. Sprinkle the meat or poultry with kosher salt and let it stand for 1 hour. Then thoroughly rinse the meat again.

Naturally, the meat absorbs some salt during this koshering process. Therefore, little or no salt needs to be added when you cook the meat.

Livers do not need soaking. Instead, they are koshered by broiling or grilling. To kosher livers, rinse them, then sprinkle them with kosher salt. For broiling, put the livers on foil so they do not come in contact with the broiler pan. Broil or grill the livers, turning them a few times, so that all sides become grilled and the livers are cooked through. You can serve them immediately as broiled liver, or let them cool and make chopped liver (see page 121).

A Note About Nutrition Calculations

Nutritionists recommend that our diet not exceed 30 percent of its calories from fat. This is not necessary for each dish, but rather over a whole day. However, to make low-fat meal planning easy, I have developed each recipe in this book so that no more than 30 percent of its calories come from fat. When the number of servings varies, the nutrition calculations are based on the higher number. When there are several options, the calculations are based on the choice that is the lowest in fat.

2

Rosh Hashanah,
The Jewish New Year

Golden Chicken Soup with Noodles, Mushrooms, and Zucchini

Baked Fish Steaks with Pistou

Baked Chicken in Spicy Tomato and Grilled Pepper Sauce

Turkey Tsimmes with Apricots and Red Wine

Orzo Pilaf with Parsley and Thyme

Braised Winter Squash with Onion

Stewed Leeks

Glazed Carrot Coins with Cranberries

Late Summer Fruit Salad

Low-Fat Honey Cake with Cocoa and Sweet Spices

THE JEWISH NEW YEAR is a fusion of solemnity and celebration. It is the beginning of the Ten Days of Awe, which focus on repentance and asking for forgiveness, and culminate in Yom Kippur, the Day of Atonement. But Rosh Hashanah is also a time of feasting, with a multicourse dinner.

Cooking for this two-day festival, which usually occurs in September, is a pleasure. Although Rosh Hashanah marks the beginning of the fall holiday season, we still have the benefit of wonderful summer produce—tomatoes, peppers, and eggplant are abundant, and there is plenty of good fruit.

When Rosh Hashanah arrives, the weather can still be quite warm. For this reason, and in order to lower the fat in our menus, more and more of us opt for lighter versions of the holiday specialties that we grew up with. For most American Jews, these dishes originated in Eastern European lands with colder climates.

Still, we want to retain the spirit of the Rosh Hashanah dinner. "Have a good and sweet New Year" is the traditional greeting and wish for Rosh Hashanah, and this is reflected in the food of the holiday.

Before the meal begins, challah is set on the table along with plates of apple wedges and bowls of honey. The Rosh Hashanah challah is different from the challah of the rest of the year. It is a round bread instead of shaped into a long braided loaf, and is a little sweeter than usual. According to the age-old Rosh Hashanah custom, the apples and challah are dipped in honey to symbolically wish for a sweet new year. Some Sephardic families begin the meal with symbolic fruits and vegetables. They eat small portions of dates, pomegranates, pumpkin, leeks, and Swiss chard and say a blessing before tasting each, a custom bearing a slight resemblance to the Passover Seder. Certain Moroccan families add sweet poached quinces to these Rosh Hashanah appetizers.

Dinner itself often includes a main course of meat with fruit, especially in Ashkenazic families, to further illustrate the hope for a good, sweet year. I grew up eating a hearty tsimmes of beef cooked with potatoes, carrots, and prunes. In recent years, I have lightened and varied this dish, and now I like to serve turkey tsimmes with dried apricots, accompanied by rice or orzo (rice-shaped pasta). Sephardic families might prepare roast chicken or braised beef accompanied by rice or couscous embellished with raisins.

Main dishes with fruit seem to have a universal appeal. Poultry and meats are paired with fruit in festive dishes of many cuisines, not only Jewish but also European and Asian, as good cooks everywhere find that fruit's sweetness is an ideal complement to meat. Of course, embellishing meat dishes with fruit does not mean serving "syrupy sweet" main courses. The fruit's taste is balanced with the subtle sharpness of spices like ginger, or with the tang of wine.

A healthful custom that I learned in Israel is to prepare several fresh vegetable salads, either as appetizers or to accompany the entree. I especially like broiled eggplant slices with fresh tomato salsa or a colorful three-bean salad with mushrooms and capers. If the weather is getting cool, you might like to serve a velvety carrot soup with parsley matzo balls; this delicious recipe is a new twist on the standard chicken soup with kneidlach.

For a fish course, prepare Baked Fish with Tomato-Garlic Sauce (page 198) or Baked Fish Steaks with Pistou (Basil Sauce) (page 13) and serve them cold. Although tradition calls for serving a fish with its head, to represent "the head of the year"—the literal meaning of the words *Rosh Hashanah*—many families skip this part and opt for fish steaks or fillets.

Honey cake flavored with cocoa, coffee, cinnamon, or other sweet spices is the dessert of choice for Rosh Hashanah. When I lived in Israel, exchanging honey cake recipes was a popular pastime of my friends and colleagues during the week before the holiday. Sometimes I vary the theme by preparing a honey-flavored apple cake instead.

Honey cake is of Ashkenazic origin; there are many similar sweets prepared throughout Europe. Today Sephardic families enjoy honey cake too, but might also serve such treats as light almond cake, filo pastries sprinkled with confectioners' sugar, or fruit-filled cookies. Whatever your family's origin, it's always a good idea to accompany dessert with an assortment of fresh seasonal fruit, for a nutritious start to a healthy new year.

Golden Chicken Soup with Noodles, Mushrooms, and Zucchini

{ m e a t }

Serving a light chicken broth with vegetables is a healthful way to begin the Rosh Hashanah dinner. For a special treat, you might like to prepare Egg Noodles (page 261), or, instead of noodles, serve the soup with Featherlight Matzo Balls (page 162).

2 pounds chicken legs or wings
Salt and freshly ground black pepper
8 to 10 cups water
1 medium onion, diced
2 celery stalks, diced
1 large carrot, diced
½ teaspoon turmeric
4 garlic cloves, chopped

¾ pound ripe tomatoes, peeled and diced
4 ounces small mushrooms, quartered
2 medium zucchini, diced
1½ cups fine noodles
2 tablespoons chopped parsley

Put the chicken wings in a heavy casserole or Dutch oven, season with salt and pepper, cover with the water, and bring to a boil. Skim off the foam. Add the onion, celery, carrot, and turmeric. Cover and cook over low heat 1½ hours or until the chicken is tender and the soup is well flavored. Remove the chicken and strain if desired. Refrigerate the soup until the fat congeals on top. Thoroughly skim the fat from soup.

Bring the soup to a simmer. Add the garlic, tomatoes, mushrooms, and zucchini. Simmer 8 to 10 minutes or until the vegetables are tender. Taste and adjust seasoning. If you like, remove some of the chicken meat from the bones, return the meat to soup, and heat through.

Cook the noodles in a large saucepan of boiling salted water about 5 minutes or until just tender. Drain and rinse with cold water.

At serving time, add noodles to each bowl of hot soup and sprinkle with parsley. Serve in shallow soup bowls.

. . . .

Makes 6 servings

Nutritional information per serving: 312 calories; 8.5 g fat—24.8% calories from fat; 2.3 g saturated fat; 101 mg cholesterol

Baked Fish Steaks with Pistou

{ p a r e v e }

Fish is a popular first course for Rosh Hashanah menus and is delicious when baked and topped with pistou, the French pesto. The classic sauce is made of garlic and fresh basil, the latter being plentiful around Rosh Hashanah time.

You can use pistou for enriching vegetable soups as well, and for tossing with pasta. It also makes a fabulous flavoring for vegetables—fresh and dried beans, corn, potatoes, and even cooked mixed frozen vegetables.

2 pounds fish steaks, such as salmon,
    halibut, sea bass, or cod, about
    1 inch thick
Salt and freshly ground black pepper
1 teaspoon dried basil
¼ cup plus 2 teaspoons extra-virgin
    olive oil

2 cups fresh basil leaves
5 garlic cloves, peeled
4 cups baby lettuce leaves (such as
    Boston or mache)
24 cherry tomatoes

Preheat the oven to 400° F. Arrange the fish steaks in a single layer in a foil-lined roasting pan. Sprinkle with salt, pepper, and dried basil. Drizzle with 1 teaspoon olive oil. Bake 10 to 12 minutes or until the fish just flakes when tested with a fork.

Meanwhile, rinse the fresh basil and pat dry. Chop the garlic in a food processor. Add the basil and chop finely. Gradually add ¼ cup plus remaining 1 teaspoon olive oil, with the motor running. Scrape down the sides and puree again so the mixture is well blended. Reserve at room temperature.

Serve the fish hot or cold. Line plates or a platter with the baby lettuce and top with the fish. Garnish with the cherry tomatoes. Spoon about 1 tablespoon pistou on each fish steak.

. . . .

Makes 6 to 8 appetizer or 4 or 5 main-course servings
Nutritional information per serving: 305 calories; 11 g fat—30% calories from fat;
1.5 g saturated fat; 49 mg cholesterol

Baked Chicken in Spicy Tomato and Grilled Pepper Sauce

{ m e a t }

Couscous or rice is a good accompaniment for this highly flavored chicken. Its sauce has roasted jalapeño and bell peppers and generous amounts of garlic and cilantro. You can make the pepper sauce ahead, or simmer it while the chicken is baking. This savory dish is based on a Moroccan-Jewish recipe, but to make it low in fat I remove the skin from the chicken.

The chicken is great not only for Rosh Hashanah but also for Shabbat. It reheats beautifully in its sauce in a covered baking dish in a low oven.

3 large green bell peppers	1 tablespoon paprika
1 large red bell pepper	2¼ teaspoons ground cumin
3 jalapeño peppers	Salt and freshly ground black pepper
5 garlic cloves, peeled	Pinch of cayenne pepper (optional)
½ cup small cilantro sprigs	4½ pounds chicken pieces, skin
1 28-ounce and 1 14½-ounce can	removed
plum tomatoes, drained	1 large onion, halved and sliced
1 tablespoon olive oil	Cilantro sprigs, for garnish

Broil the green and red bell peppers, turning every 4 to 5 minutes, until their skins are blistered and charred, a total of about 20 minutes. Meanwhile, broil jalapeño peppers, turning often, about 5 minutes in all. Transfer the peppers to a bowl and cover; or put in a plastic or paper bag and close bag. Let stand 10 minutes.

Meanwhile, mince the garlic in a food processor, add the cilantro sprigs, and mince together. Add the tomatoes and chop coarsely by pulsing.

Peel the jalapeño and bell peppers using a paring knife. (Wear gloves when handling jalapeño peppers if your skin is sensitive.) Halve the peppers; discard the seeds and ribs. Cut bell peppers into ½-inch dice. Chop the jalapeño peppers. Preheat the oven to 400°F.

In a medium sauté pan, warm the olive oil over low heat. Add 1½ teaspoons paprika and ¾ teaspoon cumin and mix well. Stir in the tomato-garlic mixture, jalapeño and bell peppers, and salt and pepper. Bring the sauce to a simmer. Cook uncovered over medium heat, stirring often, 10 minutes or until the sauce thickens. Taste and adjust the seasoning; add cayenne pepper if desired.

Put the chicken pieces in shallow roasting pan large enough to hold them in one layer. Season them on both sides with salt, pepper, remaining 1½ teaspoons cumin, and remaining 1½ teaspoons paprika. Rub spices into chicken pieces. Top chicken with sliced onion.

Cover the chicken with foil and bake 30 minutes. Uncover, turn pieces over, and bake 20 minutes. Add ⅓ cup hot water to pan juices. Spoon the pepper sauce over the chicken. Bake uncovered, basting once or twice, about 15 to 25 minutes or until the chicken is tender and the the juices run clear when the thickest part of a thigh piece is pierced with a sharp knife. Serve the chicken with sauce. Garnish with cilantro sprigs.

· ·

Makes 6 servings

Nutritional information per serving: 414 calories; 10.7 g fat—23.4% calories from fat; 2.3 g saturated fat; 194 mg cholesterol

Turkey Tsimmes with Apricots and Red Wine

{ m e a t }

Tsimmes, a traditional Rosh Hashanah entree, is usually made with beef, sweet potatoes, and prunes. In this new twist, I use turkey to create a leaner, healthier entree and pair it with a Greek-inspired sauce of red wine, onions, carrots, and a hint of cinnamon. Dried apricots impart a delicate sweetness. Serve the turkey with orzo, rice, or boiled potatoes.

1 tablespoon vegetable oil

2 pounds thick boneless turkey fillets, cut into 1-inch cubes

1 large onion, chopped

2 large carrots, peeled and diced

2 garlic cloves, chopped

1 tablespoon all-purpose flour

1 cup dry red wine

1 tablespoon tomato paste

⅔ cup chicken or turkey broth

½ teaspoon ground cinnamon

1 bay leaf

½ cup dried apricots

½ teaspoon sugar, or to taste

Salt and freshly ground black pepper

Heat the oil in a Dutch oven over medium heat. Add the turkey and sauté lightly in 2 batches, removing each batch as it colors.

Add the onion and carrots and sauté about 5 minutes. Add the garlic and sauté over low heat a few seconds. Stir in the flour and cook 30 seconds, stirring. Add the wine, stirring until smooth and scraping the bottom of the pan. Bring to a simmer. Stir in the tomato paste. Add the broth, cinnamon, bay leaf, and apricots. Mix well.

Return the turkey to the pan. Cover and cook over low heat, stirring occasionally, about 30 minutes or until the turkey pieces are tender when pierced with a knife. Remove the bay leaf. Skim as much fat as possible from the sauce.

Add the sugar to the sauce. Taste sauce and adjust seasoning, adding salt, pepper, or more sugar if needed.

. . . .

Makes 4 servings

Nutritional information per serving: 421 calories; 7.7 g fat—18.3% calories from fat;
1.6 g saturated fat; 93 mg cholesterol

Orzo Pilaf with Parsley and Thyme

{ m e a t   o r   p a r e v e }

Orzo is a tasty form of pasta that is shaped like rice. Hot pepper flakes and thyme lend zest to this pilaf, and chopped parsley contributes a fresh taste and decorative green flecks. Serve this with roasted or braised chicken or turkey. If you wish to prepare this savory pilaf for a dairy meal, substitute vegetable broth for the chicken broth.

1 ½ tablespoons olive oil

1 medium onion, minced

3 garlic cloves, minced

1 ½ cups orzo or riso (rice-shaped pasta) (about 12 ounces)

3 cups hot chicken broth or water

Salt and freshly ground black pepper

¼ teaspoon hot red pepper flakes, or to taste

1 teaspoon dried thyme

¼ cup chopped parsley

Heat the olive oil in a medium saucepan over medium heat. Add the onion and sauté, stirring often, 7 minutes, until lightly browned. Add the garlic and orzo and cook over low heat, stirring, 3 minutes. Add the broth, salt, pepper, hot pepper flakes, and thyme and bring to a boil. Cover and cook over low heat about 15 minutes or until just tender. Fluff the mixture with a fork. Add parsley and toss the mixture to combine it. Taste and adjust seasoning. Serve hot.

. . . .

Makes 4 servings

Nutritional information per serving: 233 calories; 7.7 g fat—29.8% calories from fat;
1.3 g saturated fat; 2 mg cholesterol

Braised Winter Squash with Onion

{ m e a t   o r   p a r e v e }

Sephardic menus often feature pumpkin or winter squash for Rosh Hashanah. I love to cook squash simply, as in this recipe, so its sweet, delicate flavor comes through. Braising it with onion emphasizes the squash's sweetness. I use banana or butternut squash, which are sold in cleaned pieces at some markets and have peels that are fairly easy to remove. The squash makes a tasty first course, an accompaniment for chicken, or a vegetarian dish with couscous or rice.

2 pounds winter squash, such as
   banana or butternut
2 teaspoons vegetable oil
1 large onion, diced

⅔ cup vegetable broth, chicken
   broth, or water
Salt and freshly ground black pepper

Cut off the squash peel, remove any seeds and strings, and cut squash into 1-inch pieces.

Heat the vegetable oil in a large, heavy sauté pan. Add the onion and sauté over medium heat 4 minutes or until just beginning to brown. Add the squash and broth, sprinkle with salt and pepper, and bring to a boil. Cover and cook over low heat, occasionally stirring gently, for 20 minutes or until squash is tender. If the sauce is too thin, uncover and cook 2 or 3 minutes until it thickens. Taste and adjust seasoning. Serve hot.

. . . .

Makes 4 side-dish servings

Nutritional information per serving: 139 calories; 3.5 g fat—20.4% calories from fat; 0.5 g saturated fat; 0 mg cholesterol

Stewed Leeks

{ m e a t   o r   p a r e v e }

*T*hese tender leeks are great with fish, poultry, or meat, or as an appetizer in the Sephardic Rosh Hashanah tradition. Use only the white and light green parts of the leeks for this dish. Save the tougher dark green parts to make chicken, fish, or vegetable broth.

2 pounds leeks, white and light green parts only

1 tablespoon vegetable oil

½ cup chicken or vegetable broth or water

Salt and freshly ground black pepper

Split the leeks lengthwise twice by cutting with a sharp knife, beginning about 1 inch from the root end and cutting toward the green end, leaving the root end attached. Dip the leeks repeatedly in a sinkful of cold water. Spread apart the layers to be sure they are clean. If sand remains, soak the leeks in cold water for several minutes. Then separate the leaves under running water to rinse away any clinging grit, and drain. Cut off the root ends. Cut leeks into thin slices.

In a heavy casserole, heat the vegetable oil over low heat. Add the leeks, broth, salt, and pepper. Cover and cook, stirring often, about 20 minutes or until the leeks are tender; be careful not to let them burn; add more stock or water if necessary. If the mixture is soupy, uncover and simmer until excess liquid evaporates. Taste and adjust seasoning.

. . . .

Makes 4 to 6 servings

Nutritional information per serving: 116 calories; 2.8 g fat—20.9% calories from fat; 0.4 g saturated fat; 0 mg cholesterol

Glazed Carrot Coins with Cranberries

{ p a r e v e }

Custom calls for cooked carrot slices for the Rosh Hashanah menu, as they symbolize prosperity and sweetness. Dried cranberries add a festive look to these delicious honey-glazed carrots.

1 pound carrots, peeled and sliced
  about ¼ inch thick
1 cup water
Pinch of salt

1 tablespoon sugar
1 tablespoon honey
¼ cup dried cranberries
2 teaspoons vegetable oil

Combine the carrots, water, and salt in a medium saucepan. Bring to a boil and simmer uncovered 10 minutes over medium heat. Add the sugar, honey, cranberries, and vegetable oil to the pan. Cook uncovered over medium-low heat, stirring occasionally, until carrots are very tender and liquid is absorbed, about 10 minutes. Watch so the mixture does not burn. Serve hot or at room temperature.

. . . .

Makes 4 servings

Nutritional information per serving: 152 calories; 3.4 g fat—19.6% calories from fat;
0.3 g saturated fat; 0 mg cholesterol

Late Summer Fruit Salad

{ p a r e v e }

This colorful salad of peaches, plums, and kiwis can be served on its own or alongside honey cake. Use red-fleshed plums for the prettiest result.

2 ripe kiwifruits

4 ripe peaches or nectarines

4 ripe plums, preferably red-fleshed

1 tablespoon sugar, or to taste

1 tablespoon dry red or white wine, or to taste

Peel the kiwis and cut into half-slices. Cut the peaches and plums into wedges. In a clear glass bowl, toss the fruit with the sugar and wine. Taste, and add more sugar or wine if desired. Serve cold.

· ·

Makes 4 servings

Nutritional information per serving: 112 calories; 0.7 g fat—4.9% calories from fat;
0 g saturated fat; 0 mg cholesterol

Low-Fat Honey Cake with Cocoa and Sweet Spices

{ p a r e v e }

Honey gives this cake a pleasing moist texture so that not much oil is needed. Cocoa, a favorite ingredient in honey cakes baked in Israeli homes, contributes a rich flavor and a deep brown color and complements the honey, cinnamon, and ginger.

1 $\frac{1}{2}$ cups all-purpose flour

2 tablespoons unsweetened cocoa

1 teaspoon baking powder

$\frac{1}{2}$ teaspoon baking soda

$\frac{1}{2}$ teaspoon ground cinnamon

$\frac{1}{2}$ teaspoon ground ginger

2 large eggs

$\frac{1}{2}$ cup sugar

$\frac{2}{3}$ cup honey

$\frac{1}{4}$ cup vegetable oil

$\frac{1}{4}$ cup water

$\frac{1}{4}$ cup chopped walnuts (optional)

Preheat the oven to 325°F. Lightly grease an 8 × 4-inch loaf pan, line the base and sides with parchment paper or foil, and grease the paper or foil. Sift the flour with the cocoa, baking powder, baking soda, cinnamon, and ginger.

Beat the eggs lightly with a mixer. Add the sugar and honey and beat until the mixture is very smooth and lightened in color. Gradually add the vegetable oil and beat until blended. Stir in the flour mixture alternately with the water, in 2 batches. Last, stir in the walnuts.

Pour the batter into the prepared pan. Bake about 50 minutes or until a cake tester inserted in the cake comes out clean. Cool in the pan for about 15 minutes. Turn out onto a rack and carefully peel off the paper. Wrap in foil when completely cool. (If tightly wrapped, the cake keeps 2 weeks at room temperature.) Serve in thin slices.

· ·

Makes 8 to 10 servings

Nutritional information per serving: 242 calories; 6.8 g fat—24.4% calories from fat; 1.1 g saturated fat; 43 mg cholesterol

3

Yom Kippur—Before and After the Fast

YOM KIPPUR, the most solemn holiday of the Jewish calendar, takes place ten days after Rosh Hashanah, usually in early October. Also known as the Day of Atonement, Yom Kippur is a day of repentance and fasting. The whole day is spent in prayer, with no food or drink allowed for twenty-four hours.

On the evening before Yom Kippur, a copious dinner is served before the fast begins. On many tables, the menu is similar to that of a typical Shabbat, because in religious writings Yom Kippur is called "the Sabbath of Sabbaths."

Most people dine on delicately flavored dishes and avoid salty and spicy foods that could provoke thirst during the fast. Often the main course is chicken in the pot, a whole poached chicken that also produces a rich chicken soup. There are those who claim that chicken soup helps one better withstand the fast—another of chicken soup's many merits!

Some cooks garnish the soup with kreplach, which resemble tortellini. Instead of making kreplach, you can buy them at Jewish specialty shops. Or you can follow a time-honored tradition and prepare kneidlach (matzo balls). Serve the matzo balls in the soup as a first course, followed by the chicken with vegetables as a main course.

As an accompaniment for the chicken, bake a savory kugel of noodles and veg-etables. This is a delicious dish that is always popular among children and adults.

The finale for the Yom Kippur eve dinner is fresh fruit, fruit salad, cookies, or light cake such as orange chiffon cake rather than an elaborate dessert. Tea with lemon is the standard beverage, and, in Moroccan-Jewish families, tea with fresh mint.

Following the night and day spent in prayer and remorse for sins comes a feeling of great relief. There is hope for a good year to come, and the time has finally arrived to break the fast. In our family and in many others, this means eating comfort food. Nobody worries about calories—after all, when you haven't eaten for twenty-four hours, you tend to feel virtuous from a dietary standpoint, too.

What to eat depends on each family's traditions. Some people serve a lavish meal with a main course of meat. When I was growing up, my mother would prepare a supper based on dairy foods. She felt that a leaner meal makes you feel better after fasting than a heavy one, and, besides, our family loved brunch-type foods like bagels with lox and cream cheese or scrambled eggs.

Since holiday rules prohibit cooking during Yom Kippur, the menu after the fast consists of dishes that are quick or that have been made ahead. In my parents' house, a kugel was a particular favorite for the meal. Usually my mother prepared a savory potato kugel with mushrooms and onions or an apple and noodle kugel. She baked the kugel the day before Yom Kippur and put it in the oven to reheat as soon as we returned home from Yom Kippur services. Fortunately for us, the synagogue was across the street so we didn't have to wait long!

This is still my favorite menu for the feast after the fast. In many homes, the first taste after the fast is sweet—a piece of honey cake or sponge cake, or perhaps a cinnamon roll. As children, we always opted for a slice of my mother's scrumptious sour cream coffee cake; I have developed a lower-fat version for today's lighter menus.

Before the Fast

. . . .

Chicken Soup with Potato Kneidlach

{ m e a t }

*P*otato gives these matzo balls a satisfying quality. With a touch of fresh nutmeg, they taste like *a cross between light matzo balls and Italian potato gnocchi. As these matzo balls contain no leavening, you can also prepare them for Passover.*

For the soup, use the broth from Chicken in the Pot with Fresh Herbs (page 27) or your favorite chicken soup or broth.

1 medium baking potato, peeled and coarsely grated (¾ cup grated)	Pinch of freshly ground black pepper
½ cup matzo meal	Freshly grated nutmeg to taste
1 large egg white	½ teaspoon vegetable oil
¼ cup water	4 cups chicken broth, with a few carrot slices
¼ teaspoon salt	

To make the matzo balls, mix the potato and matzo meal in a bowl. Add the egg white and mix well. Gradually mix in the water. Add salt, pepper, nutmeg, and vegetable oil and mix well.

Bring about 2 quarts salted water to a boil in a large saucepan. With wet hands, take about 1 scant tablespoon of the matzo mixture and roll it between your palms to a ball. Set balls on a plate. Reduce heat so water in pan simmers. With a rubber spatula, carefully slide the balls into the water. Return to a simmer. Cover and cook over low heat about 1 hour or until firm. Cover and keep them warm until ready to serve.

Heat the soup. With a slotted spoon, remove the potato kneidlach from the water and add to individual bowls. Add the soup with some carrot slices to each bowl and serve.

. . . .

Makes 4 servings

Nutritional information per serving: 180 calories; 3.5 g fat—17.7% calories from fat; 0.9 g saturated fat; 3 mg cholesterol

Chicken in the Pot with Fresh Herbs

{ m e a t }

Chicken in the pot is the typical entree served before the Yom Kippur fast. Although this dish is commonly referred to as "boiled" chicken, it is actually poached over gentle heat, not boiled. For Yom Kippur, the chicken is made with little or no salt, so the dish will not provoke thirst during the fast. My favorite herbs for this are thyme, dill, cilantro, and parsley, although sometimes I use fresh tarragon.

For the feast before Yom Kippur, carve the chicken into pieces with their bones, as you would a roast chicken and serve with the vegetables in shallow bowls with a bit of broth.

You can also remove the chicken meat from the bones and return it to the soup.

1 3½- to 4-pound frying or roasting chicken
1 small parsnip, peeled (optional)
2 celery stalks, including leafy tops
1 large onion, whole
2 bay leaves
4 sprigs fresh thyme, or 1 teaspoon dried
Salt and freshly ground black pepper

About 2 quarts water
4 medium carrots, peeled and cut into 1-inch slices
4 garlic cloves, coarsely chopped
4 medium zucchini, cut into thick slices
3 to 4 tablespoons chopped dill, cilantro, or parsley, or a combination

Remove the fat from the chicken. Put the chicken in a large casserole or pot. Add the parsnip, celery, onion, bay leaves, thyme, and small pinches of salt and pepper. Cover ingredients with water. Bring to a boil. Skim foam from surface. Cover and cook over low heat for 1½ hours.

Add the carrots, garlic, and zucchini and bring to a simmer. Cover and cook over low heat about 30 minutes or until the chicken is cooked through and the vegetables are tender. Skim off fat. Remove and discard the parsnip, bay leaves, and thyme sprigs. Remove skin from chicken. Carve chicken into serving pieces and return them to soup. Taste and adjust seasoning.

Serve the chicken in fairly shallow bowls with carrots and zucchini. Add dill, cilantro, or parsley to each bowl. Moisten each serving with a few spoonfuls of soup.

. . . .

Makes 4 to 6 servings

Nutritional information per serving: 328.5 calories; 6.5 g fat—18.3% calories from fat;
1.7 g saturated fat; 169 mg cholesterol

Noodle-Vegetable Kugel with Pecans

{ m e a t }

*N*oodle kugel is a traditional favorite for almost every Jewish holiday and makes a wonderful accompaniment for chicken in the pot. Pecans add a bit of crunch to the crust of this delicious kugel of noodles, sautéed mushrooms, carrots, and squash.

8 ounces medium egg noodles

1½ tablespoons vegetable oil

1 large onion, chopped

2 garlic cloves, chopped

½ pound small mushrooms, sliced

Salt and freshly ground black pepper

1 teaspoon paprika

2 large carrots, peeled and coarsely grated

1 small yellow crookneck squash, coarsely grated

1 small zucchini, coarsely grated

¼ cup chopped parsley

1 large egg

2 large egg whites

⅓ cup chicken broth

3 tablespoons finely chopped pecans

Preheat the oven to 350°F. Cook the noodles in a large pot of boiling salted water uncovered over high heat, stirring occasionally, about 7 minutes or until nearly tender but still slightly firm. Drain, rinse with cold water, and drain well. Transfer to a bowl.

Heat the vegetable oil in a large skillet over medium heat. Add the onion and sauté about 7 minutes or until golden. Add the garlic, mushrooms, pinch of salt, pinch of pepper, and ¾ teaspoon paprika. Sauté about 3 minutes, stirring often.

Add the mushroom mixture, carrots, yellow squash, zucchini, and parsley to the noodles and mix well. In a small bowl, beat the egg with the egg whites and broth, add to the noodles, and mix well. Oil a 5-cup baking dish and add the noodle mixture. Sprinkle with pecans, then with remaining ¼ teaspoon paprika. Bake 45 minutes or until set and lightly browned on top. Serve hot, from the baking dish.

· ·

Makes 4 servings

Nutritional information per serving: 381 calories; 13 g fat—29.9% calories from fat; 1.9 g saturated fat; 107 mg cholesterol

Pears in Red Wine

{ p a r e v e }

*S*erve these pears in their burgundy-colored sauce as an accompaniment for honey cake or as a light, flavorful dessert on their own.

½ cup sugar

2 cups dry red wine, such as
   Cabernet Sauvignon

1 cinnamon stick or vanilla bean

4 ripe but firm medium pears (about
   1½ pounds total)

Combine the sugar, wine, and cinnamon stick or vanilla bean in heavy, medium saucepan and heat over low heat, stirring gently, until the sugar dissolves. Raise the heat to high and bring to a boil. Reduce the heat and keep warm over very low heat.

Peel, halve, and core the pears. Bring the wine syrup to a boil and add the pears. Cover with a lid slightly smaller than the diameter of the saucepan to keep the pears submerged in the syrup. Return to a simmer. Reduce the heat to low and cook the fruit until tender when pierced with a sharp knife, about 30 minutes.

Cool the pears in the syrup, still covered with the small lid and immersed, to room temperature. Gently transfer the pears to a shallow bowl or baking dish with a slotted spoon. Bring the syrup back to a boil; simmer syrup about 5 more minutes or until thickened slightly. Cool about 5 minutes. Spoon over pears. Refrigerate the pears in the syrup for 8 hours or overnight so that they absorb color and flavor from the syrup. Serve the pears cold, adding a few tablespoons syrup to each serving.

. . . .

Makes 4 servings

*Nutritional information per serving: 282 calories; 0.7 g fat—2.8% calories from fat;
0 g saturated fat; 0 mg cholesterol*

After the Fast

. . . .

Bagels with Light Lox and Cheese Spread
{ d a i r y }

Here is a slimmed-down, economical version of the traditional bagel with lox and cream cheese. You can use reasonably priced lox trimmings to prepare the spread. Serve it on fresh or toasted bagels.

8 ounces fat-free cream cheese ("soft" type)

1 ounce lox or smoked salmon, chopped

2 teaspoons chopped chives or parsley (optional)

Freshly ground black pepper

4 bagels

4 thin slices tomato (optional)

2 thin slices red onion, separated into rings

In a small bowl, mix the cream cheese with the lox and chives or parsley. Season to taste with pepper. Halve the bagels and spread the cream cheese mixture on both cut sides. Sandwich the tomato slices and a few onion rings between the halves.

. . . .

Makes 4 servings

Nutritional information per serving: 310 calories; 2 g fat—6.8% calories from fat;
0.3 g saturated fat; 2 mg cholesterol

Cucumber Salad with Yogurt Dill Dressing

{ d a i r y }

Smoked fish is popular in many homes after the fast, and a cooling cucumber salad is a perfect complement for the fish's salty flavor. Use long cucumbers, sometimes called European or hothouse cucumbers, which have the fewest seeds, for the best taste. You can leave them unpeeled. If you are making this salad with ordinary cucumbers, peel, halve, and seed them first.

2 cups plain nonfat yogurt
1 tablespoon chopped fresh dill, or 1
   teaspoon dried
Salt and freshly ground black pepper

Cayenne pepper
1 large (European) cucumber (about
   1 pound)

Mix the yogurt with the dill, salt, pepper, and cayenne pepper to taste.

Cut the cucumber into thin slices and put in a shallow serving bowl. Add yogurt mixture and mix gently. Taste and adjust seasoning. Serve cold.

Makes 4 servings

Nutritional information per serving: 80 calories; 0.4 g fat—4.4% calories from fat;
0.2 g saturated fat; 2 mg cholesterol

Sephardic Eggplant Salad with Green Onion, Garlic, and Roasted Peppers

{ p a r e v e }

*T*his pareve vegetable spread is a terrific addition to a buffet table. Prepare it a day or two before Yom Kippur so it's ready to serve after the fast. It's also a tasty, low-fat dip to serve at parties.

2 medium eggplants (2 to
    2½ pounds total)
2 large red bell peppers
3 tablespoons finely chopped green
    onion (scallion)
2 garlic cloves, minced

1 tablespoon fresh lemon juice
1 tablespoon olive oil
Salt and freshly ground black pepper
Cayenne pepper
3 or 4 pita breads, for serving

Preheat the oven to 400°F. Pierce each eggplant a few times with a fork. Bake the whole eggplants in a large foil-lined baking dish, turning once, about 1 hour or until very tender. Let cool.

Broil the peppers about 2 inches from the heat source, turning them often, until pepper skins blister all over, 15 to 20 minutes. Transfer them to a plastic bag and close bag. Let stand 10 minutes. Peel the peppers using paring knife. Remove the core and seeds and drain any liquid from inside peppers. Dice the peppers.

Halve each eggplant lengthwise. Drain off any liquid from inside the eggplants. Use a spoon to remove eggplant flesh from the peel. Chop the eggplant in batches in a food processor, leaving a few small chunks. Transfer to a bowl.

Add the green onion and garlic and mix well. Add the lemon juice, olive oil, and salt, pepper, and cayenne pepper to taste. Stir in the diced roasted peppers. Taste and adjust seasoning. Serve cold or at room temperature, with pita bread.

. . . .

Makes 6 to 8 servings

*Nutritional information per serving: 134 calories; 2.3 g fat—14.9% calories from fat;
0.3 g saturated fat; 0 mg cholesterol*

Mashed Potato Kugel with Onions and Mushrooms

{ m e a t   o r   p a r e v e }

*O*ne of the best things that can happen to a potato is to be part of a mashed potato kugel. This irresistible dish can be served with fish, meat, or poultry, or can be a vegetarian main course. For a dairy meal, you can substitute skim milk for the broth.

2½ pounds large boiling potatoes, unpeeled

Salt and freshly ground black pepper

2 tablespoons vegetable oil

2 medium onions, chopped

½ pound small mushrooms, quartered

¼ cup chicken or vegetable broth

2 large eggs, beaten

½ teaspoon paprika

Put the potatoes in a large saucepan with water to cover and a pinch of salt and bring to a boil. Cover and simmer over low heat about 35 minutes or until very tender. Drain and leave until cool enough to handle.

In a large skillet, heat the vegetable oil, add the onions, and sauté over medium heat until light golden. Add the mushrooms and salt and pepper, and sauté over medium-high heat about 7 minutes or until browned.

Preheat the oven to 350°F. Peel the potatoes while still fairly hot. Put in a large bowl, cut each into a few pieces, and beat with a mixer at low speed until coarsely mashed. Beat in the broth, then eggs, just until blended. With a spoon, stir in ½ cup of the sautéed mushroom mixture. Add ¾ teaspoon salt and ½ teaspoon pepper, or to taste.

Grease a 6- or 7-cup casserole and add half the potato mixture (about 2½ cups). Top with the remaining sautéed mushroom mixture, then with remaining potato mixture. Smooth the top and sprinkle with paprika. Bake uncovered about 50 minutes or until top is firm and light golden at edges.

Makes 6 servings

Nutritional information per serving: 200 calories; 6.7 g fat—29.3% calories from fat; 1.2 g saturated fat; 71 mg cholesterol

Cinnamon-Swirled Coffee Cake with Light Sour Cream
{ d a i r y }

This is a lightened rendition of a cake my mother often made when I was growing up. Sour cream is replaced by its fat-free version mixed with nonfat yogurt, and vegetable oil replaces the butter. The cake is a treat for breaking the fast after Yom Kippur.

1 ½ teaspoons ground cinnamon
1 cup plus 5 tablespoons sugar
1 ¾ cups all-purpose flour
1 ½ teaspoons baking powder
½ teaspoon baking soda
1 cup nonfat sour cream

¾ cup plain nonfat yogurt
1 teaspoon vanilla extract
⅓ cup vegetable oil
2 large eggs
3 large egg whites

Position a rack in the center of the oven and preheat to 325°F. Grease a 9½ × 4-inch Bundt pan, kugelhopf mold, or fluted tube pan; grease the tube and all nooks and crannies. Mix the cinnamon with 3 tablespoons sugar. Sift the flour, baking powder, and baking soda into a bowl. In another bowl, mix the sour cream, yogurt, and vanilla.

In a large bowl, beat the vegetable oil with 1 cup sugar and 1 egg until smooth and fluffy. Beat in second egg. At low speed, stir in the flour mixture alternately with the sour cream mixture, each in 2 portions. In another large bowl, whip the egg whites until soft peaks form. Beat in the remaining 2 tablespoons sugar and whip until shiny but not dry. Fold into batter just until blended.

Pour about one-third of the batter into the prepared pan. Sprinkle with half the cinnamon mixture. Gently spoon another third of the batter in dollops over the mixture. Sprinkle with the remaining cinnamon mixture. Gently spoon the remaining batter in dollops over it. Spread gently to cover the cinnamon mixture. Bake about 60 minutes or until a cake tester inserted in the cake comes out clean. Cool in pan 15 minutes.

Run a thin-bladed flexible knife around the center tube but not around sides of pan. Invert the cake onto a rack and cool completely. (Cake can be kept, wrapped, up to 2 days at room temperature or 3 days in refrigerator.) Serve at room temperature.

. . . .

Makes 10 servings
Nutritional information per serving: 292 calories; 8.5 g fat—27.5% calories from fat;
1.2 g saturated fat; 43 mg cholesterol

4

Succot

Stuffed Tomatoes with Chicken, Rice, and Ginger

Sweet and Sour Cabbage Rolls with Turkey Stuffing

Eggplant Stuffed with Chicken, Cilantro, and Sun-Dried Tomatoes

Stuffed Peppers, Latin American Style

Sephardic Sea Bass with Sweet Peppers and Garlic

Pareve Onion Pizza

Zucchini with Corn and Tomatoes

Chicken Chasseur

Steamed New Potatoes with Parsley Oil

Double Apple Cake with Honey and Cinnamon

SUCCOT, THE FEAST OF TABERNACLES, is a week-long autumn holiday commemorating the ancient Hebrews' escape from Egypt and celebrating the harvest. Immediately after Succot are two more feast days, Shmini Atzeret, the Eighth Day of Assembly, and Simhat Torah, the Rejoicing of the Torah.

On Succot our focus is on produce and nature. The theme of appreciating the bounty of produce weaves through all the holiday customs, culinary and otherwise. Even the setting must recall the harvest: meals, entertaining, and, in some families, sleeping take place in a *succah*, a hut with a roof of leafy branches built for the occasion. The temporary nature of the succah also recalls the Israelites' wandering in the desert.

Most people build their succah in their yard or on the roof or patio of their dwelling. Helping to build and decorate the succah is a favorite activity for children of all ages. As children growing up in Washington, D.C., my brother and I looked forward eagerly to Succot. We loved to help my parents tie pears, bananas, and bunches of grapes on a string to hang inside our succah and enjoyed drawing pictures to adorn the walls. When my husband was growing up in Givatayim, Israel, the selection of fruits was different from ours; there were pomegranates, guavas, and citrus fruits, which the children picked from the family's garden to hang from their succah's ceiling. They also made colorful paper chains and paper flowers and gathered an impressive collection of pictures as succah ornaments. The family's succah even received "beautiful succah" awards from the city.

At the center of the holiday ritual is a fruit—the *etrog*, or citron. It is used during Succot synagogue prayers together with the *lulav*, a collection of palm fronds and branches of myrtle and willow. Some people believe this fragrant citrus fruit was the fruit eaten by Adam and Eve in the Garden of Eden.

Eating in the succah gives the holiday meals a special atmosphere, rather like participating in a festive picnic. The branches covering the succah are supposed to be far enough apart so you can see the stars.

Succot is not only the time to enjoy eating in the succah; it's also the period to rejoice in the fruits of the season. In ancient Israel, the grapes and olives had been picked before Succot and were in the process of being transformed into wine and olive oil. Much of the summer produce had been gathered, and our ancestors could finally have a chance to relax.

With the spotlight on produce, fruit and vegetables naturally play a major role in Succot menus. This time-honored holiday emphasis fits in perfectly with today's awareness of how important these foods are in a healthy diet.

Naturally, during Succot produce is used in a more festive fashion than for everyday meals. Vegetables become glamorous. Instead of plain boiled or steamed vegetables, stuffed vegetables are the traditional choice of many families. They are ideal as they are elegant, are easy to serve, and can be made ahead. Rice and meat is the preferred stuffing. In old-fashioned recipes beef is used, but today stuffings of lean ground turkey, as in Stuffed Peppers, Latin American Style (page 44), and meatless stuffings, as in Eggplant with Onion-Tomato Stuffing (page 294), are gaining in favor. All-vegetable stuffings of chopped mushrooms, pureed roasted peppers, and eggplant are delicious and make for a lighter dish.

Some vegetables seem to have been designed to be stuffed. Eggplant and zucchini are particularly enticing when presented in this way. They can be stuffed whole, with their insides hollowed out with a vegetable peeler to make cylinders, or can be halved lengthwise and the pulp scooped out, leaving boat-shaped shells. Onions can also be stuffed after being precooked; their centers can be removed, leaving room for stuffing, or they can instead be separated in layers and each one stuffed. In many households, cabbage leaves wrapped around a savory stuffing is a traditional dish for Succot.

The most popular flavorings for stuffed vegetables are onions and garlic. Saffron and fragrant herbs like thyme and basil also complement vegetable fillings well, as do spices like cumin and turmeric. For dairy meals, grated Parmesan or other cheeses are the quintessential seasonings for vegetable or rice fillings. Tomato sauce reigns supreme as the best-loved sauce for stuffed vegetables.

Because dining in the succah means that the dinner table is farther from the kitchen than usual, the emphasis is on dishes that are easy to serve, like casseroles, stews, and one-pot dishes, to avoid many trips to the kitchen. If you have elaborate recipes that demand last-minute attention, save them for other occasions. Avoid delicate dishes that must be rushed from the oven to the table. In our succah, I find it convenient to serve such dishes as Chicken Chasseur (page 48); Veal Chops with Piperade (page 237); or Tuscan Lamb with Peas (page 244). For dairy meals for Succot, you might like to prepare a filled savory pastry, such as a country vegetable tart.

Within the general framework of using seasonal produce to celebrate the holiday, each Jewish ethnic community has developed its own specialties. Stuffed eggplant is the most popular Sephardic dish for Succot, while stuffed cabbage is the great holiday favorite for Jews from Russia, Poland, and Hungary. Often the cabbage is cooked in a sweet and sour sauce, which might be based on tomatoes or on beef broth.

It is nice to serve appetizers in the succah as friends come to visit on the Succot holiday. Jews from Algeria might feature bites of eggplant pickled with garlic and vinegar; green olives cooked with garlic, olive oil, and lemon juice; and cumin-scented fava beans.

And pastries are often on the menu on Sephardic tables. Bourekas—savory filo dough pastries—are made with a dill-flavored meat filling by the Jews of Greece, and with meat, potatoes, or eggplant by Jews from North Africa. For dessert, filo pastries with honey-flavored nut fillings are a well-loved holiday treat. Greek Jews also prepare sweet filo pastries with fillings of pumpkin and cinnamon, and of zucchini and walnuts. Lemon-flavored almond cookies are a traditional Italian treat for this holiday, as is bollo, a yeast cake with raisins and anise. Another Italian Jewish Succot specialty is a pear torta of two layers of sweet pastry enclosing a liqueur-accented pear filling.

Ashkenazic Jews also prepare pastries for the holiday. Strudels with a wide variety of stuffings are baked in many homes. Apple strudel is the best loved, but there are also strudels stuffed with dried fruit and even a Hungarian-Jewish strudel filled with cabbage. Another Ashkenazic sweet is pfluden, which is made of a strudel-like dough layered with the filling instead of being rolled up.

Flavorful fall apples and ripe pears appear in myriad irresistible home-baked tarts and cakes. Quinces are used like apples for compotes and are also baked with meat or chicken for savory dishes. Some holiday treats, like Sephardic quince preserves, Ashkenazic honey cake, and honey sweets called teiglach, are made both for Rosh Hashanah and for Succot.

Now that my husband and I have our own vegetable garden, we can see from personal experience why this is the perfect time to celebrate the bounty of the land. Before Succot, we have usually picked so many tomatoes that we need to put several trays of them on our roof to make sun-dried tomatoes. Our bell peppers are finally turning red, so we can marinate many of them with olive oil and garlic to have on hand as holiday appetizers. We have plenty of eggplants and squash for stuffing. All this produce practically begs you to get together with your friends and family and have a big feast.

For a Succot menu, you might like to follow a Mediterranean custom and serve stuffed vegetables as the main course. Precede them with one or several salads of cooked and raw vegetables or perhaps with a warming soup, such as Minestrone with Chicken Breasts and Fresh Basil (page 162). For dessert, serve fresh seasonal fruit or prepare a luscious apple cake (page 51) or Pear Blintzes with Pear Honey Sauce (page 324).

Stuffed Tomatoes with Chicken, Rice, and Ginger

{ m e a t }

*C*hopped water chestnuts, as well as the popular Chinese seasoning trio of fresh ginger, garlic, and green onion, give an out-of-the-ordinary touch to stuffed tomatoes. These tomatoes make a tasty entree or substantial first course for Succot.

3 cups water
Salt (optional)
½ cup long-grain rice
1 tablespoon plus 2 teaspoons
  vegetable oil
2 green onions (scallions), chopped
1 tablespoon minced, peeled fresh
  ginger

2 large garlic cloves, minced
½ pound ground chicken
¾ teaspoon ground black pepper
½ cup canned water chestnuts,
  drained and chopped
2½ pounds ripe but firm tomatoes (6
  or 7 medium to large)

Preheat the oven to 400°F. Bring the water to a boil, add salt and rice, and boil the rice uncovered for 10 minutes. Rinse with cold water and drain well. Transfer to a bowl.

Heat the vegetable oil in a skillet, add the green onions, ginger, and garlic, and sauté over medium-low heat 1 minute. Add the chicken and sauté, stirring to crumble meat, about 3 minutes or until meat changes color. Add to rice. Add ¼ teaspoon salt (or to taste), pepper, and water chestnuts; mix well.

Cut off a slice from the bottom of each tomato, cutting off about one-quarter of the tomato; reserve slice as a "hat." Remove pulp and seeds from tomato with a spoon. Sprinkle the interior of the tomatoes and the cut side of hats lightly with salt.

Put tomatoes in an oiled baking dish. Fill with stuffing, mounding slightly, and cover with hats. Bake uncovered 30 to 40 minutes or until tomatoes are tender. Serve hot.

. . . .

Makes 6 or 7 servings
Nutritional information per serving: 203 calories; 7 g fat—29.8% calories from fat;
1.3 g saturated fat; 30 mg cholesterol

Sweet and Sour Cabbage Rolls with Turkey Stuffing

{ m e a t }

I*n my childhood home, stuffed cabbage was usually on a Succot menu, as it is in many other families. My mother made the stuffing the traditional way, with beef and rice. Now we both use turkey, which makes a delicious low-fat stuffing.*

1 3-pound green cabbage, cored

STUFFING
3 cups water
Salt
$\frac{1}{2}$ cup long-grain rice
2 teaspoons vegetable oil
1 medium onion, minced
2 garlic cloves, minced
1 teaspoon ground paprika
$\frac{1}{2}$ pound ground turkey
$\frac{1}{2}$ teaspoon ground black pepper
$\frac{1}{4}$ teaspoon cayenne pepper

SAUCE
1 teaspoon vegetable oil
1 medium onion, minced
$\frac{1}{2}$ teaspoon ground paprika
3 cups chicken broth
2 tablespoons tomato paste
$\frac{1}{3}$ cup raisins
1 tablespoon fresh lemon juice
$\frac{1}{2}$ teaspoon sugar
Salt and freshly ground black pepper
   (optional)

Carefully remove 15 large outer cabbage leaves by cutting them from the core. Put leaves in a large pot of boiling water and boil for 5 minutes. Transfer them carefully to a colander and rinse gently with cold water. Pat dry with a towel. Coarsely chop the remaining cabbage, add to the boiling water, and boil 2 minutes. Drain, rinse with cold water, and drain well.

To make the stuffing, bring the water to a boil in a saucepan, add salt and rice, and boil rice uncovered for 10 minutes. Rinse with cold water and drain well. Transfer to a bowl. In a nonstick skillet, heat the vegetable oil, add the onion, and cook over medium-low heat for 3 minutes. Add the garlic and paprika and cook, stirring, 1 minute. Transfer the mixture to the bowl of rice and let cool. Add the turkey, $\frac{1}{4}$ teaspoon salt, pepper, and cayenne. Knead by hand to blend ingredients thoroughly.

To make the sauce, heat the vegetable oil in a large heavy flameproof casserole, add the onion, and cook over low heat, stirring often, 2 minutes. Add the paprika and cook 1 minute. Remove from heat.

Trim the thick ribs of each cabbage leaf slightly so leaf can be easily bent. Put 2 tablespoons stuffing on the stem end of each leaf and fold stem end over it. Fold sides over stuffing to enclose it. Beginning at stem end, roll up the leaf to a neat package. If any leaves are torn, add a piece of another leaf. Arrange cabbage rolls tightly, with seam end facing down, side by side in casserole. Chop any remaining leaves and add to casserole.

Add 2¾ cups broth to casserole. Mix the tomato paste with remaining broth and add to casserole. Bring to a simmer. Cover and simmer over low heat for 1 hour and 15 minutes. Add the raisins, lemon juice, and sugar and simmer 1 minute. Season to taste with salt and pepper. When serving, spoon a little sauce over cabbage rolls.

· ·

Makes 6 servings

Nutritional information per serving: 196 calories; 6.4 g fat—29.3% calories from fat;
1.4 g saturated fat; 30 mg cholesterol

Eggplant Stuffed with Chicken, Cilantro and Sun-Dried Tomatoes

{ m e a t }

Festive stuffings for eggplant in the Middle East often include rice, nuts, and lamb. To make the stuffing leaner but still tasty, I use chicken instead of lamb and sun-dried tomatoes instead of nuts. Choose the dry-packed tomatoes rather than those that are packed in jars of oil, to ensure that the stuffing is low in fat.

2 to 2½ pounds (3 small or 2 medium) eggplants
Salt

STUFFING
3 cups water
Salt
½ cup long-grain rice, rinsed and drained
12 dry-packed sun-dried tomato halves

1 tablespoon olive or vegetable oil
1 medium onion, finely chopped
½ teaspoon ground black pepper
½ pound ground chicken
2 tablespoons chopped cilantro

SAUCE
2 tablespoons tomato paste
⅓ cup water
2 large garlic cloves, halved
1 tablespoon olive or vegetable oil

Cut the stem ends from the eggplants. Halve the eggplants lengthwise. Leave them unpeeled. Use a spoon to scoop out centers, forming boat-shaped shells. Sprinkle eggplant shells lightly with salt; let stand while making stuffing. Preheat the oven to 425°F.

To make the stuffing, bring the water to a boil in a saucepan, add salt and rice, and boil rice for 8 minutes. Add sun-dried tomatoes to the rice and boil 2 more minutes. Rinse with cold water and drain well. Transfer to a large bowl. Remove the tomato halves and dice them.

Chop the flesh removed from the eggplants. Heat the oil in a large skillet, add the onion, and cook over medium-low heat about 5 minutes. Stir in the chopped eggplant and sprinkle with ¼ teaspoon salt and the pepper. Cover and cook, stirring often, about 10 minutes or until tender. Let cool. Add to bowl of rice. Add the chicken, chopped tomatoes, cilantro, and salt and pepper to taste. Mix well.

Rinse the eggplant shells, pat them dry, and put them in a baking dish large enough to hold them side by side. Fill them with stuffing.

To make the sauce, mix the tomato paste with the water and spoon mixture over the eggplant. Add enough water to the dish to come up the side of the eggplants by one-third. Add garlic, then drizzle oil over eggplants. Cover and bake 15 minutes. Reduce the oven temperature to 350°F. and bake 15 minutes more. Uncover and bake, basting occasionally, 30 minutes or until eggplant is very tender. Serve hot.

. . . .

Makes 4 to 6 servings

Nutritional information per serving: 520 calories; 11.7 g fat—18.3% calories from fat; 2.1 g saturated fat; 36 mg cholesterol

Stuffed Peppers, Latin American Style

{ m e a t }

In Latin America, meat stuffings are often flavored with capers, raisins, and olives. The savory and sweet stuffing is delicious baked in bell peppers and perfect for Succot.

4 large red, green, or yellow bell
   peppers
1 tablespoon olive or vegetable oil
2 medium onions, chopped
¾ pound ground chicken or turkey
1 14½-ounce can diced tomatoes,
   drained
½ cup vegetable broth
1 teaspoon dried oregano
Salt and freshly ground black pepper

⅓ cup raisins
¾ cup bread crumbs
¼ cup diced green olives
2 tablespoons capers, rinsed and
   chopped
Whites of 2 hard-boiled eggs,
   chopped
1 cup tomato sauce
½ cup water

Preheat oven to 375° F. Halve 3 of the peppers lengthwise, discarding cores, seeds, and ribs, and reserve for stuffing. Core, seed, and dice remaining pepper.

Cook pepper halves in a saucepan of boiling water 3 minutes. Drain well in a colander. Lightly spray one or two shallow baking dishes with vegetable oil spray and set peppers in them, cut sides up.

Heat the oil in large nonstick skillet, add the onions and diced bell pepper, and sauté over medium heat 5 minutes. Add the chicken and sauté, stirring to crumble, until it changes color, about 5 minutes. Add the tomatoes, broth, oregano, salt and pepper, and raisins. Bring to a boil and cook over medium heat 5 minutes. Remove from the heat. Add the bread crumbs, olives, capers, and egg whites. Taste and adjust seasoning.

Divide the stuffing among the pepper halves, mounding it high. Add the tomato sauce and water to the baking dish, drizzling the sauce over the peppers. Bake uncovered 30 minutes or until peppers are very tender. Serve hot.

. . . .

Makes 6 servings

Nutritional information per serving: 299 calories; 9.7 g fat—28.7% calories from fat; 2.1 g saturated fat; 54 mg cholesterol

Sephardic Sea Bass with Sweet Peppers and Garlic

{ p a r e v e }

This is one of my favorite fish dishes. When Chilean sea bass is available, it is my first choice for preparing this easy, colorful, low-fat specialty. Serve this delectable fish as a holiday appetizer or as a main course with white or brown rice or couscous.

1½ tablespoons extra-virgin olive oil
1 medium red bell pepper, cored, seeded, and diced
1 medium yellow bell pepper, cored, seeded, and diced
4 large garlic cloves, chopped
1 green onion (scallion), chopped

2 pounds sea bass steaks or fillets, about 1 inch thick, cut into 4 pieces
½ teaspoon dried thyme
½ teaspoon dried oregano
Salt and freshly ground black pepper
Cayenne pepper
2 tablespoons chopped parsley

Preheat the oven to 400°F. Heat the olive oil in a large skillet. Add the red and yellow peppers and sauté over medium-low heat 5 minutes. Remove from the heat and stir in the garlic and green onion.

Lightly oil a baking dish large enough to hold the fish in a single layer. Set fish in dish and spoon pepper mixture over it. Sprinkle the fish evenly with the thyme, oregano, salt, pepper, and cayenne pepper to taste. Cover and bake 18 to 20 minutes or until the fish can just be flaked with a fork but is not falling apart. Taste sauce and adjust seasoning.

Serve fish hot or warm. Sprinkle with parsley, then spoon some of cooking juices with peppers over each piece.

. . . .

Makes 4 servings

Nutritional information per serving: 306 calories; 10 g fat—29.8% calories from fat;
1.8 g saturated fat; 93 mg cholesterol

Pareve Onion Pizza

{ p a r e v e }

This pizza from southern France is perfect for entertaining during the week of Succot, when you want a casual entree with a festive note. Instead of serving it as a main course, you can offer portions of this cheeseless pizza as an appetizer before a meat or dairy meal.

PIZZA DOUGH

1 envelope (¼ ounce) active dry
    yeast, or 1 cake fresh yeast
½ cup lukewarm water
1½ cups all-purpose flour
¾ teaspoon salt
2½ teaspoons olive oil

TOPPING

2 tablespoons plus 1 teaspoon olive
    oil
5 medium onions, cut into thin slices
Salt and freshly ground black pepper
2 28-ounce cans tomatoes, drained
    and chopped
1 bay leaf
1 teaspoon dried thyme
¼ cup pitted black olives, halved

To make the dough, sprinkle dry yeast or crumble fresh yeast over ¼ cup water in a cup or small bowl and let stand for 10 minutes. Stir until smooth. In a food processor fitted with a dough blade or metal blade, process the flour and salt briefly to mix them. Add the remaining water and oil to the yeast mixture. With the blades of the processor turning, gradually pour in the yeast-liquid mixture. If dough is too dry to come together, add 1 tablespoon of water and process again. Process for 1 minute to knead dough. Transfer the dough to a clean bowl and sprinkle it with a little flour. Cover with a damp towel and let rise 45 to 60 minutes or until doubled in volume.

To make the topping, heat 2 tablespoons of the olive oil in a heavy nonstick skillet over low heat. Add the onions and salt and pepper to taste. Cover and cook over low heat, stirring occasionally, about 25 minutes or until very tender; if pan becomes dry, add 1 tablespoon water to prevent burning.

Heat the remaining 1 teaspoon olive oil in another skillet or sauté pan. Add the tomatoes, bay leaf, thyme, and a little salt and pepper. Cook over medium heat, stirring occasionally, about 20 minutes or until the mixture is dry. Discard the bay leaf; taste and adjust seasoning.

Oil a 10-inch tart pan. Roll out the dough on a floured surface to a 12-inch circle and line the pan with dough, or pat dough out with oiled hands in the pan. Fill dough with the onion mixture. Spread the tomato mixture on top. Garnish with olive halves. Let rise in a warm place for 15 minutes. Preheat the oven to 375°F.

Bake the pizza for about 30 minutes or until the dough is golden brown and firm but not hard. Serve hot or warm.

. . . .

Makes 4 servings

Nutritional information per serving: 397 calories; 13.4 g fat—29.3% calories from fat;
1.6 g saturated fat; 0 mg cholesterol

Zucchini with Corn and Tomatoes
{ p a r e v e }

A colorful addition to Succot meals, this quick and easy vegetable medley is also good for Shavuot, when fresh corn is often available. It makes a lovely accompaniment for broiled fish or roast chicken.

1 tablespoon olive or vegetable oil	Kernels cut from 3 ears of corn, or 2
1 medium onion, chopped	cups frozen kernels
1 jalapeño pepper, seeded and	1 14½-ounce can diced tomatoes,
minced (optional)	drained
1½ pounds zucchini (4 medium),	Salt and freshly ground black pepper
diced	

Heat the oil in a large sauté pan over medium heat. Add the onion and sauté 5 minutes. Add the jalapeño pepper if using and sauté 30 seconds. Add the zucchini and corn and mix well. Cover and cook over medium-low heat, stirring often, 5 minutes. Add the tomatoes and cook uncovered 5 more minutes or until zucchini are crisp-tender. Season to taste with salt and pepper. Serve hot.

. . . .

Makes 4 servings

Nutritional information per serving: 118 calories; 4.4 g fat—29.2% calories from fat;
0.6 g saturated fat; 0 mg cholesterol

Chicken Chasseur

{ m e a t }

*F*resh tarragon, shallots, mushrooms, and tomatoes give this French chicken dish a luscious taste. You can lower the fat by using only chicken breast pieces; choose pieces with bones so they can simmer at length as they flavor the stew. Rice is the best accompaniment for this classic chicken entree, as it soaks up the tasty sauce so well.

2½ to 3 pounds chicken pieces
  without skin
Salt and freshly ground black pepper
1 tablespoon vegetable oil
½ pound mushrooms, quartered
3 shallots, minced
1 cup dry white wine
6 ripe plum tomatoes, peeled, seeded,
  and chopped, or 1 28-ounce can
  peeled plum tomatoes, drained and
  chopped

1 cup chicken broth
2 tablespoons cold water
1½ teaspoons potato starch or
  cornstarch
1 teaspoon tomato paste
4 teaspoons Cognac or brandy
2 teaspoons chopped fresh tarragon,
  or ¾ teaspoon dried tarragon
2 teaspoons chopped fresh parsley
6 cups cooked rice

Pat the chicken pieces dry. Sprinkle lightly with salt and pepper on all sides. Heat the vegetable oil in a large, heavy skillet over medium-high heat. Add the chicken leg and thigh pieces and brown lightly on all sides. Set on a plate, using a slotted spoon. Add breast pieces to skillet and brown lightly. Transfer to a plate.

Add the mushrooms to the skillet and brown them lightly. Stir in the shallots. Add the wine and bring to a boil. Return chicken pieces to skillet. If they do not fit in one layer, arrange breast pieces on top. Add the tomatoes. Cover and simmer over low heat about 25 minutes or until breast pieces are tender when pierced with a knife and cooked through.

Transfer the breast pieces to a platter using a slotted spoon. Cover and keep them warm. Cook the remaining chicken pieces about 10 minutes more or until tender and cooked through. Add the leg and thigh pieces to platter. Skim as much fat as possible from the sauce in the skillet.

In a small saucepan, bring the chicken broth to a boil. In a small bowl, whisk the cold water and potato starch to form a smooth paste. Whisk in the tomato paste.

Gradually pour mixture into simmering broth, whisking constantly. Bring back to a boil, whisking; simmer 1 minute if necessary, until thickened. Pour the sauce into the skillet. Add 1 tablespoon Cognac and simmer over medium heat, stirring often, until the sauce is thick enough to coat a spoon. Add the tarragon and remaining teaspoon Cognac. Taste and adjust seasoning. Spoon sauce over the chicken and sprinkle with chopped parsley. Serve with rice.

. . . .

Makes 4 or 5 servings

Nutritional information per serving: 752 calories; 20.6 g fat—26.3% calories from fat; 5.1 g saturated fat; 148 mg cholesterol

Steamed New Potatoes with Parsley Oil

{ p a r e v e }

These savory, easy-to-prepare potatoes, flavored delicately with olive oil and a squeeze of fresh lemon juice, make a good accompaniment for chicken for Succot or for Shabbat. For other meals, they are also delicious with a fish main course.

Whether to peel the potatoes is up to you. When they have attractive skins, I usually leave them on.

1 ½ pounds new potatoes
Salt and freshly ground black pepper
1 tablespoon plus 2 teaspoons olive
 oil

1 teaspoon fresh lemon juice
2 tablespoons chopped parsley

Scrub potatoes well. Peel if desired. Bring at least 1 inch of water to a boil in the base of a steamer. Boiling water should not reach holes in top of steamer. Set potatoes in the steamer top and sprinkle with salt. Cover tightly and steam over high heat about 20 minutes or until tender when pierced with a sharp knife.

Meanwhile, mix the olive oil, lemon juice, salt and pepper to taste, and 1 tablespoon parsley in a serving bowl.

When the potatoes are done, remove them from steamer, drain briefly on paper towels, and transfer to a serving bowl. Toss lightly with parsley mixture. Sprinkle with salt and pepper and toss again. Serve immediately, sprinkled with remaining tablespoon parsley.

Makes 4 servings

Nutritional information per serving: 190 calories; 5.9 g fat—27.1% calories from fat; 0.8 g saturated fat; 0 mg cholesterol

Double Apple Cake with Honey and Cinnamon

{ p a r e v e }

Layers of apple slices alternating with a honey-lemon batter ensure that this cake will be a winner. This cake is ideal for Succot or for Rosh Hashanah.

¾ cup plus 1 tablespoon sugar

1 teaspoon ground cinnamon

1½ cups all-purpose flour

1¼ teaspoons baking powder

¼ teaspoon baking soda

2 large sweet apples, such as Golden Delicious (total ¾ pound)

2 large eggs

¼ cup honey

5 tablespoons vegetable oil

¼ cup applesauce

1 teaspoon finely grated lemon rind

2 tablespoons fresh lemon juice

1 tablespoon water

2 tablespoons chopped walnuts

Preheat the oven to 350°F. Lightly oil an 8-inch square pan, line it with foil, and lightly oil the foil. Flour the foil lightly. Mix 1 tablespoon sugar with the cinnamon. Sift the flour, baking powder, and baking soda. Pare, halve, core, and slice the apples thin, under ¼ inch; set aside. With a mixer, beat the eggs with the remaining ¾ cup sugar on medium speed about 3 minutes or until light. Add the honey, vegetable oil, applesauce, and lemon rind and beat to blend. In a small cup, mix the lemon juice and water. With mixer on low speed, add the flour mixture and diluted lemon juice alternately in 3 batches. Add the walnuts and blend on low speed.

Spoon one-third of the batter into the prepared pan and spread evenly. Arrange half the apple slices on the batter and sprinkle evenly with half the cinnamon mixture. Spoon another third of the batter in dollops over the apples. Repeat with another layer of apples and cinnamon. Top with remaining batter; the apples may peek through in spots. Bake about 40 minutes or until a cake tester inserted in cake's center should come out clean. Cool cake in pan on a rack about 30 minutes. Run a metal spatula around cake and turn out onto rack. Let cool before serving.

. . . .

Makes 9 or 10 servings

Nutritional information per serving: 264 calories; 9 g fat—29.9% calories from fat; 1.2 g saturated fat; 43 mg cholesterol

5

Hanukkah

Creamy Pumpkin Soup with Green Vegetables

Potato Latke "Muffins"

Low-Fat Sweet Potato Latkes

Sephardic Hot Salsa

Hummus

Belgian Endive, Red Onion, and Orange Salad

Beef Stew with Dried Fruit

Red Cabbage Salad with Capers

Hearty Bean and Beef Soup

Easy Chicken Breast Paella

HANUKKAH IS THE MAJOR winter holiday and usually takes place in December. During this eight-day holiday, most of us feast on potato latkes, or pancakes, at least once. Israelis also indulge in *soofganiyot*, or fluffy doughnuts. These are the most popular Hanukkah treats and both are fried in oil.

Oil is associated with the holiday in a major way. Hanukkah customs relate to an event that occurred over two thousand years ago. At that time, the Jews drove the pagan army out of Jerusalem and rekindled the eternal light in the Holy Temple with pure oil. Legend says that only enough ritually clean oil for one day could be found, but it miraculously lasted for eight days, until more could be prepared. The eternal light was the symbol of religious freedom, which the foreign conquerors had been trying to deny.

A Hanukkah candle-lighting ritual commemorates this miracle. On each of the eight nights of the festival, colorful candles are lit while a blessing is recited, followed by joyous Hanukkah songs. The candles are set in a decorative *Hanukkiah*, a special Hanukkah candelabrum of eight branches and one separate branch whose candle is used to light the others. It is usually called a menorah in America (although that word in Hebrew actually means any candelabrum).

Because oil is related to the miracle, it is central to Hanukkah food customs. However, the oil does not have to be used for frying, which tends to require lavish amounts of fat. There are plenty of delicious, healthful dishes that fit in beautifully with the spirit of Hanukkah.

Still, as much as we want to eat healthy foods, most of us would be disappointed if we didn't have potato pancakes on Hanukkah. I have long been searching for savory latkes that use less fat than the traditional ones. My mother, who has always been nutrition conscious, gave me an idea. She turns vegetable pancake mixtures into kugels by baking them in individual casserole dishes. I like to bake individual potato kugels and to moisten each one with just a touch of oil. These onion-accented potato kugels taste like latkes. They taste great with the traditional latke accompaniment, applesauce, and are also attractive and delicious when topped with nonfat sour cream and chives.

Another way to reduce the fat at Hanukkah parties, even if you decide to prepare fried latkes, is to include plenty of other foods. Naturally, if your meal consists mainly of latkes, it's difficult to keep it light. Add a selection of colorful vegetable salads and an aromatic baked fish such as salmon with Sephardic Hot Salsa (page 59). Serve the latkes as an appetizer or side dish rather than the main dish of the meal or party. You will end up eating fewer latkes, and the menu becomes more balanced.

A favorite sweet for the holiday is *Hanukkah gelt,* or chocolate shaped as coins. My take-off on this custom is to prepare chocolate-dipped dried fruits, such as apricots, pears, and peaches half-dipped in semisweet chocolate, milk chocolate, or white chocolate. Since only a thin coating of chocolate adheres to the fruit, they are fairly low in fat. But with these treats, as with latkes, the best way to keep the fat down is to savor them in moderation. Decide ahead of time to eat only one or two, and enjoy every bite.

Creamy Pumpkin Soup with Green Vegetables

{ d a i r y }

Here is a good appetizer to eat before Hanukkah latkes. Bright green vegetables—peas cooked with leeks and lettuce leaves—provide a contrast of color and texture to the smooth soup. If you like, serve the soup with croutons made of squares or rounds of toasted bread.

2 pounds fresh sugar pumpkin or
　winter squash
1½ cups water
Salt and ground white pepper
1 cup milk
Freshly grated nutmeg (optional)
1 tablespoon butter or vegetable oil

2 leeks, white and light green parts,
　rinsed thoroughly and sliced
2 mild lettuce leaves, such as Boston,
　cut into thin strips
½ cup cooked fresh or thawed
　frozen green peas

Cut pumpkin or squash into pieces and cut off peel. Remove any seeds or stringy flesh. Cut pumpkin flesh into cubes. Put in a saucepan with the water and a pinch of salt. Cover and bring to a boil. Simmer, stirring often, about 20 minutes or until tender; add a bit more water if necessary.

Puree the pumpkin in a food processor, blender, or food mill. Return puree to the pan of cooking liquid. Simmer 5 minutes, stirring often. Add the milk and bring to a simmer. Cook over low heat, stirring often, 5 minutes. Season to taste with salt and white pepper, and nutmeg if using.

Heat the butter or vegetable oil in a skillet and add the leeks and some salt and pepper. Cover and cook over low heat 2 minutes. Add 2 tablespoons water and cook 5 more minutes, stirring occasionally, until tender but not browned. Add the lettuce and peas and cook just until lettuce wilts and peas are hot, about 2 to 3 minutes. Reheat the soup if necessary, ladle into bowls, and top each with green vegetable mixture.

. . . .

Makes 4 servings

*Nutritional information per serving: 175 calories; 5.4 g fat—25.5% calories from fat;
3.2 g saturated fat; 16 mg cholesterol*

Potato Latke "Muffins"

{ p a r e v e }

These savory latkes are baked instead of fried to save quite a bit of fat. If you're serving them in a meatless meal, you can substitute a small dollop of nonfat sour cream and a pinch of snipped chives for the applesauce.

2 tablespoons plus ½ teaspoon
  vegetable oil
2 medium onions, chopped
1 teaspoon paprika, plus a bit more
  for sprinkling
1¾ pounds baking potatoes, peeled

2 large eggs
1 teaspoon salt
½ teaspoon ground black pepper
1½ cups applesauce (optional), for
  serving

Preheat the oven to 400° F. Heat 1 tablespoon plus ½ teaspoon vegetable oil in a heavy nonstick skillet. Add the onions and sauté over medium-low heat until softened, about 10 minutes; if pan becomes dry during sautéing, add ½ tablespoon water. Add 1 teaspoon paprika, stir to blend, and remove from the heat. Let cool.

Coarsely grate the potatoes using the large grater disk of a food processor or a hand grater. Put the grated potatoes in a large strainer and squeeze out excess liquid. Transfer the potatoes to a bowl. Add the sautéed onions, eggs, salt, and pepper.

Oil 12 nonstick muffin pans, making sure to oil edges of bases. Using a ⅓-cup measure, add scant ⅓ cup potato mixture to each muffin pan. Smooth tops lightly. Spoon ¼ teaspoon oil over each, then shake a little paprika on top. Bake about 45 minutes or until brown at edges and firm.

Remove from oven and run a small, sturdy rubber spatula around the edges of the muffins to release them. You can then leave them in the pan 15 to 30 minutes to keep hot. Serve hot, accompanied by applesauce if desired.

. . . .

Makes 12 muffins or 4 to 6 servings

Nutritional information per serving: 312 calories; 10.6 g fat—29.7% calories from fat; 1.8 g saturated fat; 106 mg cholesterol

Low-Fat Sweet Potato Latkes

{ p a r e v e }

The trick to making these latkes low in fat is to fry them only briefly and to finish cooking them in the oven. This way they don't absorb much oil as they cook through.

Serve these yummy pancakes with applesauce for a meat meal or with nonfat sour cream for a dairy dinner.

1 ¾ pounds orange-fleshed sweet
    potatoes, peeled
1 medium onion
5 large egg whites
½ teaspoon salt

¼ teaspoon ground white pepper
⅓ cup all-purpose flour
About ¼ cup vegetable oil
1 ⅓ cups applesauce (optional),
    for serving

Preheat the oven to 450° F. Grate the sweet potatoes and onion, using grating disk of a food processor or large holes of a grater. Transfer them to a large bowl. Beat the egg whites lightly with the salt and pepper and add to the potato mixture. Mix well. Add the flour and mix well.

Heat 2 tablespoons of the vegetable oil in a heavy nonstick 10- to 12-inch skillet. Fill a ¼-cup measure with mixture, pressing to compact it, and turn it out in a mound into the skillet. Quickly form 3 more mounds. Flatten each with the back of a spoon to form a cake 2½ to 3 inches in diameter, pressing to compact it. Fry over medium heat 1½ minutes per side. Remove to a nonstick cookie sheet with a slotted spatula. Stir the potato mixture before frying each new batch and add a little more oil to pan.

Bake about 10 minutes or until golden brown. Turn over and bake 5 more minutes. Serve hot, accompanied by applesauce if desired.

. . . .

Makes about 4 servings

Nutritional information per serving: 459 calories; 14.5 g fat—27.9% calories from fat;
1.8 g saturated fat; 0 mg cholesterol

Sephardic Hot Salsa

{ p a r e v e }

This garlicky salsa makes a fresh, zesty topping for potato and other latkes, and has the advantage of having no fat or dairy products. The spicy mixture is a popular dipping sauce in Israel and is also terrific with baked or grilled fish.

2 or 3 medium jalapeño peppers
¼ cup garlic cloves, peeled
1 to 2 tablespoons water (optional)
¼ cup cilantro sprigs
¼ teaspoon salt

Freshly ground black pepper
1½ teaspoons cumin, preferably
    freshly ground
1 pound ripe tomatoes

Wear gloves when handling hot peppers. Remove the stems from the peppers, and cut away the seeds and ribs if you prefer a salsa that is less hot. Put the peppers and garlic in a food processor and puree until finely chopped and well blended. If necessary, add just enough water to enable the food processor to chop the mixture. Add the cilantro and process until blended. Add salt and pepper to taste, and the cumin. Remove mixture from the food processor.

Add the tomatoes to the processor and puree them. Stir in the jalapeño mixture. Refrigerate in a covered jar until ready to serve. Serve cold.

. . . .

Makes about 2½ cups or about 6 to 8 servings
Nutritional information per serving: 27 calories; 0.4 g fat—10.5% calories from fat; 0 g saturated fat; 0 mg cholesterol

Hummus

{ p a r e v e }

Hummus, which is a chickpea puree enriched with tahini (sesame paste or butter) and enlivened by fresh lemon juice and garlic, is a favorite spread in Israel for pita bread. It is especially useful in the kosher kitchen because it can appear in meat or dairy meals. I don't use any oil in my hummus, making it an important contribution to low-fat cooking that you can use as a light spread for bread instead of butter. By using canned chickpeas, you can whip this up in no time. Serve hummus as an appetizer at Hanukkah parties, as it is satisfying and helps prevent overindulgence of latkes!

2 large garlic cloves, peeled
2 15- to 16-ounce cans chickpeas,
   drained and rinsed
¼ cup tahini
¼ cup fresh lemon juice

About ½ cup water
Salt
Cayenne pepper
Paprika
1 tablespoon chopped Italian parsley

Mince the garlic in a food processor. Add the chickpeas and process to chop. Add the tahini, lemon juice, and ¼ cup water and puree until finely blended. Add more water if necessary so that mixture has consistency of a smooth spread. Season to taste with salt and cayenne. (The spread can be kept about 4 days in refrigerator.) To serve, spread hummus on plates and sprinkle it with paprika and chopped parsley.

· ·

Makes 2½ cups or about 8 servings

Nutritional information per serving: 177 calories; 5.3 g fat—26% calories from fat; 0.7 g saturated fat; 0 mg cholesterol

Belgian Endive, Red Onion, and Orange Salad

{ p a r e v e }

With its citrus dressing, this is a perfect salad for winter. Add it to Hanukkah or Purim menus to lend a light, lively touch.

2 tablespoons fresh lemon juice
2 tablespoons fresh orange juice
2¼ teaspoons sugar
1 tablespoon vegetable oil
1 tablespoon water
Salt and freshly ground black pepper

½ pound Belgian endive
2 navel oranges
4 cups bite-size pieces of butter lettuce or romaine
½ red onion

In a small bowl, whisk the lemon juice, orange juice, and sugar until sugar dissolves. Whisk in the vegetable oil and water. Season to taste with salt and pepper.

Wipe the endive and trim the bases. Cut the leaves in fairly thin slices crosswise. In a large bowl, combine the endive with 2 tablespoons dressing and toss. Let stand 5 minutes.

Cut the rind from the navel oranges, removing as much white pith as possible. Separate the orange into slices and place in a bowl.

Add the lettuce and red onion to the endive mixture and toss gently. Add remaining dressing and toss again. Taste and adjust seasoning. Serve topped with orange slices.

· ·

Makes 4 servings

Nutritional information per serving: 104 calories; 3.8 g fat—30% calories from fat; 0.5 g saturated fat; 0 mg cholesterol

Beef Stew with Dried Fruit

{ m e a t }

You can certainly enjoy a hearty beef stew during Hanukkah. This time-honored sweet and sour stew is embellished with prunes and dried apricots, as well as potatoes and carrots. To keep it low fat, I serve small portions of beef with plenty of vegetables.

1 ½ teaspoons vegetable oil

2 pounds beef chuck, cut into 1-inch cubes

2 large onions, coarsely chopped

1 quart water

Salt and freshly ground black pepper

3 pounds boiling potatoes

6 large carrots, peeled and cut into 1-inch chunks

4 ounces pitted prunes

6 ounces dried apricots

2 teaspoons ground ginger

⅓ cup brown sugar

⅓ cup white vinegar

2 tablespoons all-purpose flour

3 tablespoons chopped parsley

Heat the vegetable oil in a nonstick Dutch oven over medium heat. Add the meat in batches and brown lightly on all sides. Remove the meat from the pan with a slotted spoon. Add the onions and sauté until deep brown, about 10 minutes; lower the heat if they begin to turn too dark. Remove half the onions. Return the meat to the pan and add the water and a pinch of salt. Bring to a boil. Cover and simmer over low heat for 1½ hours.

Peel the potatoes and cut each into 3 or 4 chunks. Add the potatoes, carrots, and remaining browned onions to the pan and push vegetables down into the liquid. Bring to a boil. Cover and simmer 30 minutes. Meanwhile, put the prunes and apricots in a bowl, cover with hot water, and let stand for 30 minutes.

Add the ginger, brown sugar, and vinegar to the stew and stir gently. Remove the prunes and apricots from their liquid, reserving the liquid, and add the fruit to the pan. Uncover and simmer 30 minutes longer or until meat is very tender. Shake the pan occasionally; avoid stirring so ingredients do not break up.

Whisk the flour with ¼ cup fruit-soaking liquid in a bowl. Gradually stir in about 2 cups of cooking liquid from the pot, and return the mixture to the pan. Stir gently.

Simmer about 5 minutes. Add half the parsley. Season to taste with salt and pepper. Serve from a deep serving dish, sprinkled with remaining parsley.

· ·

Makes 4 to 6 servings

*Nutritional information per serving: 685.5 calories; 22.6 g fat—28.8% calories from fat;
8.6 g saturated fat; 77 mg cholesterol*

Red Cabbage Salad with Capers

{ p a r e v e }

Beets and fresh orange juice are the secrets to the sweet and tangy flavor of this tasty cabbage salad. It's great as a first course before braised beef or roast chicken, or with smoked turkey and rye bread for a quick meal.

3 tablespoons fresh orange juice

1 tablespoon fresh lemon juice

1 tablespoon vegetable oil

2 teaspoons sugar

Salt and freshly ground black pepper

1 pound red cabbage, shredded

1 16-ounce can shredded beets, drained

1 tablespoon capers, drained and rinsed

In a large bowl, whisk the orange juice with the lemon juice, vegetable oil, sugar, and salt and pepper to taste. Add the red cabbage and mix until cabbage is evenly moistened. Lightly stir in the beets. Taste and adjust seasoning. Serve sprinkled with capers.

· ·

Makes 6 to 8 servings

*Nutritional information per serving: 108 calories; 3.8 g fat—29.1% calories from fat;
0.4 g saturated fat; 0 mg cholesterol*

Hearty Bean and Beef Soup

{ m e a t }

*S*easoned in the Sephardic manner with tomatoes, saffron, and garlic, this warming soup of beans, meat, and potatoes is delicious for dinners during the week of Hanukkah or for Shabbat meals in the winter.

1 pound dried white beans (about 2½ cups)

1 tablespoon vegetable oil

3 medium onions, diced

1½ pounds beef shank or other cut of beef with bones

2 celery stalks, sliced

½ teaspoon saffron threads

7 cups water

1½ pounds boiling potatoes

Salt

1 28-ounce can diced tomatoes, drained

6 large garlic cloves, chopped

Cayenne pepper

⅓ cup chopped parsley

Sort the beans, discarding any broken ones and any stones. In a large bowl, soak the beans in cold water to generously cover overnight. Or, for a quicker method, cover the beans with 2 quarts water in a large saucepan, bring to a boil, and boil 2 minutes; cover and let stand off heat 1 hour.

Rinse the beans and drain. Heat the vegetable oil in a large saucepan, add the onions, and sauté over medium heat, stirring often, about 5 minutes. Add the beef, beans, celery, saffron, and water and bring to a boil. Cover and cook over low heat 1 hour.

Peel and halve the potatoes and add to the saucepan. Add a pinch of salt. Cook 30 minutes. Add the tomatoes and garlic, and cook 30 minutes more or until the meat is very tender. (Soup can be kept, covered, 2 days in refrigerator.)

To serve, remove the meat and dice it, then add it to the soup. Stir cayenne pepper to taste and parsley into the soup and serve.

· ·

Makes 6 to 8 servings

Nutritional information per serving: 408 calories; 8.4 g fat—18.2% calories from fat; 2.6 g saturated fat; 25 mg cholesterol

Easy Chicken Breast Paella

{ m e a t }

The most renowned dish of Spain, paella is made in many versions. It always has rice and olive oil combined with chicken, other meats, or seafood. The favorite flavorings are garlic, saffron, and tomatoes. Peas, bell peppers, and artichokes are sometimes added.

Paella is convenient for holiday dinners when you would like to serve a meal in one dish. It's great for Hanukkah, as well as for Purim or during the week of Succot. This is a low-fat dish even with the chicken skin on, but of course if you remove the skin, this paella will be even leaner.

3½ cups chicken broth
½ teaspoon saffron threads
1½ tablespoons olive oil
2¼ pounds boneless chicken breast halves, patted dry
Salt and freshly ground black pepper
1 medium onion, chopped
1 small red bell pepper, cored, seeded, and diced

1¾ cups white rice, preferably short-grain
2 ripe medium tomatoes, peeled, seeded, and chopped, or 2 canned tomatoes, drained and chopped
6 medium garlic cloves, minced
1½ cups frozen peas
2 tablespoons chopped parsley

Bring the broth to a simmer in a medium saucepan. Add the saffron and return to a simmer. Remove from the heat, cover, and let stand until ready to cook the rice.

Heat 1 tablespoon olive oil in a large, deep, heavy skillet, sauté pan, or wide flame-proof casserole over medium-high heat. Add the chicken in batches, sprinkle with pepper, and brown the pieces lightly, about 2 minutes on each side. Transfer to a plate.

Add the remaining ½ tablespoon olive oil to the skillet and heat over low heat. Add the onion and bell pepper and cook, stirring often, about 7 minutes or until softened. Add the rice and sauté over low heat, stirring, 2 minutes. Stir in hot saffron broth, tomatoes, and garlic. Add the chicken and bring to a simmer. Sprinkle with salt and pepper. Reduce the heat to low, cover, and cook, without stirring, 25 minutes. Add the peas, cover, and cook about 5 more minutes or until the chicken and rice are tender and the liquid is absorbed. Sprinkle with parsley and serve.

Makes 4 servings

Nutritional information per serving: 833 calories; 27.3 g fat—30% calories from fat;
7 g saturated fat; 133 mg cholesterol

6

Purim

Beet Salad with Creamy Mint Dressing

Aromatic Cauliflower and Potato Casserole

Spicy Chickpeas in Tomato Sauce

Bulgur Wheat Pilaf with Peas and Pecans

Eggplant Caponata

Turnips and Carrots Braised with Spinach

Turkey Breast with Mushrooms and Red Wine

Noodles with Poppy Seeds

Hamantaschen with Citrus Prune Filling

Chocolate-Dipped Apricots

THE JOYOUS JEWISH festival of Purim, which takes place around the time of Valentine's Day, originated with a royal romance. The holiday's story, related in the Book of Esther, tells of the Jewish beauty whom Ahasueros, the king of Persia, fell in love with. With the help of her wise uncle Mordecai, the new queen courageously foiled a plot by the king's wicked advisor Haman and saved the Jewish community from extermination.

Like Valentine's Day, Purim is celebrated with sweets; and like Halloween, it's enlivened with costumes. When I was growing up, all the little girls wanted to dress up as Queen Esther. I loved my long pink gown that my mother found at a bazaar and my cardboard crown embellished with glittery silver paper. The boys dressed either as Mordecai or the king, but some would opt to be Haman. Now children often dress as their favorite TV or movie characters.

Children have another reason to love Purim—they are allowed, and even encouraged, to make noise! At the synagogue, during the reading of the Book of Esther, every time the name "Haman" is chanted, the children use special noisemakers (called *groggers*) to make as much noise as possible. To this day, my husband smiles when he recalls how, as a little boy, he succeeded in making the loudest bang.

The most joyful holiday on the Jewish calendar, Purim is celebrated with a multi-course feast accompanied by wine. In Israel, turkey is often on the menu because in Hebrew it is called *tarnegol hodu* (meaning "India bird"), and alludes to the reference in the Book of Esther that King Ahasueros's rule extended all the way to India.

Purim is also the "cookie exchange" holiday. Neighbors, friends, and relatives bring each other colorful tins filled with cookies, chocolates, and bite-size pieces of cake. This is a popular custom in Israel, and often children are entrusted with this pleasant task.

The star items in Purim cookie gift boxes are hamantaschen, Purim's most famous food specialty. This filled three-cornered cookie, which means "Haman's pockets" or "Haman's ears" in Hebrew, is usually made of crisp cookie dough. The favorite fillings are poppy seeds, prunes, dates, or other dried fruit.

These fillings have their origins in the Purim story. According to tradition, Esther became a vegetarian when she moved into the king's palace. She ate only seeds and legumes in order to avoid eating food that was not kosher.

Many Jewish communities therefore observe a custom of including beans, chickpeas, poppy seeds, nuts, and dried fruits in Purim menus and sweets. North African Jews begin the holiday with a dish of couscous embellished with raisins and enriched with butter. Tunisians serve a first course of hard-boiled eggs with fava beans. At Purim banquets in Moroccan Jewish homes, a variety of colorful cooked salads is served as hors d'oeuvres. A Central European Purim favorite is noodles sprinkled with poppy seeds.

Even today Esther's solution of following a vegetarian diet is often the choice of Orthodox Jews who are traveling or in situations in which kosher food is difficult to find.

Whether you celebrate Purim with a turkey or a vegetarian feast, either is ideal for low-fat cooking. You can even include hamantaschen on a low-fat diet, if you make sure to eat only one or two!

Beet Salad with Creamy Mint Dressing

{ d a i r y }

This is a fat-free version of a salad from the land where the Purim story took place. In this delicious Persian appetizer, the delicately sweet beets are complemented by yogurt and nonfat sour cream. When you have fresh beets, steam them yourself. For quick meals, canned beets give surprisingly tasty results.

4 medium beets, about 1½ to 2
   inches in diameter, or 1 14- to
   16-ounce can sliced beets
1½ cups plain nonfat yogurt
½ cup nonfat sour cream

3 tablespoons chopped fresh mint, or
   2 to 3 teaspoons dried mint,
   crumbled
Salt and freshly ground black pepper

If using fresh beets, rinse them, taking care not to pierce their skins. Put 1 inch of water in a steamer and bring to a boil. Place the beets on a steamer rack above boiling water. Cover tightly and steam 50 to 60 minutes or until tender, adding boiling water occasionally if the water evaporates. Let cool. Run the beets under cold water and slip off the skins. Cut beets into ¾-inch dice.

If using canned beets, drain and dice them.

Mix the yogurt with the sour cream, mint, and salt and pepper to taste. Spoon into a shallow serving bowl. Fold beets partly into dressing, so that they still show. Chill and serve cold.

. . . .

Makes 4 servings

Nutritional information per serving: 103 calories; 0.3 g fat—3.2% calories from fat;
0.1 g saturated fat; 2 mg cholesterol

Aromatic Cauliflower and Potato Casserole

{ p a r e v e }

This flavorful kugel of smooth cauliflower and potato puree, accented by sautéed onion with garlic, hot peppers, and spices, is suitable for a dairy or a meat meal.

1 ¾ pounds boiling potatoes, unpeeled, halved

Salt and freshly ground black pepper

1 medium cauliflower (about 1 ½ pounds)

2 tablespoons vegetable oil

1 medium onion, chopped

4 large garlic cloves, minced

1 ½ teaspoons ground cumin

1 teaspoon turmeric

1 large egg

2 large egg whites

Cayenne pepper

½ teaspoon paprika

Preheat the oven to 375°F. Put the potatoes in a large saucepan with water to cover, add a pinch of salt and bring to a boil. Cover and simmer over low heat about 30 minutes or until very tender. Remove with a slotted spoon; leave until cool enough to handle, and reserve the cooking water. Remove peels. Mash the potatoes in a large bowl.

Divide the cauliflower into medium florets. Cut outer peel from large stalks and slice stalks. Return the potato cooking liquid to a boil and add the cauliflower; add hot water to cover if needed. Simmer uncovered about 15 minutes or until very tender. Drain well and cool. Puree the cauliflower in a food processor, leaving a few chunks.

Heat 1 ½ tablespoons vegetable oil in a medium skillet, add the onion, and sauté 5 minutes over medium heat. Add the garlic, 1 teaspoon cumin, and ½ teaspoon turmeric; sauté 1 minute.

Add the cauliflower puree to the potatoes. Blend in the egg and egg whites. Add the remaining ½ teaspoon cumin and ½ teaspoon turmeric. Season well with salt, pepper, and cayenne to taste. Stir in the onion mixture.

Oil a shallow 2-quart baking dish. Add the cauliflower mixture. Sprinkle the remaining ½ tablespoon vegetable oil over top. Sprinkle with paprika. Bake about 45 minutes or until firm on top. Serve hot.

. . . .

Makes 6 servings

Nutritional information per serving: 176 calories; 5.9 g fat—28.6% calories from fat; 0.9 g saturated fat; 35 mg cholesterol

Spicy Chickpeas in Tomato Sauce

{ p a r e v e }

Chickpeas may have been on Esther's menus, as they are favorites in Persian cooking. In this dish, cumin, coriander, and garlic give the chickpeas and their sauce an enticing aroma. Add the amount of jalapeño peppers you prefer to make the dish mild or fiery hot. I like to serve the chickpeas as a main course with rice, with a cucumber salad on the side.

2 15- or 16-ounce cans chickpeas (garbanzo beans), or 3½ to 4 cups cooked chickpeas (see Note below)

1 tablespoon olive oil

1 small onion, chopped

1 to 3 jalapeño peppers, seeded and chopped

4 large garlic cloves, chopped

1½ pounds ripe tomatoes, diced, or 1 28-ounce can diced tomatoes, drained

2 teaspoons ground cumin

1 teaspoon ground coriander

½ teaspoon turmeric

Salt

2 tablespoons tomato paste

If using canned chickpeas, drain and rinse them well.

Heat the olive oil in a sauté pan or wide saucepan, add the onion, and sauté over medium heat for 5 minutes. Add the jalapeño peppers and garlic, and sauté ½ minute. Add the tomatoes, cumin, coriander, turmeric, and salt to taste and simmer 10 minutes. Add the tomato paste and ¾ cup chickpea cooking liquid or water and bring to a boil. Add the chickpeas and simmer uncovered over medium-low heat about 10 minutes or until sauce is of desired thickness. Taste and adjust seasoning. Serve hot.

. . . .

Makes 6 main-course servings, with rice

Nutritional information per serving: 231 calories; 4.5 g fat—16.9% calories from fat; 0.5 g saturated fat; 0 mg cholesterol

N O T E :   To cook dried chickpeas, use 1½ cups dried chickpeas to obtain 3½ to 4 cups cooked chickpeas. Sort them by putting enough chickpeas on a plate to make one layer and picking over the chickpeas, discarding pebbles and broken or discolored peas. Transfer to a colander. Sort remaining chickpeas. Rinse peas.

Put chickpeas in a bowl, cover generously with cold water, and let stand 8 hours or overnight. Or, to quick-soak, put the chickpeas in a medium saucepan, add 4 or 5 cups water, bring to a boil, and boil uncovered 2 minutes. Remove from heat, cover, and let stand 1 hour. Drain and rinse.

Put the soaked chickpeas in a saucepan. Add 6 cups cold water and bring to a boil. Cover and simmer about 1½ hours, until almost tender, adding hot water occasionally to keep them covered with water. Add a pinch of salt and continue simmering 30 to 60 minutes or until tender. Reserve cooking liquid.

Bulgur Wheat Pilaf with Peas and Pecans
{ m e a t   o r   p a r e v e }

Make this pilaf with vegetable broth and serve it as a vegetarian entree accompanied by yogurt and a Mediterranean salad of diced tomatoes, cucumbers, and green onions. The pilaf also makes a good side dish with grilled or roasted chicken.

1½ cups medium bulgur wheat
3 large garlic cloves, minced
3 cups vegetable or chicken broth or
    water

Salt and freshly ground black pepper
1½ cups frozen peas
¼ cup chopped parsley
¼ cup toasted diced pecans

In a dry deep skillet, toast the bulgur with the garlic over medium heat for 2 minutes. Add the broth, salt, and pepper and bring to boil. Reduce the heat to low, cover, and cook 8 minutes. Add the peas and cook 7 minutes or until the water is absorbed.

Gently stir in the parsley. Taste and adjust the seasoning. Transfer to a serving dish, sprinkle with pecans, and serve immediately.

Makes 4 main-course or 6 side-dish servings
Nutritional information per serving: 269 calories; 5.7 g fat—18.2% calories from fat;
0.8 g saturated fat; 1 mg cholesterol

Eggplant Caponata

{ p a r e v e }

With its sweet, sour, and piquant flavors, this zesty salad is popular at Italian restaurants and delis and is perfect for the low-fat kosher kitchen. The eggplant is cooked with tomatoes, onions, and a small amount of olive oil. Vinegar and capers lend a tangy flavor, while green olives add richness. The salad is pareve, easy to make, and keeps well.

Old-fashioned versions of this dish call for deep-frying the eggplant, but I prefer to braise it instead. If your market carries Japanese eggplants, which have fewer seeds, they'll give the best flavor.

1 ½ pounds eggplant (preferably Japanese), unpeeled

2 tablespoons olive oil

1 medium onion, sliced

2 celery stalks, thinly sliced

1 small yellow or red bell pepper, cored, seeded, and diced (optional)

Salt and freshly ground black pepper

1 8-ounce can tomato sauce

1 14½-ounce can diced tomatoes, drained

2 teaspoons sugar

1 tablespoon red wine vinegar

⅓ cup pitted green olives, halved

2 tablespoons capers, rinsed

2 tablespoons raisins

6 slices crusty bread or toast, for serving

Cut the eggplant into 1-inch dice. Heat the olive oil in a large, heavy skillet or sauté pan. Add the onion, celery, and bell pepper and sauté over medium heat 5 minutes. Add the eggplant, salt, and pepper and sauté over medium-high heat, stirring, for 2 minutes. Cover and cook over medium heat, stirring occasionally, 3 minutes. Add the tomato sauce and tomatoes. Cover and cook over low heat 15 minutes. Add the sugar, vinegar, olives, capers, and raisins. Cover and simmer over low heat, stirring often, 10 minutes or until eggplant is tender. Taste and adjust seasoning. Serve cold or at room temperature, with bread.

. . . .

Makes 6 servings

*Nutritional information per serving: 199 calories; 6.7 g fat—28.6% calories from fat;
1 g saturated fat; 0 mg cholesterol*

Turnips and Carrots Braised with Spinach
{ m e a t   o r   p a r e v e }

*M*iddle Eastern cooks know that winter root vegetables taste great when simmered with garlic and with greens like spinach or Swiss chard. Serve this tasty vegetable medley with chicken or meat for Shabbat, or as a vegetarian entree with rice for Purim.

1 tablespoon olive or vegetable oil
4 garlic cloves, chopped
½ cup finely chopped spinach leaves
1 medium onion, chopped

1 ¼ cups vegetable or chicken broth
¾ pound carrots, peeled and cubed
¾ pound turnips, peeled and cubed
Salt and freshly ground black pepper

Heat 1 teaspoon oil in a deep nonstick skillet or sauté pan. Add the garlic and sauté 15 seconds. Add the spinach and sauté about 30 seconds or until dry. Remove the spinach mixture.

Add the remaining 2 teaspoons oil to the pan. Add the onion and sauté over medium heat about 3 minutes or until beginning to brown. Add the broth and bring to a boil. Add the carrots and turnips, cover, and simmer 15 minutes. Add the spinach-garlic mixture and cook 5 minutes or until vegetables are tender, adding a few tablespoons water if the pan becomes dry. Taste and adjust seasoning. Serve hot.

Makes 4 servings

Nutritional information per serving: 161 calories; 5.2 g fat—27.8% calories from fat; 0.8 g saturated fat; 1 mg cholesterol

Turkey Breast with Mushrooms and Red Wine

{ m e a t }

To celebrate Purim the Israeli way, serve turkey as a main course. It's delicious in this French-style wine sauce, flavored with onion, carrot, garlic, thyme, and chicken broth. Serve the turkey over rice or couscous, which gain great flavor from the sauce. Other good accompaniments are mashed potatoes or baked butternut squash.

2 pounds turkey breast fillets
2 tablespoons vegetable oil
1 medium onion, coarsely chopped
1 medium carrot, coarsely chopped
2 large garlic cloves, crushed
1 cup chicken broth
½ cup dry red wine
½ teaspoon dried thyme

1 bay leaf
Salt and freshly ground black pepper
3 tablespoons cold water
2 teaspoons tomato paste
1 tablespoon cornstarch, potato
    starch, or arrowroot
6 ounces mushrooms, quartered
6 cups hot cooked rice, for serving

Pat the turkey dry. Heat the vegetable oil in a heavy casserole or Dutch oven, add the turkey, and brown lightly over medium heat on all sides, about 2 minutes on each side, working in batches if necessary. Remove to a plate. Add the onion and carrot and sauté, stirring often, until well browned. Stir in the garlic.

Add the broth, wine, thyme, bay leaf, salt, and pepper and bring to a boil. Add the turkey, cover, and simmer over low heat about 30 minutes or until it is tender when pierced with a sharp knife. Remove the turkey to a board and keep it warm.

Whisk the water into the tomato paste in a small bowl. Add the cornstarch and whisk to a smooth paste. Gradually whisk the mixture into the simmering sauce. Return to a boil, whisking. Strain into a medium saucepan, pressing on vegetables, then discarding them. Add the mushrooms to the sauce and simmer 5 minutes. Taste and adjust seasoning.

Slice the turkey. Spoon the mushrooms and some sauce over the turkey. Serve remaining sauce separately. Serve turkey and sauce with rice.

. . . .

Makes 4 to 6 servings

Nutritional information per serving: 571 calories; 15.3 g fat—25.3% calories from fat; 3.4 g saturated fat; 89 mg cholesterol

Noodles with Poppy Seeds

{ d a i r y   o r   p a r e v e }

Prepare this quick and easy, slightly sweet dish to remember that Esther's diet in the Persian palace consisted largely of nuts and seeds. I like to serve this at a dairy meal with sweet vegetables like carrots and butternut squash. If you make it with pareve margarine, it's also good with chicken or turkey.

8 ounces wide noodles
Salt
2 tablespoons soft butter or
   margarine

2 tablespoons poppy seeds
2½ teaspoons sugar

Cook the noodles in a large pot of boiling salted water about 5 minutes or until tender. Drain and transfer to a serving bowl. Add the butter and toss to blend and melt the butter. Add the poppy seeds, salt to taste, and 1½ teaspoons sugar and toss again. Sprinkle with remaining teaspoon sugar and serve.

. . . .

Makes 4 servings

*Nutritional information per serving: 300 calories; 10 g fat—30% calories from fat;
4.3 g saturated fat; 69 mg cholesterol*

Hamantaschen with Citrus Prune Filling

{ d a i r y   o r   p a r e v e – d e p e n d i n g   o n   m a r g a r i n e }

*T*he dough for these delicious hamantaschen is made quickly in a food processor and is easy to roll out. To keep their shape clean, you have to resist the temptation to overfill them. I like to make small hamantaschen, as they bake more evenly and are more attractive. Besides, small sweets make perfect sense for low-fat eating.

DOUGH

1 large egg

4 tablespoons water

2½ cups all-purpose flour

½ cup confectioners' sugar

1 teaspoon baking powder

¼ teaspoon salt

7 tablespoons cold margarine, cut into small pieces

1½ teaspoons grated orange rind

FILLING

6 ounces pitted prunes

1½ tablespoons very finely chopped pecans

3 tablespoons orange marmalade

1½ teaspoons grated lemon rind

Confectioners' sugar, for sprinkling (optional)

To make the dough, beat the egg with the water. Combine the flour, confectioners' sugar, baking powder, and salt in a food processor. Process briefly to blend. Scatter the margarine pieces over the mixture. Mix using an on/off motion until mixture resembles coarse meal. Sprinkle with grated rind and pour the egg mixture evenly over the mixture in the processor. Process with on/off motion, scraping down occasionally, until the dough just begins to come together but does not form a ball. If mixture is dry, add another tablespoon water, adding it to the mixture 1 teaspoon at a time, and process briefly again between each addition.

With a rubber spatula, transfer the dough to a sheet of plastic wrap. Wrap it and push it together, shaping the dough into a flat disk. Refrigerate at least 2 hours or overnight.

To make the filling, cover the prunes with boiling water and soak 15 minutes. Drain the prunes, halve them, and puree in a food processor. Mix the prune puree with the pecans, marmalade, and lemon rind.

Grease a baking sheet. Cut the dough into 4 pieces. Roll out 1 piece on a lightly floured surface until about ⅛ inch thick. Using a 3-inch cookie cutter, cut in circles.

Brush the edges lightly with water. Put 1 teaspoon filling in the center of each circle. Pull up the edges of the circle in 3 arcs that meet in center above the filling. Close them firmly. Pinch edges to seal. Put on a greased baking sheet and refrigerate. Wrap and refrigerate scraps at least 30 minutes. Roll and shape more hamantaschen from remaining dough and from scraps. Refrigerate 1 hour or up to overnight to firm remaining dough.

Position a rack in the center of the oven and preheat to 375° F. Bake the hamantaschen about 14 minutes, or until they are light golden at edges and golden brown on bottom. Cool on a rack. If you like, serve the hamantaschen sprinkled with confectioners' sugar.

. . . .

Makes about 32 hamantaschen

Nutritional information per serving: 167 calories; 5.3 g fat—27.7% calories from fat; 0.9 g saturated fat; 13 mg cholesterol

Chocolate-Dipped Apricots
{ p a r e v e }

These candies make a beautiful and delectable sweet to add to your boxes of Purim treats. Use pareve bittersweet or semisweet chocolate so these treats can be enjoyed at any time. If you prefer to dip the apricots in white or milk chocolate, serve them at dairy meals. You can keep the dipped apricots in an airtight container in the refrigerator for one week.

12 ounces dried apricots
10 ounces fine-quality bittersweet or
   semisweet chocolate, chopped

Line 3 or 4 trays with foil or waxed paper. Melt the chocolate in a medium bowl suspended over hot water over low heat, stirring very often with a rubber spatula. Stir until smooth. Remove from the heat. Cool the melted chocolate, stirring often, until it reaches 88°F. or slightly cooler than body temperature. Set the container of chocolate in a bowl of warm water off the heat, making sure it sits squarely in the bowl and does not move around.

Holding an apricot at one end, dip half the fruit in the chocolate. Gently shake the apricot and let excess chocolate drip into the bowl. Gently wipe the apricot against the rim of the bowl to remove excess chocolate. Set the apricot on the prepared tray. Dip more fruit. If chocolate thickens, set it briefly over hot water so it becomes fluid again.

Let the dipped apricots stand at room temperature until set. If the coating does not set within 10 minutes, refrigerate the fruit about 10 minutes or until set. Carefully remove from foil.

. . . .

Makes about ¾ pound dipped fruit or about 12 servings
Nutritional information per serving: 203 calories; 7.2 g fat—28.4% calories from fat;
4.2 g saturated fat; 0 mg cholesterol

7

Passover

Haroset with Dates and Almonds

Easy Gefilte Fish

Chicken Soup with Spring Vegetables

Roasted Salmon with Asparagus

Roast Turkey Breast with Potatoes and Rosemary

Baked Chicken with Garlic, Cumin, and Tomatoes

Matzo and Vegetable Stuffing

Artichoke Hearts with Mushroom-Tomato Salad

Beet Salad with Orange Dressing

Broccoli, Carrots, and Potatoes with Lemon Herb Dressing

Glazed Carrots with a Touch of Cinnamon

Mock Noodle Kugel with Apples, Lemon, and Pecans

Matzo and Cottage Cheese Kugel with Dried Fruit

Passover Hazelnut-Almond Cake with Raspberry Sauce

Genoa Almond Cake with Poached Fruit

Walnut Meringues

"WHY IS THIS NIGHT different from all other nights?" is the question recited by Jewish children throughout the world during the Passover Seder, the ceremonial holiday dinner. The response in the *Haggadah*, the Seder book of prayers and songs, is that Passover commemorates the exodus of the ancient Hebrews from slavery in Egypt to freedom. Indeed, the time of Passover is called *zeman heiruteinu*, the time of our liberation.

Passover is an eight-day holiday that takes place in late March or early April. The Seder is prepared on the first and second nights of Passover (in Israel, on the first night only). The word *Passover*, or *Pesach* in Hebrew, comes from the story recounted in the Torah that during the Tenth Plague, in which the firstborn sons of the Egyptian oppressors were killed, the sons of the Israelites were spared, or "passed over."

Food eaten on Passover must be not only kosher but also kosher for Passover. In the broadest sense, this means it should not contain *hametz*, or leavening.

Leavening literally means yeast or baking powder. Therefore, the most important Passover food is unleavened bread, or matzo. Matzo is so central to Passover that the holiday is often called "The Matzo Holiday." This flatbread is a reminder of the bread that the Hebrew slaves ate during their hurried departure from Egypt, when they didn't have time to wait for their bread to rise.

On Passover, flour made from wheat is also prohibited because it can "leaven," or ferment, naturally upon contact with liquid (as in making sourdough starter). The only "flours" used for baking or for thickening sauces are matzo meal, which is made from already baked matzo, and potato starch. Matzos, matzo meal, and a finer version called cake meal are the basis for a variety of dumplings, stuffings, kugels, and light cakes. Matzo is even made into a sort of breakfast cereal, called *farfel*, which can also be used to make stuffings.

Ashkenazic rabbis extended the proscription against eating flour on Passover to legumes, or *kitniyot*, a term used to include beans, peas, corn, rice, and other grains; Orthodox rabbis also include green beans in this group. Thus corn oil, corn syrup, and cornstarch are not used by Ashkenazic Jews. Neither is powdered sugar, or confectioners' sugar, as it contains a small amount of cornstarch. Since many processed foods could contain ingredients that are not kosher for Passover, the easiest way to tell is to look for a "Kosher for Passover" label on the package. Supermarkets carry an increasing variety of foods that are kosher for Passover, from Passover noodles made with matzo meal and potato starch to Passover pizza mix to breakfast cereals to all sorts of cookie and cake mixes. An even greater selection can be found in kosher grocery stores.

Preparing for Passover

Before the holiday, you put away your usual dishes, flatware, and pots and take out different sets used only on Passover—one set for meat and one for dairy foods. There is a special procedure, called *kashering*, for making certain utensils used year-round suitable for Passover; for information on how to do this, consult your rabbi. In addition, the oven, burners, refrigerator, and kitchen sink must be thoroughly cleaned.

The night before Passover, the house is thoroughly searched for bread or cookie crumbs in a ceremony called "checking for hametz." The head of the house checks carefully with a candle. In fact, by this time the house has been completely cleaned, so often the children put out a few paper plates containing crumbs in obvious places, so they will be found. The next morning, this hametz is burned.

For practical purposes, most people usually have quite a few packages of food that is not kosher for Passover remaining in the house. Generally it is put in a cabinet, which is then locked during Passover. This food is symbolically sold to someone who is not Jewish through the local rabbi.

The Seder Plate

The Seder ceremony features special foods that recall the Hebrews' slavery in ancient Egypt and their escape to the desert. Small portions are displayed on an attractive Seder plate, which contains labeled sections for each food. Reddish brown *haroset*, a sweet and spicy spread made of fruits and nuts, represents the mortar and bricks the Israelite slaves were forced to make. Haroset is delicious and is the best loved of the Seder foods. *Maror*, or bitter herbs, which is freshly grated horseradish or bitter lettuce leaves, symbolizes the bitterness of the slaves' lives.

Other items on the Seder plates recall a later period in Jewish history, when the Holy Temple in Jerusalem existed. *Beitza*, a roasted hard-boiled egg, and *zeroah*, a roasted lamb bone or poultry neck, recall the sacrifices brought to the Temple.

Passover is known as the Festival of Spring. *Karpas*, a celery stalk or a parsley sprig, appears on the Seder plate as a sign of the season.

Also on the table is a plate with three matzos, covered with a decorative cloth.

The Tastings Before the Meal

During the course of the Seder, each person drinks four glasses of wine; their size can vary. The wine must be kosher for Passover, but it can be sweet or dry. Many families prefer sweet wine; others substitute grape juice.

After the first glass of wine, there is a tasting of the karpas: celery or parsley is dipped in salt water, a symbol of the tears of slavery, before it is eaten. Next the story of the *Haggadah* is read, followed by a tasting of the matzo. The ritual continues with the bitter herbs; first they are tasted alone, then with a bit of haroset, then sandwiched between pieces of matzo.

Next comes a tasting of hard-boiled eggs dipped in salt water. Finally, the meal is served, ending with a taste of the *afikoman*, a matzo that is set aside during the Seder for this purpose.

Cooking for the Seder

It's only natural that Seder menus are copious. Passover celebrations call for a lavish feast with family and friends. By the time we've read the *Haggadah*, our appetites have been stimulated by the wine and by the sight and smell of the food on the Seder plate. When it's finally time to eat, most of us are famished. No wonder we tend to overeat!

So how do we keep our Seder menus healthy? By providing plenty of light dishes, so that even if we eat them in generous quantities, we won't consume too much fat. Of course, I'm not suggesting you put your family on a diet during the Seder. Instead, reduce the fat in subtle ways. For example, cut down on the oil when you sauté onions. All you need is enough oil to barely coat the bottom of the pan.

Tradition and seasonal cooking give us the keys to a nutritious menu. Passover is the "Festival of Spring," and fresh, colorful menus with plenty of vegetables and fruit are perfect for celebrating it.

A good trick for preparing lower-fat menus is to choose highly seasoned dishes. The sweet and sour Ashkenazic favorites, the spicy Yemenite dishes seasoned with cumin and turmeric, and the Sephardic dishes enlivened with cilantro and lemon juice are all ideal candidates. When food has plenty of flavor, you will enjoy it more and miss the fat less.

In planning the Seder meal, there is also the issue of timing. You don't know exactly at what time you'll serve the meal, as it's hard to predict how long reciting the

Haggadah will take. This depends on how much of the *Haggadah* is chanted and at what length the story of Passover is actually recounted.

Therefore, most of the Passover menu should be composed of do-ahead dishes. Dishes to be served hot should reheat easily. Soups and braised dishes or stews are practical for Passover. Sautéed foods and delicate roasts or steaks that must be served the moment they're finished or done just to a specific internal temperature are not.

Chicken soup with matzo balls is a Passover favorite in many Ashkenazic families. I sometimes prepare a springtime version of the soup by adding fresh asparagus spears and chopped parsley. To make the matzo balls low in fat and extra light, I make them with egg whites and no yolks.

For a main course, I like to serve turkey breast, either roasted or braised. If I prepare a sauce, I make it from turkey broth and thicken it with potato starch. Turkey breast makes a festive, low-fat entree perfect for the Seder. As an accompaniment, I like roasted or boiled new potatoes or a light kugel. I nearly always prepare a colorful Israeli salad of diced cucumbers and tomatoes, which is a better choice than a green salad for the Seder, as it can be made several hours ahead. Appetizers of cooked vegetables, such as Artichoke Hearts with Mushroom-Tomato Salad (page 96) or Beet Salad with Orange Dressing (page 97) also help make the dinner colorful and healthful.

With the restrictions on flour and leavening, it might seem that the selection of Passover desserts and baked goods would be quite small. In fact, an astonishingly varied repertoire of Passover desserts has been developed over the centuries by Jewish women. For many families, Passover is the most eagerly anticipated holiday and Passover desserts are cherished.

Nearly all categories of desserts, cakes, and other baked goods made during the rest of the year have Passover equivalents. Matzos, matzo meal, cake meal, and potato starch are the basis for a variety of cakes, tortes, cookies, brownies, muffins, and pies. Even rolls can be made for Passover from cream puff dough made with matzo meal instead of flour. The desserts have a different flavor and texture from those of the rest of the year but are very much enjoyed as special once-a-year treats.

Coconut and almond macaroons are traditional sweets for Passover because they are flourless. Modern flourless chocolate and nut cakes are also well suited to the holiday.

The favorite dessert flavorings are citrus juice and rind, cinnamon, cocoa, nuts, coconut, and Passover wine. Many people avoid vanilla and other extracts because they are alcohol based and may not be kosher for Passover. Fortunately, kosher for

Passover chocolate is widely available. Many Passover cakes are preferred plain, but when frosting is desired, it is made of granulated or superfine sugar instead of confectioners' sugar.

Passover cakes are usually lighter than other cakes. Because matzo meal and potato starch do not have the gluten of wheat flour, they cannot hold a large proportion of fat or liquid. In many homes, Passover cakes are made without dairy products, so they will be pareve. Thus Passover cakes tend to be low in saturated fat and, compared to the average cake, low in total fat. Since they do not contain baking powder or yeast, however, they depend on eggs to make them rise. To adapt them to low-fat and lower cholesterol baking, you can replace a portion of the eggs (about half) with whipped egg whites.

The classic Passover dessert is a delicate-textured sponge cake. A light, airy cake accented with the fresh flavor of grated lemon or orange zest, it is the perfect finale for the copious Seder meals of the first two nights of Passover. Popular variations are prepared with ground almonds, hazelnuts, walnuts, or pecans. When accompanied by fresh strawberries or a strawberry sauce, a slice of one of these light cakes is the ideal springtime dessert. Meringues, whether plain or Walnut Meringues as on page 106, are traditional Passover treats that also happen to be low in fat. For sweets to enjoy with coffee, tea, or milk, prepare Chocolate-Dipped Apricots (page 80) but use chocolate that is kosher for Passover.

Haroset with Dates and Almonds
{ p a r e v e }

Haroset, one of the special foods that appears on the Seder plate, is a sweet mixture of fruit, nuts, and spices. After the ceremonial sampling of haroset, it remains on the table so everyone can enjoy it throughout the meal. Haroset is one of the few dishes made by Jews all over the world, although the recipe changes from one community to another, and there are family variations too. The majority of Jews in America are of Ashkenazic origin and many assume that their traditional haroset, made of apples, walnuts, and wine, is universal. In fact, haroset might not contain any of these ingredients. Sephardic Jews favor dried fruits, especially dates, which contribute a rich texture and intense taste. Bananas and pears appear in the haroset of Iranian Jews. The nuts in the haroset can vary, too. Sephardic Jews often include almonds or pine nuts, French Jews might use hazelnuts, and pecans are becoming increasingly popular in Israel.

When I was growing up in an Ashkenazic family in Washington, D.C., our haroset was always moistened with sweet red Passover wine. At my brother's home in Jerusalem I was amazed that the haroset included date juice. This time-honored recipe is from his wife's Indian family.

Cinnamon is the most common spice for haroset. At an Iranian Jewish market, I recently found haroset spice mixture containing cardamom, cinnamon, ginger, and nutmeg. Haroset might also be flavored with cloves, saffron, or even black pepper. Haroset's texture can range from smooth to chunky.

1 cup almonds
8 ounces pitted dates, halved and
  checked for pits
About ¼ cup sweet red wine

1 teaspoon ground cinnamon
½ teaspoon ground ginger
1 large apple, peeled
6 matzos, for serving

Finely chop the almonds in a food processor and remove to a bowl. Add the dates, the wine, and the cinnamon and ginger to the processor and grind until fairly smooth. Mix the date mixture into the bowl with the almonds. Grate the apple down to the core on the large holes of a grater. Stir into the date mixture. Add more wine by teaspoons if necessary to make a mixture that is spreadable but still thick. Serve with matzos.

Makes about 12 servings

Nutritional information per serving: 288 calories; 9.8 g fat—29.7% calories from fat;
0.9 g saturated fat; 0 mg cholesterol

Easy Gefilte Fish

{ p a r e v e }

Gefilte fish originally meant stuffed fish, but today the term refers to fish balls. They can be large or small, delicately flavored or sweet.

Making gefilte fish used to be a lot of work. I remember my grandfather and my mother chopping fish in a round wooden bowl with a small square knife; it seemed to take forever to get the fish fine enough. Today making gefilte fish is quick and easy. Instead of filleting fish, buy already filleted fish and grind it in a food processor. The mixture will be ready in a few minutes.

As for the fish, the traditional choices are pike, whitefish, and carp, but that happened only because those freshwater fish were readily available in Poland and other Eastern European countries, where the recipes developed. Use whatever fish you like. I prefer whitefish mixed with sea bass or halibut.

Classic recipes call for cooking the fish balls in broth made from the fish bones. If you don't have fish broth already made and want a quickly made broth, just cook onions and carrots with the gefilte fish to make a vegetable broth, and reinforce it with powdered pareve "chicken-flavored" broth. Serve gefilte fish balls cold, garnished with carrot slices and accompanied by horseradish prepared with beets.

1 ½ pounds whitefish fillets
¾ pound sea bass or halibut fillets
1 large egg
2 large egg whites
2 medium onions, finely chopped
Salt
½ teaspoon ground black pepper
5 tablespoons matzo meal

1 small carrot, peeled and coarsely grated
1 quart Quick Fish Broth (page 171)
2 large carrots, peeled and sliced
Horseradish prepared with beets, for serving

Check the fish fillets and remove any bones. Lightly beat the egg with the egg whites. Grind half the fish in a food processor until very fine. Add half the egg mixture, half the chopped onion, 1 teaspoon salt, and ¼ teaspoon pepper. Transfer to a large bowl. Process the remaining fish with the remaining egg mixture, onion, 1 teaspoon salt, and pepper. Add to the bowl. Add matzo meal and grated carrot and mix well.

In a large, deep saucepan or pot, bring fish broth to a simmer with sliced carrots. Season lightly with salt.

With moistened hands, shape the fish mixture into ovals or balls, using about ¼ cup mixture for each one. Carefully drop the fish balls into the simmering broth. Return to a simmer, cover, and cook over low heat about 1 hour. Let cool in broth. Refrigerate for 4 hours or overnight before serving.

To serve, garnish each fish ball with a carrot slice from the broth. Serve with horseradish.

. . . .

Makes 9 or 10 servings

Nutritional information per serving: 185 calories; 5.9 g fat—29.6% calories from fat;
1.1 g saturated fat; 85 mg cholesterol

Chicken Soup with Spring Vegetables
{ m e a t }

*P*assover is the time to celebrate spring, and what better way to do this than with this tasty thyme-scented chicken soup with asparagus and carrots? Serve the soup with the vegetables as a light first course during the Seder, and save the chicken for salads. If you prefer a heartier main-course soup during Passover week, cut the chicken into strips and serve them in the soup. You can also add Potato Kneidlach (page 26).

1 ½ pounds chicken breast, with
    bone
1 ½ pounds chicken thighs or
    drumsticks
1 large onion, whole or sliced
1 bay leaf
4 sprigs fresh thyme, or ½ teaspoon
    dried

About 2 quarts water
4 medium carrots (¾ pound total),
    peeled and cut into 2-inch lengths
1 pound medium-width asparagus,
    peeled
Salt and freshly ground black pepper
⅓ cup chopped green onions
    (scallions)

Put the chicken in a large casserole or pot. Add the onion, bay leaf, and thyme and cover ingredients generously with water. Bring to a boil. Skim foam from surface. Cover and simmer gently 1 hour.

Add carrots to the casserole, cover, and cook over low heat 45 minutes. Discard the bay leaf and thyme sprigs. Skim fat completely from soup. (This is easier to do when soup is cold.) Remove skin from chicken, remove meat from bones, and cut into strips; return the chicken to the soup. (Soup can be kept, covered, 3 days in refrigerator.)

Reheat the soup, add the asparagus, and cook about 10 minutes or until just tender. Season to taste with salt and pepper. Stir in green onions and serve.

. . . .

Makes about 6 servings

Nutritional information per serving: 328 calories; 7.5 g fat—21% calories from fat;
2 g saturated fat; 130 mg cholesterol

Roasted Salmon with Asparagus

{ p a r e v e }

This is one of the best springtime entrees and is easy to make, too. The salmon and asparagus both take less than 15 minutes to roast. I like to roast them in separate pans to make it easy to gently stir the asparagus during cooking, without disturbing the salmon.

1 pound medium-width or thick asparagus

1 tablespoon plus 2 teaspoons extra-virgin olive oil

Salt and freshly ground black pepper

1 ¼ pounds salmon fillet, preferably tail section, about 1 inch thick

1 tablespoon fresh lemon juice

1 teaspoon ground coriander

½ teaspoon dried thyme

Lemon wedges, for serving

4 large boiling potatoes, boiled, for serving

Preheat the oven to 450° F. Rinse the asparagus and cut off the tough bases, about 1 to 1½ inches. Put the asparagus in a roasting pan or large shallow baking dish so it makes one or two layers. Sprinkle evenly with 1 tablespoon olive oil and with salt and pepper to taste; toss to distribute seasonings.

Set the fish in a heavy roasting pan lined with foil. Sprinkle with lemon juice and with remaining 2 teaspoons olive oil and rub them over fish. Sprinkle the fish with coriander and thyme and rub in lightly. Sprinkle evenly with salt and pepper.

Put pan of fish and pan of asparagus in the oven. Roast the fish and asparagus uncovered, shaking asparagus dish once or twice to turn spears, about 12 minutes. When done, the asparagus should be crisp-tender; the fish should just flake and have changed color in the thickest part. Serve the fish and asparagus with lemon wedges and hot boiled potatoes.

. . . .

Makes 4 servings

Nutritional information per serving: 365 calories; 11.9 g fat—29.2% calories from fat;
1.8 g saturated fat; 89 mg cholesterol

Roast Turkey Breast with Potatoes and Rosemary

{ m e a t }

Turkey breasts make great roasts. They're easy to carve, their cooking time is not much longer than a chicken's, and their meat is white and lean. Serve this turkey for Passover, for Shabbat, or for Thanksgiving. If you like, you can turn the juices into a white wine sauce. To thicken the gravy for Passover, use potato starch rather than cornstarch or flour.

To keep this entree low in fat, serve the meat without its skin. Season the meat under the skin with thyme and rosemary, but leave the skin on during roasting so that it keeps the meat moist.

1 4-pound turkey breast with skin
  and bones

3 tablespoons olive oil

1¼ teaspoons dried leaf thyme

Salt and freshly ground black pepper

4 fresh rosemary sprigs

3 pounds medium red potatoes

⅓ cup chicken broth, for basting

SAUCE (OPTIONAL)

¾ cup dry white wine

1 cup chicken broth

1½ tablespoons potato starch,
  dissolved in 3 tablespoons water

2 tablespoons chopped parsley

Preheat the oven to 400° F. Put the turkey breast in a roasting pan. Loosen the skin. Mix 1½ tablespoons olive oil with the thyme and some pepper and rub the mixture over the meat, under the skin. Slip a few pieces of rosemary under the skin. Put the remaining rosemary in the pan under the turkey.

Halve the potatoes; you don't need to peel them. Put the potatoes around the turkey and sprinkle with salt, pepper, and remaining 1½ tablespoons oil. Stir to coat potatoes with oil.

Roast the turkey uncovered 15 minutes. Baste turkey and potatoes with pan juices; if pan is dry, use 1 or 2 tablespoons chicken broth. Reduce the oven temperature to 350° F. and roast turkey 30 minutes more. Turn the potatoes over; baste turkey and potatoes. Continue roasting about 45 minutes to 1 hour, adding 1 or 2 tablespoons of broth as necessary, or until a meat thermometer or instant-read thermometer inserted in thick part of meat, not touching the bone, registers 170° F. If potatoes are not yet tender, remove the turkey and roast them a few minutes longer.

Remove the turkey and potatoes to a board. Cover the turkey.

To make the sauce, skim the fat from the pan juices. Add the wine and bring to a simmer, scraping browned juices into wine. Pour liquid into a saucepan. Add 1 cup broth and simmer 2 or 3 minutes. Stir the potato starch mixture and whisk it into the simmering broth. Simmer 1 to 2 minutes until thickened. Stir in the chopped parsley, add the juices from the turkey board, taste the sauce, and adjust the seasoning.

Remove the turkey skin. Cut the turkey into thin slices, serve with potatoes, and garnish with fresh rosemary. Pass sauce separately.

. . . .

Makes 6 servings

Nutritional information per serving: 603 calories; 12.1 g fat—19% calories from fat; 2.5 g saturated fat; 117 mg cholesterol

Baked Chicken with Garlic, Cumin, and Tomatoes

{ m e a t }

*T*his chicken cooks with a savory tomato sauce flavored with cumin, turmeric, and plenty of garlic. It is a great holiday dish and is convenient as well, since it can be made ahead and reheated. Although the chicken pieces are baked without their skin to keep them low in fat, the sauce keeps the chicken moist.

5 pounds chicken breasts, with bones	¼ to ½ cup water
1 tablespoon vegetable oil	1 pound ripe tomatoes, or
1 large onion, chopped	1 14½-ounce can diced tomatoes,
6 large garlic cloves, chopped	drained
1 tablespoon ground cumin	1 teaspoon turmeric
1 tablespoon tomato paste	Salt and freshly ground black pepper

Preheat the oven to 375° F. Remove the skin from the chicken. Heat the vegetable oil in a large nonstick skillet. Add the onion and sauté over medium-low heat about 7 minutes. Remove from heat. Chop the garlic in a food processor; add the cumin, tomato paste, and ¼ cup water and process to blend. Add to the skillet. Coarsely chop the fresh tomatoes in the food processor. Add fresh or canned tomatoes to the skillet and heat 1 minute, stirring. Stir in the turmeric. Add a pinch of salt and pepper.

Put the chicken in a large, shallow roasting pan. Add the tomato mixture from the skillet. Mix to coat chicken thoroughly with the spice mixture. Cover with foil and bake 30 minutes. If the pan becomes dry, add ¼ cup water. Continue baking chicken covered, basting once, about 15 to 30 minutes longer or until it is tender when pierced with a sharp knife and cooked through. Serve hot.

. . . .

Makes 6 to 8 servings

Nutritional information per serving: 289 calories; 5 g fat—16.1% calories from fat;
1 g saturated fat; 132 mg cholesterol

Matzo and Vegetable Stuffing

{ m e a t }

This tasty stuffing is a good accompaniment for Baked Chicken with Garlic, Cumin, and Tomatoes (opposite) or for roasted or grilled chicken or turkey. For low-fat cooking, it's best to bake the stuffing in a separate dish rather than inside the chicken or turkey so it does not absorb fat from the bird, which otherwise will drip off during cooking.

8 matzos
1 ½ cups hot chicken broth
2 tablespoons plus 2 teaspoons
   vegetable oil
2 large onions, chopped
4 ounces mushrooms, sliced

Salt and black pepper
1 teaspoon paprika, plus a pinch for
   sprinkling
2 large carrots, grated
2 medium zucchini, grated
2 large eggs, beaten

Preheat the oven to 350° F. Crumble the matzos into a large bowl and pour hot broth over them.

Heat 2 tablespoons of the vegetable oil in a large skillet. Add the onions and sauté over medium heat, stirring often, about 7 minutes or until beginning to turn golden. Add 1 teaspoon oil, then the mushrooms, salt, pepper, and paprika, and sauté 3 minutes or until tender. Remove from the heat and stir in the carrots and zucchini. Add the vegetable mixture to the matzo mixture and let cool. Taste for seasoning. Stir in eggs.

Lightly oil a 2-quart casserole. Spoon the stuffing into the casserole. Sprinkle with remaining teaspoon oil, then with paprika. Bake for 45 minutes or until firm.

. . . .

Makes 6 to 8 servings
Nutritional information per serving: 209 calories; 7 g fat—29.6% calories from fat;
1.2 g saturated fat; 54 mg cholesterol

Artichoke Hearts with Mushroom-Tomato Salad

{ p a r e v e }

*S*ymbols of spring, artichokes are a perfect beginning for an elegant meal and are traditional Passover fare among North African and French Jews. These artichoke hearts are filled with a colorful but simple salad of fresh white mushrooms and diced tomatoes.

4 large artichoke hearts	2½ teaspoons olive oil
1 lemon	1 teaspoon fresh lemon juice
4 ounces mushrooms, sliced	½ teaspoon dried thyme
2 fresh plum tomatoes, diced	Salt and freshly ground black pepper

Prepare the artichoke bottoms (see page 158) but do not cook them. Squeeze any juice remaining in the lemon into a large saucepan of boiling salted water. Add the artichokes. Cover and simmer over low heat 15 to 20 minutes or until tender when pierced with a knife. Cool to lukewarm in liquid. Using a teaspoon, scoop out the hairlike choke from the center of each artichoke to make a cup for filling.

Mix the mushrooms and tomatoes. In a small cup, whisk the olive oil with the lemon juice, thyme, salt, and pepper. Mix with the mushroom salad; taste and adjust seasoning. Sprinkle the artichoke hearts with salt and pepper. Fill with the mushroom salad. Serve cold or at room temperature.

. . . .

Makes 4 servings

Nutritional information per serving: 87.7 calories; 3.3 g fat—29.3% calories from fat; 0.5 g saturated fat; 0 mg cholesterol

Beet Salad with Orange Dressing

{ p a r e v e }

Beets are a popular Passover vegetable, and their delicate sweet flavor is well complemented by a light citrus dressing. For a colorful appetizer, serve the beets on a bed of baby lettuce.

14 small beets (about 1 ½ inches in
   diameter)
2 tablespoons fresh orange juice
Salt and freshly ground black pepper

1 tablespoon plus 2 teaspoons
   vegetable oil
½ teaspoon grated orange rind

Rinse the beets, taking care not to pierce the skin. Put 1 inch of water in a steamer and bring to a boil. Place the beets on a steamer rack or on another rack or in a colander above the boiling water. Cover tightly and steam 50 to 60 minutes or until tender, adding boiling water occasionally if water evaporates. Let cool. Rinse beets with cold water and slip off skins.

In a small bowl, whisk the orange juice with salt and pepper. Whisk in the vegetable oil and orange rind. Taste and adjust seasoning.

Dice the beets. Put in a bowl and add the dressing. Toss gently. Taste and adjust seasoning.

. . . .

Makes 6 servings

*Nutritional information per serving: 118 calories; 4.1 g fat—29.8% calories from fat;
0.5 g saturated fat; 0 mg cholesterol*

Broccoli, Carrots, and Potatoes with Lemon Herb Dressing

{ p a r e v e }

Commonplace vegetables gain a lively new flavor when sprinkled with olive oil, fresh lemon juice, and a touch of oregano. Serve this vegetable medley cold as a salad or hot as an accompaniment to baked fish or roasted chicken or turkey.

3 large boiling potatoes
Salt and freshly ground black pepper
4 large carrots, peeled and diagonally sliced ¼ inch thick
2 tablespoons olive oil
1 tablespoon lemon juice

1 teaspoon fresh oregano leaves, or ½ teaspoon dried
1¾ pounds broccoli, cut into bite-size florets
2 tablespoons chopped parsley

Peel the potatoes if desired and cut into 1-inch chunks. Put the potatoes in a large saucepan with enough water to generously cover them. Add a pinch of salt and bring to a boil. Cover and cook over medium-low heat 5 minutes. Add the carrots and return to a boil. Cover and cook over medium-low heat 15 minutes.

In a small bowl, whisk the olive oil with the lemon juice, oregano, salt, and pepper.

Add the broccoli to the saucepan of vegetables, adding additional hot water if necessary, and return to a boil. Cook, uncovered, about 5 minutes or until all of the vegetables are tender. Drain well. Transfer vegetables to a bowl. Add the lemon dressing and mix gently. Taste and adjust seasoning. Serve warm or at room temperature. Sprinkle with parsley just before serving.

. . . .

Makes 4 servings
Nutritional information per serving: 215 calories; 7.7 g fat—29.3% calories from fat; 1.1 g saturated fat; 0 mg cholesterol

Glazed Carrots with a Touch of Cinnamon

{ p a r e v e }

Even children will eat their vegetables when you serve them these sweet carrots with a hint of cinnamon in the glaze. These are perfect for Passover, Rosh Hashanah, Succot, or any other festive occasion and are delicious with chicken, turkey, beef, or lamb.

1 pound fairly thin carrots, peeled
1 cup water
1 cinnamon stick

Pinch of salt
1 tablespoon sugar
2 teaspoons vegetable oil

Quarter the carrots lengthwise and cut into 3-inch lengths. Combine the carrots, water, cinnamon, and salt in a medium sauté pan. Cover, bring to a boil, and simmer 7 minutes over medium heat.

Add the sugar and oil to the pan. Cook uncovered over medium heat, stirring occasionally, until the carrots are tender and the liquid is absorbed, 8 or 9 minutes. Watch so mixture does not burn. Discard the cinnamon stick. Serve hot or at room temperature.

. . . .

Makes 4 servings

Nutritional information per serving: 81 calories; 2.5 g fat—26.2% calories from fat; 0.3 g saturated fat; 0 mg cholesterol

Mock Noodle Kugel with Apples, Lemon, and Pecans
{ p a r e v e }

*M*atzos cut into strips create the illusion of noodles in this tasty kugel, in which the matzo strips are layered with sliced apples and cinnamon. Serve it as a sweet accompaniment for chicken or turkey. For a dairy meal, it's also good with nonfat yogurt.

5 matzos

2 large eggs

2 large egg whites

2½ tablespoons pareve margarine, melted

Pinch of salt

2 teaspoons grated lemon rind

6 tablespoons sugar

½ teaspoon ground cinnamon

4 medium-size sweet apples, such as Golden Delicious

1 tablespoon lemon juice

1 tablespoon water

3 tablespoons chopped pecans

Lightly grease a shallow 2-quart baking dish. Preheat the oven to 350°F.

Break the matzos into quarters and put in a large bowl. Pour boiling water over them to cover. Turn the matzos over to be sure all are lightly moistened. Immediately drain in a colander, tossing a few times so water drains quickly. Cut the matzos into strips about ¾ inch wide. Put in a large bowl. In a small bowl, beat the eggs with the egg whites to combine. Add to the matzos and mix well. Add 1½ tablespoons melted margarine, the salt, lemon rind, and 4 tablespoons sugar.

Mix the remaining 2 tablespoons sugar with the cinnamon. Peel, halve, and core the apples and slice very thin. Mix the apples with the lemon juice, cinnamon mixture, and water. Add to the matzo mixture. Add pecans and mix lightly.

Spoon the matzo mixture into the prepared baking dish. Sprinkle remaining tablespoon melted margarine over top. Bake for about 45 minutes or until kugel is firm and apples are tender. Serve hot or warm.

. . . .

Makes 4 servings
Nutritional information per serving: 438 calories; 14 g fat—28.1% calories from fat; 2.5 g saturated fat; 106 mg cholesterol

Matzo and Cottage Cheese Kugel with Dried Fruit

{ d a i r y }

*S*erve this rich-tasting, sweet kugel as a milchig *main dish during the week of Passover or as a satisfying dessert.*

1 pound fat-free cottage cheese
   (about 2 cups)
½ cup plain nonfat yogurt
2 large eggs
2 large egg whites
½ teaspoon salt
⅓ cup sugar
1 tablespoon fresh lemon juice

Grated rind of 1 lemon (about
   1 teaspoon)
½ cup diced dried apricots
½ cup raisins
4 matzos
2 tablespoons butter or margarine,
   melted

Preheat the oven to 350°F. In a large bowl, mix the cottage cheese, yogurt, eggs, egg whites, salt, sugar, lemon juice, lemon rind, apricots, and raisins. Soak whole matzos in a bowl of hot water to cover until slightly softened but not mushy, about 1 minute. Drain well. Cut matzos into strips about 3 inches by 1 inch. Add to cottage cheese mixture and mix lightly.

Pour 1 tablespoon margarine into a 2-quart baking dish and brush a bit of the butter up the sides of the dish. Spoon the matzo and cottage cheese mixture into the dish. Sprinkle with the remaining tablespoon butter. Bake for about 50 minutes or until set and top is browned. Serve hot or lukewarm.

. . . .

Makes 6 servings

Nutritional information per serving: 390 calories; 12.1 g fat—27.7% calories from fat; 4.7 g saturated fat; 86 mg cholesterol

Passover Hazelnut-Almond Cake with Raspberry Sauce

{ p a r e v e }

This light cake combines the flavors of almonds and toasted hazelnuts. To turn it into an elegant dessert, spoon a ribbon of ruby red raspberry sauce on each serving plate, top with a slice of cake, and garnish with a ring of banana slices for a stylish presentation.

HAZELNUT-ALMOND CAKE
1 cup hazelnuts
⅔ cup whole unblanched almonds
¼ cup matzo meal
1 cup sugar
4 large eggs, separated
1½ teaspoons grated lemon rind

RASPBERRY SAUCE AND GARNISH
6 cups fresh raspberries, or
    2 12-ounce packages frozen
    unsweetened or lightly sweetened
    raspberries, thawed
¾ cup sugar
8 medium bananas, peeled and sliced
    (optional)
Additional fresh raspberries
    (optional)

To make the cake, preheat the oven to 350°F. Toast the hazelnuts in a shallow baking pan in the oven for about 8 minutes or until the skins begin to split. Transfer to a strainer. Rub the hot hazelnuts energetically with a towel against the strainer to remove some of skins. Cool nuts completely. Leave oven on. Grease a 9-inch springform pan with margarine.

Grind the hazelnuts and almonds with the matzo meal and ¼ cup sugar in a food processor until fine. Beat the egg yolks with ½ cup sugar at high speed of an electric mixer until light and fluffy. Beat in lemon rind just until blended. Set aside.

In a clean bowl, whip the egg whites with a pinch of salt until they form soft peaks. Gradually beat in the remaining ¼ cup sugar, beating until stiff and shiny.

Alternately fold the whites and nut mixture into the yolk mixture, in 3 batches. Transfer to baking pan and bake about 35 minutes or until a cake tester inserted in center of cake comes out clean. Cool 5 minutes. Run a metal spatula gently around the cake and remove the sides of the springform. Cool on a rack. Cake will sink slightly. (Cake can be kept, covered, 1 day at room temperature or in refrigerator.) Serve at room temperature.

To make the sauce, puree the berries with the sugar in a food processor until very smooth. Strain into a bowl, pressing on the pulp; use a rubber spatula to scrape the mixture from the underside of strainer. Cover and refrigerate 30 minutes to 1 day.

Serve the cake in wedges on dessert plates, surrounded by sauce and sliced bananas and/or raspberries, if desired.

. . . .

Makes 8 servings

Nutritional information per serving: 533 calories; 18.8 g fat—29.9% calories from fat; 2.3 g saturated fat; 106 mg cholesterol

Genoa Almond Cake
with Poached Fruit

{ d a i r y   o r   p a r e v e }

Pain de genes, *or Genoa almond bread, is a classic French cake created in honor of a battle won by Napoleon's army in Genoa, in northern Italy. When I published a recipe for this cake in the* Los Angeles Times, *readers called and asked if this dessert could be made for Passover. This turned out to be a good idea. Since the original cake contained just a small amount of cornstarch and flour, this Passover version made with potato starch tastes very similar. A combination of fresh pears poached with prunes or dried apricots is a perfect companion for a slice of the tasty almond cake.*

Almonds are rich, but most of their fat is unsaturated. Besides, they contain protein, calcium, iron, riboflavin, vitamin E, and fiber.

ALMOND CAKE

4 tablespoons unsalted butter or
   margarine (see Note)
¾ cup whole blanched almonds
½ cup plus 1 tablespoon sugar
3 large eggs
2 tablespoons orange liqueur
¼ cup potato starch, sifted

POACHED PEARS WITH PRUNES
OR APRICOTS

2 pounds pears
1 lemon
1 cup sugar
1 quart water
1 cup prunes or dried apricots

To make the cake, grease an 8-inch round cake pan about 2 inches deep. Line the base with a round of waxed paper or foil; grease the paper or foil with a bit of margarine. Preheat the oven to 375°F.

Melt the margarine in a small saucepan over low heat; let cool. Grind the almonds with the sugar in a food processor until a fine powder.

Beat 1 egg with the almond mixture at low speed of an electric mixer until blended, then at high speed for 2 minutes or until the mixture is thick and smooth. Add the remaining 2 eggs one by one and beat at high speed about 3 minutes after each. Beat in the liqueur. Sprinkle the potato starch over the almond mixture and fold it in gently. Gently fold in the melted margarine in a fine stream.

Transfer batter immediately to the cake pan. Bake for 28 to 30 minutes or until the cake comes away from pan and a cake tester inserted into center of the cake comes out clean. Carefully turn the cake out onto a rack. Gently remove paper. Turn cake over again so smooth side is down. Let cool.

To poach fruit, cut the rind from the lemon in strips. Halve the lemon; squeeze out 1 tablespoon juice from one half; set the remaining lemon half and juice aside.

Combine the sugar, water, and lemon rind strips in a large, heavy saucepan and heat over low heat, stirring gently, until the sugar dissolves. Raise the heat to high and bring to a boil. Remove from heat. Peel the pears. Rub them well with the cut lemon half. Halve the pears lengthwise. With the point of a peeler, remove the flower end and core of each pear, including the long stringy section that continues to stem.

Bring the syrup to a boil. Add the pears, prunes, and tablespoon of lemon juice. Cover with a lid slightly smaller than the diameter of the saucepan to keep the pears submerged. Reduce the heat to low and cook the fruit until tender when pierced with a sharp knife, about 12 minutes. Cool the fruit in the syrup, still covered with the small lid, to room temperature. Refrigerate for 30 minutes.

Slice the cake and serve slices with fruit, topped with a little of the poaching syrup. Serve remaining syrup separately.

. . . .

Makes 8 servings

Nutritional information per serving: 444 calories; 15.3 g fat—29.4% calories from fat; 2.3 g saturated fat; 80 mg cholesterol

N O T E : If butter or dairy margarine is used, this recipe is dairy.

Walnut Meringues
{ p a r e v e }

*S*weet, crunchy meringues are a popular Passover treat with coffee, tea, or milk and are especially good when studded with nuts. Be sure to use very fresh, good-tasting walnuts.

Matzo cake meal, for flouring pan	1⅔ cups sugar
4 large egg whites, at room temperature	1 cup coarsely chopped walnuts

Preheat the oven to 275°F. Lightly grease the corners of 2 large or 3 small baking sheets with margarine or oil and line sheets with foil. Grease and lightly flour the foil with matzo cake meal.

Whip the egg whites in a large bowl until almost stiff. Gradually beat in ⅔ cup sugar at high speed and whip until whites are very shiny.

Gently fold in the remaining cup sugar in 2 batches as quickly as possible. Quickly fold in the walnuts until evenly distributed. Spoon the mixture in irregular mounds onto prepared baking sheets, using 1 mounded tablespoon for each and spacing them about 1½ inches apart.

Bake 30 minutes. Reduce the oven temperature to 250°F. and bake 30 minutes more or until meringues are firm to touch, dry at bases, and can be easily removed from foil. They will be light beige.

Transfer the meringues to a rack and cool. Put them in an airtight container as soon as they are cool. (Meringues can be kept in airtight containers at room temperature up to 1 week in dry weather. If they become sticky from humidity, they can be baked in a 200°F. oven for about 30 minutes to recrisp.)

. . . .

Makes about 36 meringues

Nutritional information per serving: 179 calories; 5.9 g fat—28.4% calories from fat; 0.4 g saturated fat; 0 mg cholesterol

8

Shavuot

Cucumber Salad with Dried Cranberries and Yogurt

Salad of Baby Greens, Corn, and Red Pepper

Creamy Broccoli-Noodle Kugel

Spinach Crepes with Morel Cream Sauce

Penne with Zucchini, Garlic, and Feta Cheese

Light Blueberry and Cheese Blintzes

Low-Fat Lemon Cheesecake

THE JEWISH HOLIDAY of Shavuot takes place in late May or in June. It's a one-day festival in Israel and two days elsewhere. *Shavuot* means "weeks" in Hebrew because the festival comes seven weeks after Passover. The holiday commemorates the Israelites' receiving the Torah when Moses ascended Mount Sinai.

In religious writings, Shavuot is often referred to as the "Festival of the First Fruits" and the "Feast of the Harvest" because, in ancient Israel, the first fruits of the season, as well as loaves of bread made from the recently harvested grain, were brought to the Holy Temple in Jerusalem. Although these customs ceased when the Temple was destroyed and have not given rise to any culinary ones, it is fitting to highlight fruits and grains in Shavuot menus.

In many homes, dairy delicacies are the traditional foods served for Shavuot. Some popular ones are baked noodle kugel with cottage cheese, sour cream, and either vegetables or fruits; bourekas, Sephardic pastries made of filo dough with a savory cheese or spinach and cheese filling; and cheese blintzes. But the favorite holiday food is undoubtedly cheesecake.

There is no commandment saying "Thou Shalt Eat Cheesecake," nor did the ancient Hebrews bake cheesecakes in the desert! The custom of celebrating Shavuot by eating dairy foods evolved in remembrance of the Hebrews' having avoided meat on the day before Moses received the Holy Scriptures.

My mother, who moved to Jerusalem from Washington, D.C., almost three decades ago, has always made great cheesecakes for Shavuot. A few years ago, she noticed that some of her friends had to say no to cheesecake for health reasons. She came up with a low-fat version, to her friends' delight. The last time I visited her, I tasted her new creation and loved it. When I came back home to the United States, I tried to re-create the cake. Because the cheeses, sour cream, and yogurt here are different from those in Israel, I had to experiment for a while in order to make a similar cheesecake using dairy products readily available in our markets. I used nonfat cream cheese and nonfat sour cream and was very pleased with the result.

At parties, everybody is amazed at how delicious and creamy Low-Fat Lemon Cheesecake (page 117) is. Nobody can tell it is made with nonfat cheese instead of full-fat cream cheese.

Cucumber Salad with Dried Cranberries and Yogurt

{ d a i r y }

The humble cucumber is transformed into a colorful holiday salad when combined with a creamy herb dressing and garnished with bright red dried cranberries, pecans, and chopped parsley.

2 medium cucumbers
1 cup plain nonfat yogurt
½ cup nonfat sour cream
¼ cup chopped red onion
1 tablespoon chopped fresh dill

4 tablespoons dried cranberries
⅓ cup chopped parsley
Salt and freshly ground black pepper
2 tablespoons coarsely chopped
   pecans

Peel and coarsely grate the cucumbers. Drain the grated cucumber in a strainer for a few minutes. Mix the yogurt with the sour cream until blended. Stir in the onion, dill, and cucumber. Reserve 2 tablespoons cranberries and 2 tablespoons parsley for garnish.

Add the remaining cranberries and parsley to the salad. Season to taste with salt and pepper. Serve cold in a bowl, garnished with pecans and with reserved cranberries and parsley.

. . . .

Makes 4 servings

Nutritional information per serving: 173 calories; 3.8 g fat—21.3% calories from fat;
0.3 g saturated fat; 1 mg cholesterol

Salad of Baby Greens, Corn, and Red Pepper

{ p a r e v e }

For this lively salad, the greens are topped with corn kernels and diced fresh red bell peppers, then enhanced by a light sprinkling of toasted pine nuts. Mixed baby lettuces are the most colorful and festive, but if you don't have them, the salad is also good with torn butter lettuce (also called Boston lettuce), red leaf lettuce, or a mixture of romaine and iceberg lettuces.

1 tablespoon pine nuts
4 cups mixed baby lettuces
1 tablespoon extra-virgin olive oil
1½ teaspoons wine vinegar

Salt and freshly ground black pepper
2⅓ cups corn kernels, cooked
1 medium red bell pepper, cored, seeded, and diced

Preheat the toaster oven or oven to 350°F. Toast the pine nuts on a tray in the oven about 3 minutes or until lightly browned, but not too dark. Transfer to a plate.

In a salad bowl, toss the lettuces with the olive oil, vinegar, salt, and pepper. Taste and adjust seasoning. Top with corn and diced red pepper, and toss lightly, leaving some of corn and peppers on top. Sprinkle with pine nuts.

· ·

Makes 4 servings

Nutritional information per serving: 147 calories; 5.5 g fat—29.7% calories from fat; 0.8 g saturated fat; 0 mg cholesterol

Creamy Broccoli-Noodle Kugel

{ d a i r y }

A kugel of noodles baked with cottage cheese has always been one of my favorite dairy entrees for Shavuot. This healthful version is enriched with nonfat sour cream and accented with broccoli, sautéed onions, and garlic.

1 pound broccoli, divided into
  florets
8 ounces medium egg noodles or
  pasta bow ties
2 tablespoons vegetable oil
1 large onion, chopped
2 large garlic cloves, chopped

1 teaspoon paprika, plus a bit more
  for sprinkling
Salt and freshly ground black pepper
2 large eggs, beaten
½ cup nonfat sour cream
½ cup fat-free cottage cheese

Preheat the oven to 350°F. Boil the broccoli in a large pot of boiling salted water about 4 minutes or until crisp-tender. Remove with a slotted spoon and transfer to a strainer. Rinse with cold water and drain well. Chop the broccoli coarsely. Add the noodles to the pot of boiling water and boil uncovered over high heat about 4 minutes for noodles or 8 minutes for bow ties; they should be nearly tender but firmer than usual. Drain, rinse with cold water, and drain well. Transfer to a large bowl.

In a skillet, heat 1 tablespoon plus 2 teaspoons vegetable oil. Add the onion and sauté over medium heat, stirring, about 5 minutes or until beginning to turn golden. Add the garlic and sauté 1 minute. Remove from the heat. Stir in the paprika. Add the broccoli, sprinkle with salt and pepper, and mix well.

Add the eggs, sour cream, and cottage cheese to the noodles and mix well. Season with salt and pepper.

Lightly oil a 2-quart baking dish with oil spray and add half the noodle mixture. Top with the broccoli mixture, then with the remaining noodles. Sprinkle with the remaining teaspoon oil, then with paprika. Bake uncovered 40 minutes or until set and lightly browned. Serve from baking dish.

. . . .

Makes 3 main-course or 6 side-dish servings

Nutritional information per serving: 246 calories; 8 g fat—29.9% calories from fat;
1.4 g saturated fat; 102 mg cholesterol

Spinach Crepes with Morel Cream Sauce

{ d a i r y }

*M*orel cream sauce is one of the most luscious of French creations. This milchig entree, in which the crepes are rolled around a spinach filling before being coated with the sauce, makes an elegant and indulgent-tasting Shavuot feast.

To make tasty low-fat crepes, I use skim milk, egg whites, and whole eggs.

CREPES

2 large eggs

2 large egg whites

1 ¼ cups skim milk

¾ cup plus 2 tablespoons all-purpose flour

½ teaspoon salt

1 teaspoon vegetable oil

About 1 teaspoon vegetable oil, for brushing pan

SPINACH FILLING AND MUSHROOM SAUCE

2 10-ounce packages cleaned spinach leaves

1 ½ ounces dried morels or shiitake mushrooms, soaked in hot water for 20 minutes

2 tablespoons butter or margarine

4 tablespoons all-purpose flour

2 cups skim milk, plus 2 tablespoons more if needed

½ cup fat-free sour cream

Salt and freshly ground black pepper

Freshly grated nutmeg

To make the crepes, combine the eggs, egg whites, milk, flour, and salt in a blender. Blend on high speed about 1 minute or until the batter is smooth; scrape down once or twice. Cover and refrigerate about 1 hour or up to overnight.

Whisk 1 teaspoon vegetable oil into crepe batter. The batter should have the consistency of heavy cream. If it is too thick, gradually add more milk, about 1 teaspoon at a time. If the crepe batter is too thin, sift 2 tablespoons all-purpose flour into another bowl and gradually stir batter into it.

Heat a nonstick crepe pan or skillet with a 6- to 6½-inch base over medium heat. Sprinkle with a few drops of water. If the water immediately sizzles, the pan is hot enough. Remove the pan from the heat and hold it near the bowl of batter. Using a brush, dab the pan very lightly with oil. Working quickly, fill a ¼-cup measure three-fourths full of batter (to easily measure 3 tablespoons) and add the batter to one edge of the pan, quickly tilting, swirling, and shaking the pan until its base is covered with a thin layer of batter. Immediately pour any excess batter back into the bowl.

Return the pan to medium heat. Loosen the edges of the crepe with a metal spatula. Cook until bottom browns lightly, about 2 minutes. Turn carefully with the spatula. Cook until second side browns lightly in spots, 1 to 2 minutes. Slide the crepe onto plate. Reheat the pan a few seconds. Continue making crepes, stirring the batter occasionally. If the first crepes are too thick, whisk a teaspoon of milk into the batter. Adjust the heat and dab the pan with more oil if necessary. Pile the cooked crepes on a plate. (Crepes can be refrigerated, covered tightly, up to 3 days.)

To make the filling and sauce, in a large saucepan of boiling salted water, cook the spinach, uncovered, over high heat, pushing leaves into water often, about 3 minutes, or until very tender. Rinse with cold water and drain. Squeeze by handfuls until dry. Chop coarsely. Remove the soaked mushrooms from the water. Rinse them and cut into small pieces; if using shiitake mushrooms, discard the stems.

Melt the butter in a medium saucepan, add the flour, and cook over low heat, whisking, 2 minutes. Off the heat, gradually pour in 1¼ cups milk, whisking and making sure to whisk in any flour adhering to sides of pan. Bring the sauce to a boil, whisking. Cook over low heat, whisking often, for 2 minutes.

Return the chopped spinach to the pan it was cooked in and cook over medium heat, stirring, 1 minute, to evaporate any liquid. Remove from heat and stir in ½ cup of the sauce, then ½ cup sour cream. Season to taste with salt, pepper, and nutmeg.

Reheat the remaining sauce and slowly whisk in ¾ cup milk. Bring to a boil, whisking. Add the morels and cook uncovered over low heat, stirring often, 5 minutes or until tender.

Preheat the oven to 350°F. Lightly oil 2 shallow baking dishes. On the lower third of the less attractive side of each crepe, spoon about 3 tablespoons spinach filling and roll up in a cigar shape, beginning at the edge with the filling. Arrange the crepes in one layer in the baking dish. Very lightly dab the crepes with a bit of sauce (without mushrooms) to moisten. Bake the crepes about 15 minutes, or until the filling is hot.

Reheat the morel sauce, stirring. If the sauce is too thick, gradually whisk in 1 or 2 tablespoons milk and return to a simmer. Taste and adjust seasoning. Serve crepes with a little mushroom sauce spooned over center of each one.

. . . .

Makes 5 or 6 servings

Nutritional information per serving: 270 calories; 7.9 g fat—27.4% calories from fat; 3.3 g saturated fat; 83 mg cholesterol

Penne with Zucchini, Garlic, and Feta Cheese

{ d a i r y }

Toppings of diced ripe tomato, crumbled feta cheese, and fresh herbs quickly turn this easy pasta dish into an eye-catching vegetarian entree. Use the diagonal-cut macaroni called penne or mostaccioli, or substitute elbow macaroni.

1 pound small zucchini

4 cups penne or mostaccioli

2 tablespoons olive oil

2 large garlic cloves, minced

1 large ripe tomato, diced

Salt and freshly ground black pepper

½ cup crumbled feta cheese

2 tablespoons shredded fresh basil, or 2 teaspoons fresh thyme

Quarter the zucchini lengthwise and cut each piece into 2-inch lengths.

Cook the pasta in a large saucepan of boiling salted water over high heat, stirring occasionally, 7 minutes. Add the zucchini and cook 2 to 3 minutes or until penne are just tender, al dente. Pour the pasta and zucchini into a strainer.

Heat the olive oil in the saucepan that was used to cook the pasta. Add the garlic and sauté over low heat about 30 seconds or until softened but not brown. Add the drained pasta and zucchini mixture to the garlic in the pan, then add the diced tomato and toss over low heat for about 30 seconds. Season to taste with salt and pepper. Serve the penne topped with feta and sprinkled with basil or thyme.

· ·

Makes 3 or 4 main-course servings

Nutritional information per serving: 512 calories; 11.7 g fat—20.6% calories from fat; 3.3 g saturated fat; 13 mg cholesterol

Light Blueberry and Cheese Blintzes

{ d a i r y }

I't's not easy to decide which blintzes are better, blueberry or cheese. These low-fat blintzes combine both—a creamy cheese filling studded with fresh blueberries. The filling of the blintzes is made with fat-free cottage cheese, and they are topped with honey-flavored nonfat sour cream.

Crepe batter (page 112)
About 1 teaspoon vegetable oil

CHEESE FILLING
2½ cups fat-free cottage cheese
1 large egg
4 tablespoons sugar, or to taste
1 teaspoon vanilla extract
1 teaspoon grated lemon rind

2 tablespoons nonfat dry milk
1 cup sliced blueberries

2 tablespoons butter or margarine,
   melted
1½ cups nonfat sour cream
3 tablespoons honey
Blueberries, for garnish

Prepare the batter for crepes as directed on page 112.

Heat a nonstick crepe pan or skillet with a 6- to 6½-inch base over medium heat. Sprinkle with a few drops of water. If the water immediately sizzles, the pan is hot enough. Remove the pan from the heat and hold it near the bowl of batter. Using a brush, dab the pan very lightly with oil. Working quickly, fill a ¼-cup measure three-fourths full of batter (to easily measure 3 tablespoons) and add the batter to one edge of pan, quickly tilting, swirling, and shaking pan until its base is covered with a thin layer of batter. Immediately pour any excess batter back into the bowl.

Return the pan to medium heat. Loosen the edges of the crepe with metal spatula, discarding any pieces of crepe clinging to the sides of the pan. Cook until the bottom browns lightly. Slide the blintz onto a plate. Reheat the pan a few seconds. Continue making blintzes with the remaining batter, stirring it occasionally. If the first blintzes are too thick, whisk a teaspoon of milk or water into the batter. Adjust heat and dab pan with more oil if necessary. Pile the blintzes on plate as they are done.

To make filling, in a bowl combine the cottage cheese, egg, and sugar. Mix well. Stir in the vanilla, grated lemon, and dry milk. Last, stir in the blueberries.

Spoon 2½ tablespoons filling onto the brown side of each blintz near one edge.

Fold over edges of blintz to right and left of filling so that each covers about half of filling; roll up the blintz, beginning at edge with filling.

Preheat the oven to 400°F. Arrange the blintzes in one layer in a shallow, lightly buttered baking dish. Lightly brush the blintzes with melted butter. Bake for about 20 minutes, or until heated through and lightly browned.

To prepare the topping, mix the sour cream with the honey. Serve the blintzes with a tablespoon of topping on the center of each. Garnish with a few blueberries. Serve the remaining topping on the side.

Makes 4 to 6 servings

Nutritional information per serving: 283 calories; 8.2 g fat—25.6% calories from fat; 3.4 g saturated fat; 118 mg cholesterol

Low-Fat Lemon Cheesecake

{ d a i r y }

Most people look forward to eating cheesecake for Shavuot. There's no need to give up this sweet tradition when you do low-fat cooking. You'll be amazed at what a delicious, creamy-textured cheesecake you can make with fat-free cheese and nonfat sour cream.

CRUMB CRUST

5 ounces graham crackers (20 squares)

2 tablespoons sugar

½ teaspoon grated lemon rind (yellow part only)

¼ cup vegetable oil

CHEESE FILLING

1 15-ounce container fat-free ricotta cheese

¾ cup nonfat sour cream

¾ cup sugar

2 large eggs, separated

2 tablespoons all-purpose flour

2 teaspoons grated lemon rind (yellow part only)

2 teaspoons fresh lemon juice

TOPPING

1 ½ cups nonfat sour cream

3 tablespoons sugar

½ teaspoon grated lemon rind (yellow part only)

1 teaspoon fresh lemon juice

½ teaspoon vanilla extract

GARNISH (OPTIONAL)

1 medium lemon, sliced ⅛ inch thick

⅔ cup sugar

½ cup water

Julienned lemon rind (optional)

To make the crust, preheat the oven to 350°F. Process the crackers in a food processor to fine crumbs. Measure 1¼ cups crumbs and mix them with the sugar and lemon rind. Add the vegetable oil and mix well. Lightly oil a 9-inch springform pan. Using the back of a spoon, press the crumb mixture in an even layer on the bottom and about 1 inch up the sides of the pan. Bake 8 minutes. Let cool completely. Leave oven at 350°F.

To make the filling, beat the ricotta with the sour cream at low speed until smooth. Gradually beat in the sugar. In this order, beat in the egg yolks, flour, lemon rind, and juice. Whip the egg whites in a small bowl until stiff. Fold the whites into the cheese mixture. Carefully pour the filling into the cooled crust. Bake about 55 minutes or until the top center is just firm but shakes slightly when you gently move the pan; cracks will form in the top of the cake. Cool the cake 15 minutes; the center will sink, making room for the topping. With a metal spatula, release any bits of cake from the upper part of the pan. Raise the oven temperature to 425°F.

To make the topping, mix the sour cream with the sugar, lemon rind, lemon juice, and vanilla. Spoon the topping evenly over the cake in spoonfuls. Carefully spread the topping in an even layer, without letting it drip over edge of cake. Bake 10 minutes. Cool the cake to room temperature. Refrigerate 4 hours or overnight before serving.

To make the garnish, put the lemon slices in a small, heavy saucepan and cover with water by about 1 inch. Bring to a boil, then boil 1 minute. Drain the lemon slices. Add the sugar and water to the saucepan and cook over medium-low heat, stirring, until the sugar dissolves. Add the lemon slices. Cover and cook over very low heat, so that the syrup simmers very gently for 30 minutes, or until the peel of the lemon slices is translucent. Uncover and cook 5 minutes over low heat. Cool 20 minutes in syrup. Carefully remove the slices from syrup with a slotted spoon. Use the tip of a small knife to remove any pits. Garnish the cake with whole lemon slices placed in an overlapping ring in the center, or around the edges. Decorate with lemon rind, if desired.

· ·

Makes 8 to 10 servings

Nutritional information per serving: 331 calories; 7.9 g fat—23.1% calories from fat; 1.3 g saturated fat; 43 mg cholesterol

9

Shabbat

Lighter Chopped Liver

Light Carrot Soup with Parsley Matzo Balls

Chicken-Noodle Soup with Cilantro and Green Onion

Carrot and Sugar Snap Pea Salad with Raspberry Vinaigrette

Broiled Eggplant Slices with Fresh Tomato Salsa

Israeli Salad

Marinated Cauliflower with Mushrooms and Tomatoes

Corn with Peppers and Peas

Sea Bass in Tomato Sauce with Bell Peppers and Garlic

Golden Roast Chicken with Corn and Cilantro Stuffing

Yemenite Chicken Cholent

Winter Fruit Salad

Orange Chiffon Cake

OVER THEIR LONG HISTORY, the Jews have developed dishes to suit the special requirements of the weekly day of rest, the Sabbath, or *Shabbat*, as it is called in Hebrew. Since no cooking is allowed after sunset on Friday, cooks have created dishes like cholent. This time-honored entree of meat and beans tastes good when made ahead and left over low heat all night for the Saturday midday meal. To keep the cholent warm, the oven is left on its lowest setting. Some people instead use a hot plate, called a *blech* (in Yiddish) or a *plata* (in Hebrew) and leave it on a very low gas flame or a very low setting for electric *blechs*. This cooking technique also produces an aromatic, delicious dish because the ingredients slowly exchange flavors and turn their cooking liquid into a savory sauce. It is probable that cholent inspired similar classics, from French cassoulet to American baked beans. Because the oven can be left on but not turned off during Shabbat, foods for the Shabbat midday meal are cooked, refrigerated, then warmed in the oven or on the heating pad. Water for making tea and coffee also keeps hot this way.

In many homes, Shabbat is welcomed like royalty, and the metaphor of "Shabbat the Queen" appears in songs and hymns. The table is festive, with fresh flowers, a pretty tablecloth, and Shabbat candles in beautiful candlesticks. There are wineglasses and a special goblet for kiddush, the holiday prayer over wine. Two golden braided challah breads are set on the table, covered with a decorative cloth. The family's best flatware and finest dishes appear on the table. Families who don't dine together every night make a point of enjoying a Shabbat family meal on Friday night and Saturday noon.

The meal itself is a feast, usually of several courses. Saving the best of everything for Shabbat is a popular custom. If you find fresh fish or beautiful fruit at the market, you buy them for Shabbat. You keep your best clothes and shoes for this special day. Everything is done to make the holiday a joyous occasion, which is looked forward to and prepared for during the rest of the week.

The Friday night meal generally begins with a fish appetizer, chopped liver, or marinated vegetables. Roast chicken or turkey is a typical main course, served with seasonal vegetables and with potatoes, stuffing, rice, or a kugel. Salad is a popular element of Shabbat meals, either as an appetizer or with the main course. A colorful salad such as Israeli salad of tomatoes, cucumbers, and onion is especially welcome if the entree is substantial.

Baking a cake for Shabbat is almost a ritual in many Jewish kitchens, either to serve as dessert or with coffee or tea when friends come to visit. Since Shabbat is a day to relax, it is a traditional time for getting together with friends and relatives. Because many Orthodox Jews who have eaten meat wait six hours before eating any food containing dairy products, the cake is generally made dairy-free.

{above} *Passover Hazelnut-Almond Cake with Raspberry Sauce, page 102.* {opposite} *Golden Roast Chicken with Corn and Cilantro Stuffing, page 130, and Asparagus and New Potatoes with Chives, page 291.* {following page} *Low-Fat Lemon Cheesecake, page 117.*

Lighter Chopped Liver

{ m e a t }

Chopped liver should be rich in flavor, but it does not have to be high in fat. Contrary to popular belief, it does not need schmaltz (chicken fat) to be delicious. The key to its good taste is to thoroughly sauté the onions in a little vegetable oil. To further reduce the fat, I add a secret ingredient: ground chickpeas. You don't notice their taste, but they contribute a smooth texture and lower the fat content of the mixture. You can serve chopped liver in a small scoop or as a spoonful on lettuce leaves and garnish it with radish or tomato slices for an attractive individual first course.

Unlike other meats, livers are koshered not by being salted and soaked but by being broiled or grilled.

½ pound chicken livers
Kosher salt
2 tablespoons vegetable oil
2 medium onions, chopped
1 15-ounce can chickpeas, rinsed, or
   1⅔ cups cooked chickpeas

4 or 5 tablespoons chicken broth
1 hard-boiled egg, grated
Salt and freshly ground black pepper
8 slices bread, for serving

Preheat the broiler with the rack about 3 inches from the heat. Put the livers on a foil-lined broiler pan and sprinkle with kosher salt. Broil 3 minutes or until the top is light brown. Turn the livers over and broil 3 more minutes or until cooked through and color is no longer pink; cut to check. Cool livers slightly.

Heat the vegetable oil in a large, heavy skillet over medium-low heat. Add the onions and sauté, stirring often, 15 to 20 minutes or until brown.

Grind the chickpeas and 4 tablespoons broth in a food processor. Transfer to a bowl. Chop the liver in a food processor. Add the onions and chop with on/off pulses until blended in. Return the chickpeas to the processor and pulse to blend, adding 1 tablespoon broth if needed. Transfer to a bowl. Lightly mix in egg. Season well with salt and pepper. (Chopped liver can be kept, covered, 2 days in refrigerator.) Serve cold, with bread.

. . . .

Makes 8 appetizer servings
Nutritional information per serving: 205 calories; 6.7 g fat—29.4% calories from fat; 1.2 g saturated fat; 151 mg cholesterol

Light Carrot Soup with Parsley Matzo Balls

{ m e a t }

*T*his is a very pretty soup, of a bright orange color with green-flecked white matzo balls. In spite of being low in fat, it has a wonderful smooth texture thanks to the pureed carrots and rice.

1 tablespoon vegetable oil

2 medium onions, chopped

1 1/2 pounds carrots, peeled and diced

Approximately 5 1/4 cups canned or homemade chicken broth

3 tablespoons uncooked rice

Salt and freshly ground black pepper

1/2 teaspoon dried thyme, crumbled

1 bay leaf

Pinch of sugar (optional)

MATZO BALLS

1/4 cup packed parsley sprigs

2 large eggs

2 teaspoons vegetable oil

1/2 teaspoon salt

1/2 cup matzo meal

2 tablespoons water

Heat the vegetable oil in a large, heavy saucepan. Add the onions and sauté over medium-low heat, stirring often, 7 minutes or until soft but not brown. Add the carrots, 4 cups broth, the rice, salt, pepper, thyme, and bay leaf. Stir and bring to a boil. Reduce the heat to low, cover, and cook about 30 minutes or until the carrots and rice are very tender. Discard the bay leaf. Let soup cool 5 minutes.

Pour the soup into a blender and puree until very smooth. Return to saucepan. Bring to a simmer, stirring often. Add about 1 1/4 cups broth, or enough to bring soup to desired consistency. Bring to a boil, stirring. Taste and adjust seasoning; add pinch of sugar if desired. (Soup can be kept, covered, 2 days in refrigerator; reheat over medium-low heat, stirring, before serving.)

To make the matzo balls, chop the parsley in a food processor. Combine the eggs, vegetable oil, and salt in a bowl. Lightly beat until blended. Add the matzo meal and beat until batter is well blended. Beat in the water, then the chopped parsley. Transfer the batter to a bowl, cover, and refrigerate for 20 minutes.

Bring about 2 quarts salted water to a boil in a large saucepan. With wet hands, take about 1 teaspoon matzo ball mixture and roll it between your palms to a ball; mixture will be soft. Set the balls on a plate. Reduce the heat so water simmers. With a rubber spatula, carefully slide the balls one by one into the simmering water. Cover and simmer over low heat about 30 minutes or until the matzo balls are firm. Cover and keep them warm until ready to serve.

When serving soup, use a slotted spoon to add 3 to 6 matzo balls to each bowl.

. . . .

Makes 6 servings

Nutritional information per serving: 251 calories; 8.3 g fat—29.6% calories from fat; 1.7 g saturated fat; 73 mg cholesterol

Chicken-Noodle Soup with Cilantro and Green Onion

{ m e a t }

For a change of pace from the traditional chicken soup, try this bright, fresh soup inspired by Vietnamese cuisine. It's very easy to make, once you have good chicken broth. You simply add a few strips of cooked chicken, some fresh cilantro, and green onion to the soup at the last moment, and serve the soup with a plate of bean sprouts and lime wedges. Each person sprinkles in some bean sprouts and squeezes in a bit of lime juice to have a light and tasty soup.

1 cup fine noodles
6 cups chicken broth
1 cup cooked chicken or turkey, cut
   into strips
Salt and freshly ground black pepper
⅓ cup thinly sliced green onions
   (scallions)

¼ cup cilantro leaves
2 cups bean sprouts, rinsed and
   drained, for serving
4 lime wedges, for serving

Cook the noodles in a pot of boiling salted water about 5 minutes or until just tender, al dente. Rinse with cold water. Drain well.

Heat the chicken broth. Add the chicken and noodles and heat through. Season to taste with salt and pepper. Just before serving, stir in the green onion and cilantro. Serve with a platter of bean sprouts and lime wedges.

. . . .

Makes 4 servings

Nutritional information per serving: 179 calories; 4.3 g fat—21.8% calories from fat; 1.2 g saturated fat; 39 mg cholesterol

Carrot and Sugar Snap Pea Salad with Raspberry Vinaigrette

{ p a r e v e }

Sugar snap peas are one of the best of the relatively new vegetables available in our markets. As with snow peas, you eat the whole pod, but sugar snap peas are sweet like green peas. Combined with carrots and the fruity sweetness of raspberry vinegar, they make a light and colorful Shabbat appetizer. This salad is also great for Rosh Hashanah, Succot, or Shavuot.

2 large carrots (about 10 ounces), peeled

8 ounces sugar snap peas, rinsed, ends removed

2 teaspoons raspberry vinegar

2 teaspoons vegetable oil

Salt and freshly ground black pepper

Cut the carrots into chunks of about same length as sugar snap peas. Cut each chunk in lengthwise slices about ¼ inch thick. Cut any especially wide slices in half lengthwise to form sticks. Put the carrot sticks in a medium saucepan, then add water to cover and a pinch of salt. Bring to a boil, cover, and simmer 5 minutes or until just tender; drain well.

Add the sugar snap peas to a medium saucepan of boiling salted water and boil uncovered over high heat 3 minutes or until crisp-tender. Drain in a colander, rinse with cold water, and drain well.

Whisk the vinegar and vegetable oil to blend. Add salt and pepper to taste. Toss the dressing with carrots. Add sugar snap peas just before serving. Taste and adjust seasoning.

· ·

Makes 4 servings

Nutritional information per serving: 79 calories; 2.6 g fat—29% calories from fat;
0.2 g saturated fat; 0 mg cholesterol

Broiled Eggplant Slices with Fresh Tomato Salsa

{ p a r e v e }

Fried eggplant is a popular appetizer in Israel. To make a low-fat version, broil the eggplant instead and top it with a zesty red salsa dotted with fresh hot peppers and cilantro. The salsa is also delicious stirred into cooked beans or rice or as a topping for summer squash or potatoes.

I usually remove the seeds from hot peppers to moderate their heat, but if you like them really hot, leave the seeds in. Remember that if you're not used to handling hot peppers or if your skin is sensitive, it's best to wear gloves.

SALSA
¾ pound ripe tomatoes, chopped
2 fresh jalapeño or serrano peppers,
    seeded and minced
½ cup chopped cilantro
2 large green onions (scallions),
    chopped, or ½ to ⅔ cup minced
    white onion

¼ teaspoon salt
Cayenne pepper (optional)

2 medium eggplants, unpeeled
About 4 teaspoons olive oil
Salt and freshly ground black pepper

To make the salsa, combine the tomatoes, jalapeño peppers, cilantro, and green onions in a bowl. Add the salt; season to taste with cayenne pepper if desired. Add 2 or 3 tablespoons water if mixture is dry; it should have a chunky, saucelike consistency.

Preheat the broiler. Cut the eggplant into slices ¼ inch thick. Arrange the eggplant on a foil-lined broiler pan. Brush lightly with olive oil and sprinkle with salt and pepper. Broil about 8 minutes. Turn over and broil about 7 minutes or until tender.

Serve the eggplant hot, warm, or at room temperature, topped with a small spoonful of salsa at room temperature. Serve more salsa separately.

. . . .

Makes 4 to 6 servings

Nutritional information per serving: 107 calories; 3.7 g fat—27.5% calories from fat;
0.5 g saturated fat; 0 mg cholesterol

Israeli Salad

{ p a r e v e }

This colorful salad adds a fresh touch to any meal. In its most basic version, diced tomatoes and cucumbers, I prepare it almost every day, a habit I picked up when I lived in Israel. For Shabbat, I prepare a slightly more elaborate variation and add chopped fresh parsley, green onions, and sweet bell peppers. The bell peppers are not traditional, but they make the salad even more delicious. It is especially beautiful with yellow bell peppers. Generally I season the salad with a touch of extra-virgin olive oil, but you can omit the oil for a fat-free version.

1 large cucumber

9 plum tomatoes

1 medium yellow or red bell pepper,
   cored and seeded

2 green onions (scallions), chopped

2 tablespoons chopped Italian
   parsley (optional)

$3\frac{1}{2}$ teaspoons extra-virgin olive oil
   or vegetable oil

2 teaspoons lemon juice

Salt and freshly ground black pepper

Dice the cucumber, tomatoes, and bell pepper very small, at most ½ inch. In a glass bowl, mix the diced vegetables with the green onions and parsley. Add the oil, lemon juice, and salt and pepper to taste.

. . . .

Makes 6 to 8 servings

Nutritional information per serving: 71 calories; 2.6 g fat—29.3% calories from fat;
0.3 g saturated fat; 0 mg cholesterol

Marinated Cauliflower with Mushrooms and Tomatoes

{ p a r e v e }

This appetizer originated in Provence, in southern France. Unlike many marinated vegetables, these are not aggressively sour from vinegar. Rather, they have a gentle sweet and sour taste from the balance of tomatoes, white wine, fresh lemon juice, and raisins. Serve these vegetables as a starter or an accompaniment.

1 medium cauliflower, divided into
   small florets
1½ tablespoons olive oil
1 medium onion, minced
1 pounds ripe tomatoes, peeled,
   seeded, and chopped, or 1 28-
   ounce can diced tomatoes, drained
Salt and freshly ground black pepper
½ pound small mushrooms,
   quartered

3 celery stalks, cut into thin
   crosswise slices
2 teaspoons fresh thyme leaves,
   or ½ teaspoon dried
½ cup dry white wine
1 cup (1 8-ounce can) tomato sauce
¼ cup dark raisins
1 tablespoon fresh lemon juice

Add the cauliflower to a medium saucepan of boiling salted water and boil uncovered over high heat 2 minutes. Drain, rinse with cold water, and drain thoroughly.

Heat 1 tablespoon olive oil in a medium sauté pan over medium heat. Add the onion and cook about 5 minutes or until light golden. Add the tomatoes, salt, and pepper and cook over medium heat, stirring occasionally, about 12 minutes or until the tomatoes are soft and most of their liquid has evaporated.

Add the remaining ½ tablespoon oil to the tomato mixture and bring to a boil, stirring. Stir in the mushrooms, celery, and thyme and cook over high heat 2 minutes. Stir in the wine, tomato sauce, and raisins and bring to a boil. Add the cauliflower. Reduce the heat to low, cover, and cook about 10 minutes or until the cauliflower is tender.

Remove from the heat. Add the lemon juice. Taste and adjust the seasoning. Transfer to a bowl and cool completely. Serve cold or at room temperature.

. . . .

Makes 8 servings

Nutritional information per serving: 94 calories; 3.2 g fat—29.6% calories from fat;
0.4 g saturated fat; 0 mg cholesterol

Corn with Peppers and Peas

{ p a r e v e }

This lively vegetable medley is at its best in summer, when all three vegetables are in season, but you can make it with frozen vegetables during the rest of the year. It makes a colorful accompaniment for roast chicken for Shabbat or for grilled fish or lamb chops at other occasions.

3 ears fresh corn, husked, silk
    removed carefully (about 1 ½ cups
    kernels), or 1 ½ cups frozen
    kernels
1 ½ pounds fresh peas (about
    1 ½ cups shelled), or 1 ½ cups
    frozen small peas

2 tablespoons vegetable or olive oil
2 medium red bell peppers, seeded,
    cored, and cut into strips
1 ½ teaspoons chopped fresh
    marjoram or oregano, or
    ½ teaspoon dried
Salt and freshly ground black pepper

Holding one end of a corn cob, cut off about 3 rows of kernels at a time, using a sharp knife. Repeat with second ear of corn.

In a medium saucepan, boil enough lightly salted water to cover the peas generously. Add the peas and boil uncovered until barely tender, about 5 minutes for fresh or about 2 minutes for frozen.

With a slotted spoon, transfer the peas to a strainer. Return cooking liquid to a boil. Add the corn and boil uncovered for 2 minutes. Drain thoroughly.

Heat the oil in a heavy skillet over medium-low heat. Add the peppers and sauté, stirring occasionally, 5 minutes. Add the corn, cover, and cook, stirring often, 5 minutes or until corn and peppers are tender; add 1 or 2 tablespoons water if pan becomes dry. Stir in the peas and marjoram, and heat for 1 or 2 minutes. Season to taste with salt and pepper.

· ·

Makes 4 servings

Nutritional information per serving: 241 calories; 8 g fat—28.6% calories from fat;
1 g saturated fat; 0 mg cholesterol

Sea Bass in Tomato Sauce with Bell Peppers and Garlic

{ p a r e v e }

Sautéed red bell peppers, garlic, and parsley give this Moroccan-Jewish holiday specialty a fine flavor and an attractive color. In some families, this dish is cooked with dried hot peppers. It is a popular dish for Rosh Hashanah, but it's also great for Shabbat because it's delicious cold and so is easy to prepare ahead. I love it best when made with Chilean sea bass.

1 tablespoon plus 1 teaspoon olive
    or vegetable oil
2 medium red bell peppers, cored,
    seeded, and diced
8 large garlic cloves, minced
1 pound ripe tomatoes, peeled,
    seeded, and diced

4 fillets (1½ pounds) Chilean sea
    bass or halibut, about 1 inch thick
Salt and freshly ground black pepper
1 teaspoon paprika
1 cup water
½ cup chopped parsley
Pinch of cayenne pepper

In a medium sauté pan, heat the oil and add the bell peppers. Sauté over medium heat 2 minutes. Add the garlic and cook over low heat, stirring, 1 minute. Stir in the tomatoes. Add the fish and sprinkle it with salt, pepper, and paprika. Add water to the pan and bring to a simmer over high heat. Reduce the heat to low, cover, and cook about 10 minutes or until the fish is tender; when checked in thickest part, its color should be opaque.

Transfer the fish to a deep platter, using a slotted spatula. Add the peppers to the platter. Boil the cooking liquid, stirring occasionally, until only about ¾ cup remains. Stir in the parsley and cayenne pepper. Taste liquid for seasoning and pour it over fish. Serve hot or cold.

Makes 4 to 6 first-course servings or 3 to 4 main-course servings
Nutritional information per serving: 180 calories; 5.9 g fat—28.9% calories from fat;
1.1 g saturated fat; 47 mg cholesterol

Golden Roast Chicken with Corn and Cilantro Stuffing

{ m e a t }

*O*n many tables, roast chicken is a must for Shabbat. Turmeric gives the standard weekend fowl a lovely golden color. Along with the cumin, it imparts a delicately spicy flavor to the bird. In our family, roast chicken is often accompanied by a savory stuffing.

This recipe includes extra stuffing, as a chicken never has room to hold enough stuffing for everyone. Actually, the stuffing will be lower in fat if you bake it separately (see Note below), as it won't absorb fat that drips from the chicken during roasting. Besides, a chicken that is roasted without stuffing cooks faster. Make the stuffing from plain white bread rather than challah, as it is lower in fat.

CORN AND CILANTRO STUFFING
8 cups cubed day-old or stale bread
1 tablespoon vegetable oil
2 medium onions, chopped
½ cup chopped celery
1 medium zucchini, coarsely grated
½ teaspoon dried oregano
Salt and freshly ground black pepper
1½ cups frozen corn kernels, thawed
½ cup chopped cilantro

½ cup chicken or vegetable broth

1 3½-pound chicken
¼ teaspoon black pepper
½ teaspoon paprika
½ teaspoon turmeric
½ teaspoon ground cumin
Additional ¼ to ½ cup chicken
   broth, for basting

To make the stuffing, put bread cubes in a large bowl.

Heat the vegetable oil in a large skillet. Add the onions and sauté over medium heat, stirring occasionally, until the onions brown, about 10 minutes. Stir in the celery, zucchini, oregano, salt, and pepper. Remove from heat.

Add onion mixture, corn, and cilantro to the bread and toss lightly until blended. Gradually add the broth, tossing lightly. The mixture may appear dry, but will become much moister from the juices in the bird. For baking separately, most of the bread should be very lightly moistened; if dry, gradually add more broth by tablespoons. Taste and adjust seasoning. (Stuffing can be refrigerated up to 1 day in covered container. Do not stuff bird in advance.)

Preheat the oven to 375°F. Discard any excess fat from the chicken. Mix the pepper, paprika, turmeric, and cumin. Rub the chicken all over with mixture. Spoon the stuffing lightly into the chicken. Fold the skin over stuffing; truss or skewer closed if desired. Set chicken in a roasting pan.

Grease a 2-quart baking dish and spoon the remaining stuffing into it. Cover the dish.

Roast the chicken 50 minutes. Then put the pan of extra stuffing in the oven and roast both together about 40 minutes, basting chicken occasionally with pan juices if desired, and basting stuffing occasionally with a few tablespoons broth. To check whether the chicken is done, insert a skewer into the thickest part of a drumstick; it should be tender and juices that run from the chicken should be clear. If juices are pink, roast the chicken a few more minutes and check it again. Also insert a skewer into the stuffing inside the chicken; it should come out hot.

Transfer the chicken to a carving board or platter and remove any trussing strings. Carve the chicken and serve hot, with stuffing.

. . . .

Makes 6 to 8 servings

Nutritional information per serving: 822 calories; 26.8 g fat—29.7% calories from fat;
7.2 g saturated fat; 125 mg cholesterol

N O T E :   To bake all of the stuffing separately, lightly oil a 2½-quart casserole and spoon the stuffing into it. Cover and bake 1 hour, basting twice with ¼ cup broth. Uncover for last 10 minutes for a crisper top.

Yemenite Chicken Cholent
{ m e a t }

Cholent, known in Hebrew as hamin, is one of the most famous dishes in Jewish cooking. It evolved from the rules for Shabbat meal preparation and is made in various forms by most Jewish ethnic groups. Basically it is a casserole of meat and beans that is made ahead and kept hot overnight, because cooking is prohibited on Shabbat. It is cooked in a very low oven or in a pot set on a metal heating pad set on low. Cholent is served as the main course at the Saturday midday meal. Depending on the season and what time you eat, it cooks for about 15 to 19 hours.

At Mahane Yehuda, the central market of Jerusalem, vendors sell several kinds of beans for making cholent: large white beans for Ashkenazic hamin, medium white beans for Sephardic hamin, and pink beans for Persian hamin. Sephardic Jews often mix chickpeas with the white beans, as in this version.

Cholent can be made with poultry. This lighter version makes use of skinless chicken thighs and is seasoned generously with cumin and garlic to give it a rich, lively flavor. The meat becomes deep brown and so tender it falls off the bones; and even the bones become soft. A favorite Yemenite and Sephardic custom is to set whole eggs on top of the stew so they brown slowly inside and acquire a fabulous flavor.

For the Shabbat that falls during Passover, cholent is made in some families with matzo balls instead of the beans.

4 pounds whole chicken legs

3 ½ teaspoons ground cumin

2 teaspoons turmeric

½ teaspoon ground black pepper

1 cup large dried white beans

1 ½ cups dried chickpeas

1 ½ pounds boiling potatoes

2 large onions, sliced

6 large garlic cloves, chopped

½ teaspoon salt

7 cups water

3 to 6 eggs in shells, rinsed
   (optional)

Preheat the oven to 180 to 200°F. Pull the skin and excess fat off the chicken. Put the chicken in a 6-quart flameproof casserole and sprinkle with cumin, turmeric, and pepper. Sort through and rinse the beans and chickpeas; you don't need to soak them. Peel the potatoes and cut each in half if they are large. Add the beans, chickpeas, potatoes, onions, and garlic to the casserole. Sprinkle with salt. Add the water and bring to a boil. Cover and cook over very low heat 45 minutes. Set eggs gently on top of stew and push them slightly into liquid.

Cover tightly and bake mixture, without stirring, overnight. Serve the stew from the casserole or carefully spoon it into a heated serving dish. Shell and halve the eggs lengthwise; set them on top for a garnish.

. . . .

Makes 6 servings

Nutritional information per serving: 667 calories; 2.8 g fat—17.7% calories from fat; 2.8 g saturated fat; 198 mg cholesterol

Winter Fruit Salad

{ p a r e v e }

Dried cherries soaked in orange liqueur add spirit (pun intended) to this melange of oranges, pears, and kiwis. If you like, add a sliced banana or a ripe persimmon. Serve the salad within half an hour after adding the pears or bananas so they won't turn brown.

2 tablespoons orange liqueur or
  orange juice
3 tablespoons dried cherries or
  raisins

2 navel oranges
2 kiwifruits
2 ripe pears
1 tablespoon sugar

Combine the orange liqueur and dried cherries in a small jar. Cover and let stand for about 30 minutes.

Cut the rind from the orange, removing most of the white pith. Cut the orange into segments. Peel the kiwis, cut in half lengthwise, then cut each half in slices. Transfer the orange and kiwi slices to a serving bowl. Core and slice the pears; add to serving bowl. Add the dried cherries with their liquid and toss. Add the sugar and toss again. Serve cool or cold.

. . . .

Makes 4 servings

*Nutritional information per serving: 163 calories; 0.6 g fat—3.4% calories from fat;
0 g saturated fat; 0 mg cholesterol*

Orange Chiffon Cake
{ p a r e v e }

Chiffon cakes are popular with kosher cooks because they are pareve. This is one of my mother's favorite cakes. I have adapted the recipe so it has less oil and fewer yolks than traditional chiffon cakes but still is tender and flavorful. Serve it with strawberry or raspberry sauce.

2 cups cake flour
1 tablespoon baking powder
½ teaspoon salt
1½ cups sugar
2 large egg yolks
6 tablespoons vegetable oil

⅔ cup orange juice
Grated rind of 1 large orange
  (1 tablespoon)
1 teaspoon vanilla extract
7 large egg whites

Preheat the oven to 325°F. Have ready a 10 × 4-inch tube pan with removable tube; do not butter it. Do not use a nonstick pan. Sift the flour, baking powder, and salt into a large bowl. Add 1 cup sugar; stir until blended. In another bowl, combine the egg yolks, vegetable oil, and juice; beat until smooth. Beat in the orange rind and vanilla.

Make a large well in the bowl of dry ingredients; pour in the egg yolk mixture. Gently stir dry ingredients into yolk mixture.

In a large bowl, beat the egg whites to soft peaks. Gradually beat in the remaining ½ cup sugar. Beat at high speed until whites are stiff and shiny but not dry. Fold about one-fourth of the whites into the yolk mixture until nearly blended. Gently fold the yolk mixture into the remaining whites. Transfer batter to tube pan.

Bake about 1 hour or until a cake tester inserted in cake comes out clean. Invert pan on its "feet" or on a heatproof funnel or bottle; let stand until completely cool, about 1½ hours. Run a metal spatula gently around side of cake. Push up the tube to remove the side of pan. Run a thin-bladed knife around the tube. Run a metal spatula carefully under cake to free it from the base; turn out carefully onto a platter. (Cake can be kept, wrapped, 2 days at room temperature.)

. . . .

Makes 10 to 12 servings

Nutritional information per serving: 259 calories; 7.9 g fat—27.1% calories from fat; 1.1 g saturated fat; 35 mg cholesterol

10

Appetizers and Salads

Vegetarian Bean and Walnut Pâté

Jerusalem Eggplant Mushroom Spread

Moroccan Hot and Sweet Pepper and Tomato Salad

Red Cabbage Salad with Pears

Cucumber-Tomato Salad with Yogurt

Grilled Marinated Peppers with Garlic and Thyme

Three-Bean Salad with Mushrooms and Capers

Diced Summer Vegetable Salad with Chickpeas

Provençal Potato, Green Bean, and Pepper Salad

Summer Tomato and Pepper Salad

Spicy Potato Salad with Cilantro and Red Onion

Pasta Salad with Lima Beans, Corn, and Tomatoes

Greek Pasta Salad with Spinach, Feta Cheese, and Tomatoes

Artichoke Salad with Jicama, Corn, and Sun-Dried Tomatoes

Coleslaw with Cranberries and Water Chestnuts

Vegetables with Sour Cream and Herb Dip

Light Moroccan Zucchini and Eggplant Salad

Grilled Bell Peppers

Cooked Artichoke Bottoms

WHEN I WAS GROWING UP, we always had appetizers for Shabbat and holiday meals. As in most Ashkenazic families, this appetizer usually was chopped liver or homemade gefilte fish. The liver was served in a scoop, on a bed of lettuce leaves. The gefilte fish was garnished with a slice of cooked carrot and served with red horseradish. We loved them and could not imagine Shabbat meals without them.

Later I realized that in Sephardic homes the appetizers were different. Garlicky spreads of grilled eggplant, spicy carrot salads with cilantro, hot pepper salsas, and tomato dips all appear as a selection of first courses to enjoy.

In my home, I love to prepare appetizers in both styles. Occasionally I prepare gefilte fish or a reduced-fat version of chopped liver. I find, however, that vegetable spreads and salads are the best appetizers for low-fat cooking. Pâtés and spreads made from vegetables such as eggplant, peppers, and beans not only are terrific as starters but are also convenient to have on hand for spreading on bread instead of butter.

Appetizers might be reserved for holidays or special dinners, but salads are important for everyday meals. When I lived in Israel, I prepared a salad of diced tomatoes and cucumbers every day, like most of my neighbors. There it was called Israeli salad (page 126); here in America, it's often known as Mediterranean chopped salad. I find that preparing such a salad daily is a healthful habit. The vegetables look so pretty that they usually tempt children, too. The salad is traditionally flavored with chopped onion, vegetable or olive oil, lemon juice, salt, and pepper, but some people omit the onion or the oil. There are many other tasty variations. Italian parsley or cilantro are sometimes added, as are minced jalapeño pepper, diced radish, diced sweet bell peppers, or shredded red cabbage.

Another important type of salad is one based on lettuce or other salad greens. You might like to toss the greens with sliced fresh mushrooms, grated carrot, sliced cucumbers, or tomatoes. Occasionally you might top the greens with strips of smoked fish or turkey, or perhaps sprinkle them with bean sprouts.

Cooked vegetables also make wonderful salads. Potato salads can be low in fat and still delicious, as on page 150. With little effort, mixtures of cooked vegetables can be turned into flavorful salads, such as Three-Bean Salad with Mushrooms and Capers (page 146).

Salads are easy to make low in fat—just be parsimonious with the dressing. A salad that's swimming in dressing is not only high in fat, it's unappetizing. I prefer oil and vinegar or oil and lemon juice dressings, although to make them low in fat I use less oil than in the classic vinaigrette proportions of 3 tablespoons oil for every tablespoon vinegar. For most salads, I find that 1½ or 2 tablespoons oil for each tablespoon vinegar is fine. For sweet ingredients like carrots or beets, or for green salads that contain fruit, I often use equal amounts of oil and vinegar.

Experiment with the interesting vinegars now available, such as raspberry vinegar and balsamic vinegar. They make tasty dressings even when combined with just a little oil.

To keep your fat intake down, avoid heavy dressings like ordinary mayonnaise. Reduced-fat and low-fat mayonnaise, when combined with fresh lemon juice, herbs, and other seasonings, can make fine dressings. For dairy meals, include nonfat sour cream or yogurt in your dressings.

Have fun serving appetizers. Use ingredients that might not appear in everyday meals. Experiment with mixed baby lettuces instead of sticking to the familiar iceberg, butter, and romaine lettuces. For an elegant touch, garnish the plates with lox, sprigs of fresh herbs, small pickled vegetables, pear tomatoes or other baby vegetables, or even edible flowers.

Other Appetizers and Salads

Cucumber Salad with Yogurt Dill Dressing (page 31) · Sephardic Eggplant Salad with
Green Onion, Garlic, and Roasted Peppers (page 32) · Hummus (page 60)
Belgian Endive, Red Onion, and Orange Salad (page 61) · Red Cabbage Salad with
Capers (page 63) · Beet Salad with Creamy Mint Dressing (page 70)
Eggplant Caponata (page 74) · Easy Gefilte Fish (page 88) · Artichoke Hearts with
Mushroom-Tomato Salad (page 96) · Beet Salad with Orange Dressing (page 97)
Cucumber Salad with Dried Cranberries and Yogurt (page 109) · Salad of Baby Greens,
Corn, and Red Pepper (page 110) · Carrot and Sugar Snap Pea Salad with
Raspberry Vinaigrette (page 124) · Israeli Salad (page 126) · Marinated Cauliflower
with Mushrooms and Tomatoes (page 127)

Vegetarian Bean and Walnut Pâté

{ p a r e v e }

A popular appetizer at dairy meals is a "mock" or "pretend" chopped liver. These vegetarian versions of chopped liver are made from vegetables—usually eggplant, green beans, or peas ground with a generous amount of nuts. In this low-fat pâté, I use chickpeas and green beans and a small proportion of walnuts. The secret ingredient is well-sautéed onions. Serve this pâté as a spread for bread or matzo, or on a bed of lettuce and garnished with tomato.

2 tablespoons vegetable oil
2 large onions, chopped
¾ pound green beans, broken in
   half, ends removed
3 cups cooked chickpeas, or 2
   15-ounce cans, drained and rinsed

¼ cup walnuts
¼ cup vegetable broth
1 hard-boiled egg, coarsely grated
Salt and freshly ground black pepper
8 to 10 slices bread, for serving

Heat the vegetable oil in a large skillet, add the onions, and sauté over medium heat until golden brown, about 10 minutes.

Cook the green beans in a large pan of boiling salted water about 10 minutes or until very tender. Rinse with cold water and drain well.

In a food processor, chop the beans. Add the chickpeas, onions, walnuts, and broth and process until smooth. Transfer to a bowl. Lightly stir in the chopped hard-boiled egg. Season to taste with salt and pepper. Serve cold, with bread.

. . . .

Makes 8 to 10 servings

Nutritional information per serving: 223 calories; 6.9 g fat—27.2% calories from fat;
0.9 g saturated fat; 23 mg cholesterol

Jerusalem Eggplant Mushroom Spread

{ p a r e v e }

My mother and I often prepare this appetizer when we are together because it has become a family favorite. Neither of us can remember when we started making it. I think I learned it from her, and she says she learned it from me! Basically it's made of finely diced eggplant cooked thoroughly with sautéed onions and mushrooms until the three vegetables blend into a pâté.

2 tablespoons vegetable oil
2 medium onions, chopped
1 ½ pounds eggplant, peeled and cut into small cubes
Salt and freshly ground black pepper

½ pound mushrooms, diced
½ teaspoon dried thyme
White of 1 hard-boiled egg, chopped
Parsley sprigs, for garnish
8 slices bread, for serving

Heat the vegetable oil in a large skillet. Add the onions and sauté 8 minutes or until soft and beginning to brown. Add the eggplant, salt, and pepper. Sauté 5 minutes over medium heat. Cover and cook over low heat, stirring often, about 15 minutes or until very tender. Add the mushrooms and thyme. Cover and cook, stirring often and mashing the vegetables occasionally with a wooden spoon, 15 minutes or until vegetables are very tender. Transfer to a bowl and let cool. Lightly stir in the egg white. Spoon into a shallow serving bowl and garnish with parsley. Serve cold, with bread.

. . . .

Makes 8 servings

Nutritional information per serving: 135.5 calories; 4.6 g fat—29.6% calories from fat; 0.7 g saturated fat; 0 mg cholesterol

Moroccan Hot and Sweet Pepper and Tomato Salad

{ p a r e v e }

This spicy mélange of cooked vegetables is known in Israel as a salad, but it's really a dip. If you like, you can substitute parsley for the cilantro.

½ cup small cilantro sprigs

6 large garlic cloves, peeled

3 jalapeño peppers, seeds and ribs removed (see Note below)

2½ tablespoons olive oil

2 large green bell peppers, cored, seeded, and diced

3 medium red bell peppers, cored, seeded, and diced

3 pounds ripe tomatoes, peeled, seeded, and diced, or 3 28-ounce cans plum tomatoes, drained and diced

Salt

8 slices fresh bread or toast, for serving

Chop the cilantro in a food processor. Remove and reserve. Chop the garlic and remove. Quarter the jalapeño peppers and chop in food processor.

Heat the olive oil in a large, wide, deep pan, such as a Dutch oven, over medium-low heat. Add both types of bell peppers and sauté until softened, about 10 minutes. Remove with a slotted spoon.

Add the tomatoes to the pan, sprinkle with salt to taste, and bring to a boil. Cook uncovered over medium heat about 20 minutes or until thickened. Add the sautéed peppers, chopped jalapeño peppers, and garlic and cook over medium heat, stirring often, 10 to 15 minutes or until peppers are tender and mixture is thick. Add the cilantro and cook 2 minutes. Taste and adjust seasoning. Refrigerate 1 hour or up to 3 days. Serve at room temperature with bread. Stir before serving.

. . . .

Makes 8 servings

Nutritional information per serving: 167 calories; 5.9 g fat—29.8% calories from fat;
0.9 g saturated fat; 0 mg cholesterol

N O T E : Wear rubber gloves when handling hot peppers if your skin is sensitive to them, or if you've never used them before.

Red Cabbage Salad with Pears

{ p a r e v e }

Red cabbage blends very well with fruit. In Northern Europe, red cabbage braised with apples is a classic dish. I also love red cabbage as a salad with pears and a sweet and sour dressing. For a quick summertime meal, serve it with smoked turkey and a pasta salad.

1 tablespoon vegetable oil
1 ½ tablespoons red wine vinegar
1 tablespoon sugar
1 tablespoon water

Salt and freshly ground black pepper
4 cups shredded red cabbage
  (8-ounce package)
2 large pears

In a large bowl, whisk the vegetable oil with the vinegar, sugar, water, salt, and pepper. Add the red cabbage and mix well, until cabbage is evenly moistened. Peel the pears and cut into ½-inch dice. Add to the salad and toss. Taste and adjust seasoning.

. . . .

Makes 4 servings

Nutritional information per serving: 107 calories; 3.9 g fat—29.8% calories from fat; 0.4 g saturated fat; 0 mg cholesterol

Cucumber-Tomato Salad with Yogurt

{ d a i r y }

I learned to prepare this salad when I lived in Israel. It's a creamy version of the standard Israeli salad of cucumbers and tomatoes, and is a perfect accompaniment for Israeli Rice and Lentil Stew with Cumin and Garlic (page 269), plain white or brown rice, and dried bean dishes. I find it delightful for many occasions. In fact, I love it for brunch and even for breakfast.

1 cup plain nonfat yogurt
Pinch of cayenne pepper
Salt and freshly ground black pepper
2 cups finely diced cucumbers

6 plum tomatoes, diced
1 tablespoon chopped parsley or
    mint, or 1 teaspoon dried mint

Mix the yogurt with the cayenne pepper, salt, and black pepper. Lightly stir in the cucumbers, tomatoes, and parsley. Taste and adjust seasoning. Serve cold.

Makes 4 servings

*Nutritional information per serving: 76 calories; 0.8 g fat—8.4% calories from fat;
0.2 g saturated fat; 1 mg cholesterol*

Grilled Marinated Peppers
with Garlic and Thyme
{ p a r e v e }

Popular all around the Mediterranean, these peppers are wonderful as an appetizer with French or Italian bread, as part of a party buffet, or as an accompaniment for grilled chicken.

6 large red bell peppers, or 3 red and
   3 green bell peppers
3½ teaspoons extra-virgin olive oil
2 teaspoons fresh lemon juice or
   wine vinegar

Salt and freshly ground black pepper
2 large garlic cloves, cut into
   quarters
½ teaspoon dried thyme
6 slices bread, for serving

Grill and peel the peppers (see page 157). Remove the cores and seeds. Cut the peppers into wide strips. Pat dry, then put the peppers in a shallow serving dish. Whisk the olive oil with the lemon juice and salt and pepper to taste. Pour over the peppers and add the garlic. Sprinkle the peppers with the thyme. Let stand at room temperature, turning occasionally, for 30 minutes, or refrigerate overnight. Remove the garlic. Serve the peppers at room temperature, accompanied by bread.

Makes 6 servings

Nutritional information per serving: 111 calories; 3.7 g fat—29.2% calories from fat; 0.6 g saturated fat; 0 mg cholesterol

Three-Bean Salad with Mushrooms and Capers

{ p a r e v e }

This colorful, robust dish makes a great appetizer for a Shabbat meal and adds a bright touch to a buffet dinner. If you're making this savory salad ahead, slice and add the mushrooms at the last minute so they will remain white.

1 10-ounce package frozen lima beans

8 ounces green beans, ends removed, cut in half

1 15-ounce can white beans, drained and rinsed

1 cup sliced fresh mushrooms

1 medium red bell pepper, cored, seeded, and cut into thin strips

2 green onions (scallions), chopped

3 tablespoons extra-virgin olive oil

1½ tablespoons tarragon vinegar

½ teaspoon dried oregano

Salt and freshly ground black pepper

1 tablespoon capers, drained

Add the lima beans to a medium saucepan of boiling salted water, cover, and bring to a boil. Cook 5 minutes. Add the green beans and return to a boil. Cook uncovered over high heat about 5 minutes or until both beans are tender. Drain, rinse with cold water, and drain well.

In a bowl, combine the cooked beans with the white beans, mushrooms, bell pepper, and green onions. Add the olive oil, vinegar, oregano, salt, and pepper and mix well. Sprinkle with capers. Serve cold or at room temperature.

. . . .

Makes 4 servings

Nutritional information per serving: 360 calories; 11.1 g fat—26.5% calories from fat; 1.6 g saturated fat; 0 mg cholesterol

Diced Summer Vegetable Salad
with Chickpeas

{ p a r e v e }

I like to serve this easy summer appetizer as a first course for the Friday night or Shabbat after-
noon meal, as a fresh counterpoint to a hearty chicken dinner.

1 15- or 16-ounce can chickpeas,
  drained and rinsed, or 1 ½ to
  2 cups cooked chickpeas

4 teaspoons fresh lemon juice

2 to 3 teaspoons extra-virgin olive
  oil

1 cup finely diced cucumber

1 medium red or green bell pepper,
  cored, seeded, and diced
  (optional)

6 ripe plum tomatoes, diced

¼ cup chopped green onions
  (scallions)

Salt and freshly ground black pepper

Mix the chickpeas with the lemon juice and olive oil. Add the cucumber, bell pepper, tomatoes, and green onion. Season to taste with salt and pepper. Serve cold or at room temperature.

. . . .

Makes 4 servings

Nutritional information per serving: 195 calories; 4.2 g fat—18.1% calories from fat;
0.5 g saturated fat; 0 mg cholesterol

Provençal Potato, Green Bean, and Pepper Salad

{ p a r e v e }

This pretty appetizer has been popular in my cooking classes on summer salads. In the French manner, the potatoes are tossed with a simple white wine marinade immediately after cooking because they absorb seasonings best when they are still warm. You can serve the vegetables mixed together, or in three mounds as three separate salads.

1 ½ pounds red-skinned potatoes, scrubbed

Salt and freshly ground black pepper

2 tablespoons dry white wine

2 tablespoons plus 2 teaspoons extra-virgin olive oil

¾ pound green beans, ends removed, cut into 2-inch pieces

1 tablespoon fresh lemon juice

1 teaspoon water

½ teaspoon fresh thyme leaves (optional)

2 medium red bell peppers, grilled and peeled (page 157), cored, seeded, and cut into thin strips

2 green onions (scallions), chopped

1 tablespoon chopped parsley

Put the potatoes in a large saucepan, cover with water by about ½ inch, and add salt. Bring to a boil. Cover and simmer over low heat about 25 minutes or until tender enough so that largest potato falls from knife when lifted; check by cutting the largest potato at widest point. Drain the potatoes in a colander and peel while hot, with the aid of a paring knife. Cut the potatoes into medium dice (about ½ inch).

Put the potatoes in a large bowl. Combine the wine, 1 tablespoon olive oil, salt, and pepper in a small bowl and whisk until blended. Pour over the potatoes. Toss or fold gently to mix thoroughly. Cool slightly so potatoes are still warm, or cool to room temperature.

Cook the beans in a saucepan of boiling salted water about 7 minutes or until just tender but still crisp. Drain, rinse with cold water until cool, and drain well.

In a cup, whisk the remaining 1 tablespoon plus 2 teaspoons olive oil with the lemon juice and water. Add the thyme and a pinch of salt and pepper.

Transfer the roasted peppers to a bowl. Add 1 teaspoon dressing. Toss 2 tablespoons dressing with the potatoes and add the green onions and parsley.

Just before serving, add the remaining 2 teaspoons dressing to the beans. Taste each mixture for seasoning. Serve vegetables side by side or lightly mixed, at room temperature.

. . . .

Makes 4 servings

Nutritional information per serving: 284 calories; 9.6 g fat—29.1% calories from fat;
1.2 g saturated fat; 0 mg cholesterol

Summer Tomato and Pepper Salad

{ p a r e v e }

Summer vegetables at their peak taste best very simply prepared, as in this salad from Spain, which combines fresh tomatoes and roasted peppers. Serve it with Italian sesame bread or crusty French or sourdough bread.

1 large ripe tomato, sliced
1 medium red bell pepper, grilled
   and peeled (page 157), cored,
   seeded, and quartered lengthwise
1 medium green bell pepper, grilled
   and peeled (page 157), cored,
   seeded, and quartered lengthwise

1 teaspoon sherry vinegar or
   balsamic vinegar
2 teaspoons extra-virgin olive oil
Salt and freshly ground black pepper
4 to 6 thin slices French bread, for
   serving

Arrange the tomato and peppers on a platter. Whisk the vinegar with the olive oil in a small bowl. Pour over vegetables. Sprinkle with salt and pepper and serve, accompanied by the bread.

. . . .

Makes 2 or 3 servings

Nutritional information per serving: 186 calories; 4.7 g fat—22.7% calories from fat;
0.8 g saturated fat; 0 mg cholesterol

Spicy Potato Salad with Cilantro and Red Onion

{ p a r e v e }

*C*umin, cayenne pepper, and the pungent flavor of fresh cilantro give this potato salad a vivid *flavor so you don't need a rich dressing. If you like, substitute a diced fresh or roasted red bell pepper for the tomatoes. You might like to serve the salad as part of a selection of salads for Succot or for the weekly Friday night meal.*

2 pounds red-skinned potatoes,
   scrubbed but not peeled
Salt and freshly ground black pepper
2 tablespoons fresh lemon juice
2 teaspoons ground cumin
½ teaspoon paprika
Cayenne pepper

1 tablespoon water
2½ tablespoons extra-virgin olive oil
⅓ cup chopped red onion
¼ cup chopped cilantro
4 plum tomatoes, cut into small dice
   (optional)

Put the potatoes in a large saucepan, cover with water by about ½ inch, and add salt. Bring to a boil. Cover and simmer over low heat about 25 minutes, or until a knife can pierce the center of the largest potato easily and potato falls from knife when lifted.

In a bowl large enough to contain the potatoes, whisk the lemon juice with the cumin, paprika, cayenne pepper to taste, and water. Add the olive oil and whisk again.

Drain the potatoes and leave just until cool enough to handle. Peel them and cut into 1-inch dice. Add to the bowl. Add the red onion. Fold gently but thoroughly with dressing. Let cool. Fold in 3 tablespoons cilantro, then gently fold in the tomatoes if desired. Serve at room temperature, sprinkled with remaining chopped cilantro.

. . . .

Makes 4 servings

Nutritional information per serving: 296 calories; 9.4 g fat—27.3% calories from fat;
1.3 g saturated fat; 0 mg cholesterol

Pasta Salad with Lima Beans, Corn, and Tomatoes

{ p a r e v e }

The delectable dressing of fresh basil, olive oil, and fresh lemon juice gives this colorful salad a lively flavor so it is sure to please. It's a tasty accompaniment for any meats, from cold cuts to roast chicken. You can also serve it for Shavuot, accompanied by a little feta, goat cheese, or cottage cheese, or as the center of a vegetarian dinner.

1 10-ounce package frozen baby lima beans

1½ cups fresh or frozen corn kernels, thawed

8 ounces medium pasta shells (about 3 cups), cooked, drained, and rinsed

⅓ cup finely chopped red onion

8 ounces ripe tomatoes (about 2), diced

2 tablespoons chopped fresh basil leaves, or 2 teaspoons dried

2 tablespoons fresh lemon juice

4 tablespoons extra-virgin olive oil

Salt and freshly ground black pepper

¼ cup sliced black olives (optional)

Add the lima beans to a medium saucepan of enough boiling water to cover them generously and cook uncovered over medium-high heat until just tender, about 5 minutes. Add the corn, return to a boil, and cook 2 minutes or until beans and corn are tender. Drain well.

Combine the lima beans, corn, pasta, onion, tomatoes, and basil in a large bowl and toss lightly.

In a small bowl, whisk the lemon juice with the olive oil and salt and pepper to taste. Add to the salad and toss until ingredients are coated. Add the olives if desired. Taste and adjust the seasoning. Serve warm or at room temperature.

. . . .

Makes 3 main-course or 6 side-dish servings

Nutritional information per serving: 338 calories; 10.9 g fat—28.2% calories from fat;
1.5 g saturated fat; 0 mg cholesterol

Greek Pasta Salad with Spinach, Feta Cheese, and Tomatoes

{ d a i r y }

*G*reek salad is often made of lettuce or spinach topped with ripe tomatoes, feta cheese, black olives, and an olive oil vinaigrette. This pasta version is more substantial and is suitable for a light main course. Serve it as part of a salad buffet or for a dairy meal for Shavuot or during Succot.

8 ripe plum tomatoes, diced

2 teaspoons chopped fresh oregano, or ¾ teaspoon dried

3 tablespoons extra-virgin olive oil

1 tablespoon red wine vinegar

Salt and freshly ground black pepper

8 ounces medium pasta shells (about 3 cups)

4 ounces spinach, stems removed, leaves rinsed well and patted dry (about 5 cups leaves)

½ small red onion, cut into thin slices, divided into slivers

⅔ cup crumbled feta cheese

¼ cup sliced black olives

Combine the tomatoes, oregano, olive oil, and vinegar in a large bowl. Season with freshly ground pepper and a small pinch of salt.

Cook the pasta uncovered in a large pot of boiling salted water over high heat, stirring occasionally, about 8 minutes or until tender but firm to the bite. Meanwhile, cut the spinach leaves into thin strips. Drain the pasta, rinse with cold water, and drain well. Add the spinach and onion to the pasta in the strainer and toss.

Add the pasta-spinach mixture to the tomato mixture and toss. Add half the feta cheese and toss lightly. Taste and adjust seasoning; salt may not be needed if cheese is salty. Serve warm or at room temperature. Serve salad topped with remaining feta cheese and with the black olives.

· ·

Makes 4 main-course or 6 to 8 appetizer servings

Nutritional information per serving: 254 calories; 8.6 g fat—30% calories from fat; 2.3 g saturated fat; 8 mg cholesterol

Artichoke Salad with Jicama, Corn, and Sun-Dried Tomatoes

{ p a r e v e }

*I*n the spirit of California cooking, this recipe borrows from several culinary cultures. The artichoke is braised with garlic and turmeric in the Moroccan style. It is then tossed with sun-dried tomatoes, a staple of southern Italy; corn, a favorite American native; and jicama, a crunchy, fresh-tasting root vegetable from Mexico. The result is an easy salad with an interesting medley of textures and flavors.

4 large artichokes

2 teaspoons chopped garlic

1 tablespoon plus 1 or 2 teaspoons fresh lemon juice

¼ teaspoon turmeric

1½ cups diced peeled jicama

1 cup fresh or frozen corn kernels, cooked

6 oil-packed sun-dried tomato halves, drained and diced

⅓ cup chopped red onion

1½ teaspoons extra-virgin olive oil

Salt and freshly ground black pepper

Prepare the artichoke bottoms (see page 158), but do not cook them. Add the garlic, 1 tablespoon lemon juice, and the turmeric to a medium saucepan of boiling salted water. Add the artichoke bottoms. Cover and simmer over low heat until tender when pierced with knife, 15 to 20 minutes. Cool to lukewarm in liquid. Using a teaspoon, scoop out the hairlike "choke" from center of each artichoke.

Cut the artichokes in slices. Toss with jicama, corn, sun-dried tomatoes, and onion. Add the olive oil, 1 or 2 teaspoons lemon juice, and salt and pepper to taste. Mix lightly. Serve cold or at room temperature.

Makes 4 servings

Nutritional information per serving: 425 calories; 15.5 g fat—30% calories from fat; 2.1 g saturated fat; 0 mg cholesterol

Coleslaw with Cranberries and Water Chestnuts

{ p a r e v e }

Nutritionists urge us to find as many ways as possible to add cruciferous, or cabbage family, vegetables to our menus. Instead of a heavy, mayonnaise-laden coleslaw, try this lean sweet and sour version, in which bright red dried cranberries and water chestnuts are combined with cabbage and carrots.

2 tablespoons red wine vinegar

1 tablespoon sugar

1 tablespoon plus 1 teaspoon
   vegetable oil

Salt and freshly ground black pepper

1 tablespoon water

4 cups shredded green cabbage or
   coleslaw mix

½ cup shredded peeled carrots

¼ cup dried cranberries, cherries, or
   raisins

8 ounces water chestnuts, drained
   and sliced

In a large bowl, whisk the vinegar with the sugar, vegetable oil, salt, pepper, and water. Add the green cabbage and carrots. Mix well to moisten cabbage evenly. Add the cranberries and water chestnuts, and mix well. Taste and adjust seasoning.

. . . .

Makes 4 servings

*Nutritional information per serving: 165 calories; 5.8 g fat—30% calories from fat;
0.6 g saturated fat; 0 mg cholesterol*

Vegetables with Sour Cream and Herb Dip
{ d a i r y }

You don't need to give up creamy dips on a low-fat menu. Just make them with low-fat mayonnaise lightened with nonfat sour cream and enlivened with fresh herbs. Serve the dip with a colorful selection of fresh vegetables and, if you like, with fat-free crackers or matzo.

DIP
¾ cup nonfat sour cream
½ cup low-fat or nonfat mayonnaise
1 tablespoon fresh lemon juice, or to taste
1 tablespoon chopped parsley
1 tablespoon thinly sliced chives
1 tablespoon chopped tarragon leaves
Salt and freshly ground black pepper

About 6 cups of a selection of the following:
Jicama, peeled and cut into sticks
Small radishes
Cucumber, cut into sticks
Carrot sticks
Celery sticks
Cauliflower florets
Broccoli florets
Zucchini, cut into sticks
Mushrooms, cut into thick slices
Cherry tomatoes

To make dip, mix the sour cream with the mayonnaise in a bowl until smooth. Stir in the lemon juice, parsley, chives, and tarragon. Taste and adjust seasoning. Spoon into a small serving bowl. Cover and refrigerate until ready to serve.

Arrange the vegetables on a platter around the dip, grouping each type together and alternating colors.

. . . .

Makes 6 to 8 servings
Nutritional information per serving: 93 calories; 3.2 g fat—30% calories from fat;
0.5 g saturated fat; 4 mg cholesterol

Light Moroccan Zucchini and Eggplant Salad

{ p a r e v e }

Unlike most eggplant recipes, in this light salad the vegetable is cooked briefly with the zucchini in water to save time, then continues cooking with tomatoes and roasted peppers. The salad has plenty of flavor, thanks to a fresh hot pepper, cilantro, and a generous amount of garlic.

1 tablespoon olive oil

6 garlic cloves, chopped

½ to 1 jalapeño or serrano pepper, seeded and chopped, or cayenne pepper, to taste

4 to 5 ripe tomatoes (about 2 pounds), peeled, seeded, and diced

3 tablespoons chopped parsley

2 teaspoons paprika

Salt

1 small eggplant (about 1 pound), peeled

2 zucchini (about ½ pound), unpeeled

2 medium green bell peppers, or 1 red and 1 green bell pepper, grilled and peeled (page xxx), cored, seeded, and diced

2 tablespoons chopped cilantro (optional)

Heat the oil in a large skillet. Add the garlic and hot pepper and sauté ½ minute. Add tomatoes, 1 tablespoon chopped parsley, paprika, and salt to taste. Cook uncovered over medium-high heat, stirring often, 15 minutes.

Cut the eggplant into 1-inch cubes and the zucchini into 1-inch slices. Put the eggplant in a large pan of boiling salted water and boil 2 minutes. Add zucchini and boil about 5 minutes or until both vegetables are nearly tender. Drain well.

Add the peppers to the tomato mixture and simmer about 5 minutes. Add the eggplant and zucchini and cook over low heat 5 to 10 minutes or until all ingredients are very tender and the mixture is thick. Stir in the remaining parsley and the cilantro. Taste and adjust seasoning. Serve hot, room temperature, or cold.

· ·

Makes 4 servings

Nutritional information per serving: 141 calories; 4.8 g fat—26.4% calories from fat; 0.7 g saturated fat; 0 mg cholesterol

Grilled Bell Peppers

{ p a r e v e }

*S*weet red, yellow, and green peppers are delicious when grilled and peeled, either for serving as an accompaniment to grilled meats or fish or for marinating (see page 145) and serving as an appetizer. I find their flavor is best when they are grilled on the barbecue, but they are also good broiled. Whenever I am barbecuing, I try to have some peppers on hand to put on the grill. I prepare enough for several meals, as they keep well in the refrigerator.

6 large red bell peppers, or a mixture
 of red, yellow, and green bell
 peppers

Preheat a barbecue or broiler. Put the peppers on the barbecue or broiler rack about 4 inches from heat. Grill or broil the peppers, turning every 4 or 5 minutes with tongs, until pepper skins are blistered and charred, 15 to 20 minutes total. Transfer to a bowl and cover tightly, or put in a bag and close the bag. Let stand until cool enough to handle. Peel using a paring knife. Halve the peppers; be careful, as there may be hot liquid inside. Discard the tops, seeds, and ribs. Pat dry if desired; do not rinse. Cut the peppers into wide strips. Serve hot, cold, or at room temperature.

. . . .

Makes 6 servings

Nutritional information per serving: 20 calories; 0.1 g fat—5.5% calories from fat;
0 g saturated fat; 0 mg cholesterol

Cooked Artichoke Bottoms

{ p a r e v e }

*A*rtichoke bottoms make a luxurious addition to salads and to pasta dishes. You can stuff them with marinated peppers, page 145, or with mushroom-tomato salad for serving cold, as on page 96, or with stewed tomatoes, page 304, for serving hot.

2 lemons   Salt
4 artichokes

Squeeze the juice of ½ lemon into a medium bowl of cold water. Break off the stem of 1 artichoke and the large leaves at the bottom. Put the artichoke on its side on a board. Holding a very sharp knife or serrated knife against the side of the artichoke (parallel to leaves), cut the lower circle of leaves off, up to the edge of the artichoke heart; turn the artichoke slightly after each cut. Rub the cut edges of the artichoke with the cut side of a lemon. Cut off the artichoke leaves under the base. Trim the base, removing all dark green areas. Rub again with lemon. Cut off the central cone of leaves just above the heart. Put the artichoke in the bowl of lemon water. Repeat with the remaining artichokes. Keep artichokes in lemon water until ready to cook them.

To cook the artichoke bottoms, add 1 tablespoon lemon juice to a medium saucepan of boiling salted water. Add the artichokes. Cover and simmer over low heat until tender when pierced with knife, 15 to 20 minutes. Cool to lukewarm in the cooking liquid. Using a teaspoon, scoop out the hairlike "choke" from the center of each artichoke.

. . . .

Makes 4 servings

Nutritional information per serving: 60 calories; 0.2 g fat—2.4% calories from fat;
0 g saturated fat; 0 mg cholesterol

11
Soups

CHICKEN SOUP IS a standard on the menu for Shabbat and all major holidays in many Jewish homes. It is hard to improve on the classic dish: a rich-tasting chicken broth delicately flavored with onions, carrots, celery, and bay leaves and served with fluffy matzo balls. Some people add dill or cilantro; both are a nice touch if added discreetly. Noodles, rice, or kreplach (a filled pasta resembling ravioli) are also popular in chicken soup, but matzo balls remain the favorite.

There are other time-honored holiday soups. In Yemenite homes, for example, beef soup is often served for Shabbat instead of chicken soup. The tempting soup does not contain matzo balls, but is golden from turmeric and zesty from the addition of freshly ground cumin seeds. The soup is served with fresh pita bread, hot pepper chutney (zehug), and fenugreek dip (hilbeh).

Soup recipes are easy to adapt to kosher cooking, whether you wish to prepare creamy French velouté soups, Chinese chicken soups, or Italian minestrone. If you're preparing a soup with dairy products, use vegetable broth as the cooking liquid. If you're serving the soup at a meat meal, you can use vegetable broth if you wish, or you can vary the flavor by using chicken, turkey, beef, or veal broth. Of course, long-cooking soups made with meat or poultry do not need prepared broth, as the main ingredients turn water into a flavorful soup.

When you're looking for a low-fat first course or main course, soup is a wonderful solution. In summer, begin your Shabbat meals with a refreshing bowl of gazpacho. Cook a pot of hearty Bean Soup with Winter Squash and Garlic (page 165) as a rib-sticking entree during the week of Hanukkah. A pareve Parslied Potato Soup (page 168) is versatile enough to appear at any meal, whether the main course is meat, fish, or vegetarian.

Vegetable and fish broths are naturally low in fat. When you prepare poultry or meat broth, for low-fat cooking it is essential to skim the fat from the surface as thoroughly as possible. When you can, refrigerate the broth for several hours or overnight, so the fat congeals on top and is easy to remove.

Other Soups

Golden Chicken Soup with Noodles, Mushrooms, and Zucchini (page 12) · Chicken Soup with Potato Kneidlach (page 26) · Creamy Pumpkin Soup with Green Vegetables (page 56) · Hearty Bean and Beef Soup (page 64) · Chicken Soup with Spring Vegetables (page 90) · Light Carrot Soup with Parsley Matzo Balls (page 122) Chicken-Noodle Soup with Cilantro and Green Onion (page 123)

Israeli Chicken Soup

{ m e a t }

In Israel, leeks and winter squash are favorite enhancers of chicken soup. Along with the custom-ary onions and carrots, some people add cumin and cilantro for extra zest and turmeric to give the soup a golden color. Other popular additions are a few whole tomatoes or 1 or 2 dried hot peppers.

If you would like to have cooked chicken in your soup, use a whole bird or meaty chicken pieces to make the soup. If you need only broth, it's more economical to use back, neck, and small wing pieces, which then are discarded.

Serve the soup with small bow ties, fine noodles, or other delicate pasta shapes, matzo balls (see page 162), packaged soup almonds, white or brown rice, or good crusty bread.

1 3-pound chicken, or 2½ to 3 pounds chicken pieces	Salt and freshly ground black pepper
1 large onion, whole or sliced	2 teaspoons ground cumin (optional)
4 medium carrots, peeled and cut into 2-inch lengths	1 teaspoon turmeric (optional)
1 parsley root or parsnip (optional)	8 to 10 cups water
2 large leeks, trimmed, split lengthwise, and rinsed thoroughly	1 ¾- to 1-pound piece winter squash, peeled and cubed
1 bay leaf	2 tablespoons chopped cilantro, parsley, or dill (optional)

Remove the fat from the chicken. Put the chicken in a large casserole or pot. Add the onion, carrots, parsley root, leeks, bay leaf, salt, pepper, cumin if desired, and turmeric if desired. Cover ingredients with water. Bring to a boil, then skim foam from surface. Cover and cook over low heat 1 hour. Add the squash, bring to a sim-mer, cover, and cook 30 minutes or until chicken and vegetables are tender.

Thoroughly skim off the fat. (This is much easier to do when soup is cold.) Taste and adjust seasoning. Either strain soup or serve it with carrots and squash. If desired, remove meat from chicken and add to the soup. Add the herbs if desired to soup just before serving.

. . . .

Makes about 6 servings

Nutritional information per serving: 318 calories; 7.3 g fat—21% calories from fat; 2 g saturated fat; 102 mg cholesterol

Featherlight Matzo Balls

{ m e a t   o r   p a r e v e − d e p e n d i n g   o n   s o u p }

Chicken soup with matzo balls is welcome as the beginning for any festive meal, not just for the Jewish holidays. At the house of my cousin Marlene, it is the standard first course for the Thanksgiving dinner and is always made by her father, my uncle Herman. These superlight matzo balls are fat free—they are made without egg yolks, chicken fat, or oil. For the best flavor, they depend on good chicken soup or vegetable soup.

4 large egg whites   ⅔ cup matzo meal
½ teaspoon salt

Whip the egg whites with the salt until soft peaks form. Fold in the matzo meal until blended. Cover and refrigerate for 20 minutes.

Bring about 2 quarts salted water to a boil in a large saucepan. With wet hands, take about 1 teaspoon matzo ball mixture and roll it between your palms to a ball; mixture will be soft. Set balls on a plate. Reduce heat so the water simmers. With a rubber spatula, carefully slide the balls one by one into the simmering water. Cover and simmer over very low heat about 30 minutes or until the matzo balls are firm. Cover and keep them warm until ready to serve.

. . . .

Makes about 6 servings

Nutritional information per serving: 69 calories; 0.2 g fat—3% calories from fat;
0 g saturated fat; 0 mg cholesterol

Minestrone with Chicken Breasts and Fresh Basil

{ m e a t }

An Italian-Jewish favorite for Succot is minestrone made with dried beans and a broad selection of seasonal vegetables. In this version, the hearty, delectable soup becomes a meaty main course because chicken cooks right in it. Basically you can think of this minestrone as chicken noodle soup with lots of vegetables.

The fresh basil and garlic added to this colorful main-course soup at the last minute are responsible for its bold flavor. Other good vegetables to include, according to the season, are winter squash, spinach, Swiss chard, or green beans. If you have cooked dried beans of any kind, add 1½ to 2 cups of them instead of the canned beans.

When it suits your schedule, cook the chicken in the soup a day ahead. After the soup has been chilled, it's so much easier to remove the fat.

For other meals, prepare the soup without chicken as a vegetarian entree and accompany it with a bowl of grated kosher Parmesan cheese for sprinkling lightly on each portion.

2 tablespoons olive oil
2 medium onions, chopped
2 celery stalks, cut into thin slices
1 28-ounce can diced tomatoes, drained
½ teaspoon dried oregano
2 pounds chicken breasts, with skin and bones
2 small carrots, peeled and diced
1 large potato, peeled and diced

7½ cups water
Salt and freshly ground black pepper
4 small yellow summer squash or zucchini (about 1 pound), diced
½ pound peas, shelled, or ½ cup frozen peas
1 cup medium or fine noodles
4 large garlic cloves, finely minced
1 15-ounce can white beans, drained
½ cup chopped fresh basil

Heat the olive oil in a large saucepan over low heat, add the onions, and sauté about 10 minutes. Add celery, tomatoes, and oregano and cook over medium heat 5 minutes.

Add the chicken, carrots, potato, water, and a pinch of salt and pepper and bring to a boil. Cover and cook over low heat 45 minutes or until the chicken is tender. Remove the chicken and skim the fat from the broth (or chill the broth and remove the fat from the top once it solidifies.) Discard the chicken skin and bones; return meat to pot.

Add the squash, peas, and noodles to the soup and simmer until just tender, about 5 minutes. Add the garlic and canned beans and heat through. Stir in half the basil. Taste, and add salt and pepper if needed. Sprinkle more fresh basil on each portion when serving.

. . . .
Makes 6 main-course or 8 to 10 appetizer servings
*Nutritional information per serving: 266 calories; 5.8 g fat—19.3% calories from fat;
1.1 g saturated fat; 47 mg cholesterol*

Split Pea Soup with Vegetables, Turkey Sausage, and Dill

{ m e a t }

*T*his satisfying soup makes a great lunch or supper entree. Serve it during the week of Hanukkah or for other winter meals, with whole wheat or pumpernickel bread.

10 cups water

1 6-ounce package split pea soup mix (¾ to 1 cup dry mix)

2 medium onions, chopped, or 2 leeks, split, cleaned, and sliced

3 large carrots, diced

3 small boiling potatoes, diced

6 ounces turkey frankfurters, cut into ½-inch slices

3 small zucchini, diced

3 garlic cloves, minced

¼ cup snipped fresh dill

Salt and freshly ground black pepper

Bring the water to a boil and add the soup mix. Begin cooking the soup according to package directions, adding the onions and carrots during the last 45 minutes of cooking. Add the potatoes for the last 30 minutes of cooking. Ten minutes before serving, add the franks, zucchini, and garlic and simmer, covered, over low heat. Remove from the heat and add the dill. Season with salt and pepper to taste. Serve hot.

. . . .

Makes 4 to 6 main-course servings

Nutritional information per serving: 145 calories; 3.4 g fat—22.4% calories from fat; 0.8 g saturated fat; 17 mg cholesterol

Bean Soup with Winter Squash and Garlic

{ p a r e v e }

I t's hard to believe that this filling soup is fat free! To save time, I make it with bean soup mix, which has several kinds of beans packaged together. Served with hearty whole-grain bread, it makes a great vegetarian supper in winter. For a meaty variation, you can slice 6 to 8 ounces of low-fat beef or turkey frankfurters and simmer them in the soup for 10 minutes.

10 cups water
1 6-ounce package bean soup mix
    (¾ to 1 cup dry mix)
2 large onions, diced
1½ pounds winter squash, such as
    butternut or acorn

3 celery stalks, diced
3 large garlic cloves, chopped
¼ to ½ cup chopped cilantro or
    parsley
Salt and freshly ground black pepper

Bring the water to a boil and add the soup mix. Begin cooking the soup according to package directions, adding the onions during the last 45 minutes of cooking.

Meanwhile, prick the squash 5 or 6 times. Microwave on high about 3 minutes to soften the skin. Let squash cool, then cut off peel. Halve the squash or cut it into pieces. Remove the seeds with a spoon. Dice the squash meat.

Add the squash and celery to the soup during last 30 minutes of cooking. Add the garlic in the last 15 minutes. Just before serving, stir in the cilantro or parsley. Season with salt and pepper to taste. Serve hot.

. . . .

Makes 6 main-course servings

*Nutritional information per serving: 66.4 cal calories; 0.5 g fat—5.8% calories from fat;
0.1 g saturated fat; 0 mg cholesterol*

Creamy Turnip Soup

{ d a i r y }

Homemade soups are becoming an uncommon treat; many people don't often prepare soups at home because they perceive them as time-consuming. In fact, many vegetable soups are quick and easy to make. You simply cook the vegetables in vegetable broth, which you can purchase to save time, and then puree them in a food processor or blender. The vegetable puree gives the soups body, but you can further thicken the soup with potatoes, rice, or oatmeal that cook along with the vegetables, or with a quick roux of flour and a little bit of butter.

Although classic recipes call for cream, butter, or egg yolks for enrichment, I find that even low-fat milk, which is much more healthful, gives soups a creamy taste and color, as in this delight-ful recipe.

Serve the soup with the best French or Italian bread you can get or, if you like, with croutons. For a fresh touch, sprinkle each portion with a pinch of chopped chives.

1 tablespoon vegetable oil, butter, or margarine
1 small or medium onion, chopped
4 medium turnips (1 ½ pounds), peeled, quartered, and sliced about ¼ inch thick

2 medium boiling potatoes (½ pound), peeled, quartered, and sliced about ¼ inch thick
2 cups vegetable broth
Salt and ground white pepper
1 ½ cups low-fat or skim milk

Heat the vegetable oil in a medium sauccpan. Add the onion and sauté over medium-low heat about 5 minutes or until soft but not brown. Add the turnip and potato slices, broth, salt, and pepper. Stir and bring to a boil. Cover and simmer about 25 minutes or until vegetables are very tender. Puree the soup in batches in a blender or food processor. Return to a cleaned pan.

Heat the soup gently. Gradually stir in the milk. Heat but do not boil. Taste and adjust seasoning. Serve in heated bowls.

. . . .

Makes 4 or 5 servings
Nutritional information per serving: 196 calories; 5.9 g fat—26.4% calories from fat; 1.6 g saturated fat; 6 mg cholesterol

Tomato and Cucumber Gazpacho

{ p a r e v e }

Gazpacho is ideal for the kosher kitchen, as it is pareve and thus can begin any meal. My husband calls this "Israeli salad in soup form" because it contains the same ingredients as Israeli salad and in fact is garnished with some of the diced vegetables.

In Spain, there are many versions of gazpacho. Some don't even contain tomatoes and are green or white. Certain gazpachos are thickened with ground almonds, pine nuts, hazelnuts, or bread crumbs, while others contain no thickener, and some contain bits of chicken or meat. For flavorings, they may include onion, garlic, parsley, or fresh mint.

This light version gets a burst of flavor from fresh, ripe tomatoes, cucumbers, and peppers. For a quicker recipe, and one that can be made year-round, substitute a 28-ounce can of tomatoes for those used in the soup, but use fresh ones for the garnish.

2 pounds ripe tomatoes

2 small cucumbers, peeled

2 medium red or green bell peppers, or 1 of each kind, halved, cored, and seeded

½ red onion, finely diced

2 tablespoons wine vinegar

2 teaspoons olive oil

1 cup cold water

Salt and freshly ground black pepper

Finely dice ½ pound of the tomatoes, 1 cucumber, and half the bell peppers. Add the diced red onion, stir to mix, and set aside.

Peel and seed the remaining tomatoes, reserving the juice. Put in a blender. Strain the reserved juice from the tomatoes and add to the blender. Add the remaining cucumber, remaining bell pepper, vinegar, olive oil, and water. Blend until smooth. Pour into a bowl and season to taste with salt and pepper. Refrigerate 1 or 2 hours.

When serving soup, add some diced vegetables to each bowl.

. . . .

Makes 4 servings
Nutritional information per serving: 106 calories; 3.3 g fat—24.6% calories from fat; 0.5 g saturated fat; 0 mg cholesterol

Parslied Potato Soup

{ m e a t o r p a r e v e }

*Here is a satisfying, flavorful, and virtually fat-free soup based on the familiar parslied pota-
toes. Its creamy texture does not come from cream or milk, but from the pureed potatoes. For a
pareve dish, use vegetable broth for cooking the potatoes. If you wish, top each portion with a
spoonful of nonfat sour cream for* milchig *meals. For a* fleishig *meal, you can use chicken broth.*

1 ½ pounds russet potatoes, peeled
   and diced
2 cups vegetable or chicken broth
2 cups water
2 medium onions, diced

1 bay leaf
10 parsley stems (without leaves)
1 cup small parsley sprigs
Salt and freshly ground black pepper
   (optional)

Put the potatoes in a saucepan with the broth and water and bring to a boil. Add the
onions to the pot. Add the bay leaf and parsley stems. Cover and cook over low heat
for 20 minutes or until potatoes are tender. Discard the bay leaf and parsley stems.

Chop the parsley sprigs in a food processor. Add the soup to the processor and
puree, leaving a few chunks of potato. Taste and add salt and pepper if desired.
Serve hot.

. . . .

Makes 4 servings

*Nutritional information per serving: 186 calories; 1.7 g fat—7.8% calories from fat;
0.5 g saturated fat; 1 mg cholesterol*

Fat-Free Butternut Squash and Barley Soup

{ m e a t   o r   p a r e v e }

T*his hearty soup has a pleasing texture and a delicately sweet taste from the vegetables. I like it as a winter lunch or supper, accompanied by coarse brown bread. If you make the soup with vegetable stock, you can top each portion with a dollop of nonfat sour cream. If you prefer a meaty version, use chicken stock and stir in 1 or 2 cups diced cooked chicken or turkey about 5 minutes before the soup is ready.*

2 cups chicken or vegetable broth

6 cups water

½ cup pearl barley

½ butternut squash (about 1 to 1 ¼ pounds)

1 ½ cups peeled baby carrots or diced large carrots

1 celery stalk, diced

1 medium onion, diced

2 garlic cloves, chopped

1 ½ teaspoons snipped fresh dill, or ½ teaspoon dried

Salt and freshly ground black pepper

Bring the broth and water to a simmer in a large saucepan. Add the barley. Cover and cook over low heat 30 minutes.

Cut the peel from the squash and discard. Remove the seeds with a spoon. Cut the squash in about ¾-inch cubes.

Add the squash, carrots, celery, onion, and garlic to the soup. Cover and simmer about 20 to 30 minutes or until all the vegetables and the barley are tender. Add dill. Season to taste with salt and pepper.

. . . .

Makes 4 servings

Nutritional information per serving: 267 calories; 2.9 g fat—9.2% calories from fat; 0.6 g saturated fat; 1 mg cholesterol

Cucumber Velouté Soup

{ d a i r y }

Don't just think of cucumbers for salads. In Eastern Europe, they are sautéed or made into soups, like this one. The creamy soup contains a puree of lightly cooked cucumbers and a garnish of rice and diced cucumber. Serve the soup with fat-free crackers or with toasted cubes of French bread.

1 ½ cups water
Salt and ground white pepper
⅓ cup long-grain rice
2 ½ tablespoons butter or margarine
3 tablespoons all-purpose flour
4 cups vegetable broth

3 medium cucumbers (total
   1 ½ pounds), peeled
⅔ cup skim milk
Pinch of cayenne pepper
1 tablespoon chopped fresh chives or
   parsley

In a medium saucepan, bring the water to a boil with a pinch of salt over medium-high heat. Add the rice and simmer about 14 minutes or until just tender. Drain well and reserve.

Melt the butter in a heavy, medium saucepan over low heat. Whisk in the flour. Cook over low heat, whisking constantly, until the mixture turns light beige, 2 to 3 minutes. Remove from the heat. Gradually ladle 3 cups broth into the flour mixture, whisking. Bring to a boil, whisking, over medium-high heat. Add a pinch of salt and white pepper. Reduce heat to medium-low and simmer, uncovered, whisking often, for 5 minutes.

Halve 2 cucumbers and remove the seeds. Cut into thin slices. Bring the remaining 1 cup vegetable broth to a boil in a medium skillet over low heat and add the cucumber slices. Bring to a simmer, cover, and cook over low heat about 7 minutes or until cucumbers are very tender.

Puree the cooked cucumbers and cooking liquid in a blender or food processor until very smooth. Add the puree to the soup and simmer uncovered over medium heat, stirring often, for 5 minutes. Stir in the milk and bring to a boil. Add the cayenne pepper. Simmer, stirring, about 2 minutes or until the soup thickens. Taste and adjust seasoning.

Halve the remaining cucumber and remove the seeds. Cut the cucumber into small dice. Add to a medium saucepan of boiling salted water and boil uncovered about 2 minutes or until just tender. (Soup can be kept, covered, 1 day in refrigerator;

refrigerate diced cucumber and rice in separate containers. Reheat the soup over medium-low heat, stirring. Reheat the diced cucumber in a pan of boiling water ½ minute; drain well.)

Stir the rice into the hot soup and heat briefly. Ladle the soup into shallow bowls and garnish with diced cucumber and chopped chives or parsley.

. . . .

Makes 4 servings

Nutritional information per serving: 342 calories; 11.5 g fat—29.8% calories from fat; 5.5 g saturated fat; 22 mg cholesterol

Quick Fish Broth

{ p a r e v e }

Classic fish broth contains sautéed onions, but this herb-scented version is easier to make and has no added fat. It is perfect for fish soups, such as Mediterranean Fish Soup with Linguine (page 206), and sauces, such as the one in Sole with Tarragon-Scented Mushroom Sauce (page 204). Use the heads, tails, and bones of any kosher fish except strong-flavored ones like tuna and mackerel. You can also use this broth for cooking gefilte fish.

1 pound fish bones, heads and tails	1 sprig fresh thyme
1 medium onion, chopped	6 cups water
1 bay leaf	

Rinse the fish bones or pieces and put in a large saucepan. Add the onion, bay leaf, thyme, and water and bring to a boil; skim off the foam. Simmer uncovered over low heat, skimming occasionally, 20 minutes. Strain into a bowl. (Broth can be kept up to 2 days in refrigerator; or it can be frozen.)

. . . .

Makes 4½ to 5 cups

Nutritional information per serving: 23 calories; 0.2 g fat—7% calories from fat; 0 g saturated fat; 0 mg cholesterol

Vegetable Broth

{ p a r e v e }

You can buy pareve chicken-flavored broth or vegetable broth in powdered and cube form, but when you have time, this natural vegetable broth will give your soups greater depth of flavor, and can be used in vegetarian meals. It should have a relatively neutral taste because it is a base for a great number of dishes, and it should not clash with the taste of other ingredients. Thus you don't use such assertive vegetables as cabbage or turnips.

Broth is almost effortless to make. Many cooks freeze dark green parts of leeks and small pieces and trimmings of onions, carrots, mushrooms, and celery in freezer bags for the purpose of making broth. Basically when you have enough trimmings, you cover them with water, add garlic and herbs, and simmer them to make broth.

3 medium onions, coarsely chopped

1 medium carrot, diced

2 celery stalks, chopped

Dark green part of 1 leek, rinsed
   thoroughly and sliced (optional)

6 cups water

1 bay leaf

2 sprigs fresh thyme, or ½ teaspoon
   dried

3 medium garlic cloves, peeled and
   crushed

5 parsley stems (optional)

½ teaspoon black peppercorns

1½ to 2 cups mushroom stems or
   sliced mushrooms (optional)

Pinch of salt (optional)

Combine all the ingredients in a large saucepan. Bring to a boil, reduce heat to medium low, and simmer uncovered 1 hour. Strain the broth, pressing on the ingredients in a strainer; discard ingredients in strainer. (Broth can be kept up to 3 days in refrigerator; or it can be frozen.)

· ·

Makes about 1 quart

Nutritional information per serving: 25 calories; 0.2 g fat—7% calories from fat;
0 g saturated fat; 0 mg cholesterol

Chicken Broth

{ m e a t }

Good broth is especially important in low-fat cooking because its flavor often compensates for the reduced fat. If you prepare chicken broth with a whole chicken or with a generous amount of meaty chicken pieces, as in Israeli Chicken Soup (page 161), you will get the richest and most flavorful broth. When you don't use a whole chicken, you can also make a tasty broth from chicken or turkey bones, necks, backs, wing tips, and giblets, but do not use the liver. Use your broth to make soups and sauces and as a flavorful cooking liquid for chicken pieces, rice, and vegetables.

3 pounds chicken wings, bones, backs, necks, and giblets (no livers)

2 medium onions, quartered

2 medium carrots, quartered

1 celery stalk, with leaves (optional)

2 bay leaves

12 parsley stems, without leaves (optional)

About 4 quarts water

2 sprigs fresh thyme, or ½ teaspoon dried

Combine the chicken, onions, carrots, celery, bay leaves, and parsley in a large pot. Add enough water to cover the ingredients. Bring to a boil, skimming froth. Add the thyme. Reduce the heat to low so that broth bubbles very gently, partially cover, and cook, skimming foam and fat occasionally, 2 or 3 hours.

Strain the broth into large bowls. If not using immediately, cool to lukewarm. Refrigerate until cold and skim fat off top. (Broth can be kept 3 days in refrigerator; or it can be frozen.)

. . . .

Makes about 2½ quarts

Nutritional information per serving: 78 calories; 1.8 g fat—23.8% calories from fat; 0.4 g saturated fat; 2 mg cholesterol

Turkey Broth: Substitute turkey wings, bones, and giblets for the chicken. Cook broth for 3 hours.

Beef Broth

{ m e a t }

Beef broth adds a meaty flavor to soups and sauces, and is great for cooking rice and vegetables when you'll be serving them for fleishig meals. It's especially useful for low-fat cooking because it enables you to add a meaty taste to meals but serve less meat. Of course, skimming the fat thoroughly is essential to keep the broth low in fat. The taste is superior to that of broth made from powders or cubes. Homemade broth is much lower in sodium than commercially prepared versions. In fact, it's best to make it without any salt in case it will be used in a recipe with salty ingredients.

If you don't have beef soup bones, you can use any bony cut of beef. Roasting the bones and vegetables gives the broth a deep color and richer flavor, although you can skip this step. The broth keeps for several months in the freezer.

5 pounds beef soup bones, chopped
    into pieces by butcher if possible
2 medium onions, rinsed but not
    peeled, root end cut off, quartered
2 medium carrots, scrubbed but not
    peeled, quartered crosswise

2 celery stalks, cut into 3-inch pieces
    (optional)
2 bay leaves
4 large garlic cloves, unpeeled
About 4 quarts water
2 sprigs fresh thyme, or ½ teaspoon
    crumbled dried

Preheat the oven to 450°F. Roast the bones in a large roasting pan, turning them over once, about 30 minutes or until they begin to brown. Add the onions and carrots and roast about 30 minutes or until browned.

With a slotted metal spatula, transfer the bones and vegetables to a large pot. Discard any fat from the roasting pan. Add the celery if desired, bay leaves, garlic, and enough water to cover the ingredients. Bring to a boil, skimming froth. Add the thyme, partially cover, and cook over very low heat, so broth bubbles very gently, skimming foam and fat occasionally. During the first 2 hours of cooking, add hot water occasionally to keep the ingredients covered. Cook broth for 6 hours. Strain broth, cool, and refrigerate until cold, then skim solidified fat off top.

. . . .

Makes about 2 quarts
Nutritional information per serving: 78 calories; 2.3 g fat—28.5% calories from fat;
0.7 g saturated fat; 2 mg cholesterol

Brown Veal Broth: Substitute veal knuckle bones for the beef bones.

12

Dairy and Egg Dishes

Pasta Shells with Broccoli, Red Peppers, and Feta Cheese

Noodle Casserole with Creamy Mushroom Sauce and Vegetables

Low-Fat Macaroni and Cheese

Fettuccine with Parmesan, Porcini, and Peas

Spinach and Rice Gratin

Kosher Mushroom-Tomato Pizza

Country Vegetable Tart

Cauliflower and Corn Soufflé

Poached Eggs with Zucchini, Tomatoes, and Mushrooms

Scrambled Eggs with Green Onions and Tomatoes

SHAVUOT IS THE HOLIDAY most associated with *milchig*, or dairy, menus. Custom dictates that Shabbat and the other major holidays be observed with meat as the main course.

There are plenty of other special occasions in which egg or dairy dishes star on the menu. Often a Bar Mitzvah or Bat Mitzvah is celebrated with a festive brunch menu of creamy noodle kugels, egg dishes, pastries with a quiche-like filling such as Country Vegetable Tart (page 186), and, of course, bagels with lox and cream cheese.

Milchig cooking is also important for everyday meals. In many families, several weekday suppers are meatless. Dairy meals are appealing because they are lighter and easier to prepare. In Israel, dairy meals are loved for entertaining as well. They are favorites at our house. We like them so much that I wrote a whole cookbook on dairy meals called *Aruhot Halaviot* in Hebrew and published it in Israel.

For a quick supper, I like to serve a diced salad with a small portion of feta cheese, cottage cheese, or yogurt, accompanied by fresh bread. Occasionally I prepare an omelet or an egg and vegetable dish such as Scrambled Eggs with Green Onions and Tomatoes (page 191). To lower the fat in egg dishes, I replace part of the eggs with egg whites or egg substitutes.

Many observant Jews like dairy meals because these are the occasions to enjoy a creamy dessert. Children and adults alike are delighted to be able to eat ice cream or cheesecake, which, of course, cannot be served as dessert after a meat meal.

A greater variety of kosher cheeses are available than before. Some well-stocked supermarkets carry several types, especially ricotta, cottage cheese, mozzarella, Muenster, Swiss, Parmesan, and feta, but you'll find the greatest selection, including some delicious Israeli cheeses, at kosher markets. Fortunately, more reduced-fat kosher cheeses are becoming available too and are useful for sprinkling lightly on pasta dishes, vegetables, and vegetable soups.

Other Dairy and Egg Dishes

Noodle-Vegetable Kugel with Pecans (page 28) · Bagel with Light Lox and Cheese
Spread (page 30) · Mock Noodle Kugel with Apples, Lemon, and Pecans (page 100)
Matzo and Cottage Cheese Kugel with Dried Fruit (page 101) · Creamy
Broccoli-Noodle Kugel (page 111) · Spinach Crepes with Morel Cream Sauce
(page 112) · Light Blueberry and Cheese Blintzes (page 115)

Pasta Shells with Broccoli, Red Peppers, and Feta Cheese

{ d a i r y }

*This colorful dish is good for Succot or for weekday suppers. When I make it in Israel, I use
oorda, a low-fat, low-salt cheese with a texture like that of feta. If your kosher market carries
Israeli cheeses, try it in this dish.*

3 tablespoons olive or vegetable oil
1 large onion, chopped
1 large red bell pepper, cored, seeded, and diced
2 large garlic cloves, minced
1 teaspoon dried thyme

12 ounces large pasta shells or pasta button shapes (orecchiette) (about 4½ cups)
1½ pounds broccoli, divided in large florets
⅔ cup crumbled feta cheese
Salt and freshly ground black pepper

Heat the oil in a large skillet. Add the onion and red pepper and sauté over medium-low heat, stirring often, about 10 minutes or until soft but not brown. Add the garlic and thyme and sauté about 10 seconds. Remove from heat.

Cook the pasta in a large saucepan of boiling salted water over high heat, stirring occasionally, 5 minutes. Add the broccoli and cook 5 minutes or until the pasta is just tender, al dente. Pour the pasta and broccoli into a strainer. Rinse briefly with hot water.

Remove the broccoli florets and dice them. Reheat the onion mixture, add the broccoli, and heat through. Transfer the pasta to a large heated bowl, add the broccoli mixture, and toss well. Add feta and toss. Season to taste with salt and pepper.

. . . .

Makes 4 servings

*Nutritional information per serving: 518 calories, 16.2 g fat—27.5% calories from fat,
4.5 g saturated fat; 17 mg cholesterol*

Noodle Casserole with Creamy Mushroom Sauce and Vegetables

{ d a i r y }

The idea for this one-dish meal came from my sister-in-law, Nirit Levy. It tastes wonderfully rich, but in fact it gets less than 25 percent of its calories from fat. Begin the meal with Israeli salad or a cabbage salad, serve fresh fruit for dessert, and you'll have a healthy, satisfying supper.

3 tablespoons butter, margarine, or
 vegetable oil
⅓ cup minced onion
12 ounces mushrooms, sliced
Salt and freshly ground black pepper
¼ cup all-purpose flour
2½ cups skim milk
Freshly grated nutmeg

Cayenne pepper
1 10-ounce package frozen mixed
 vegetables or peas and carrots
14 ounces to 1 pound fine noodles
 (depending on package size)
2 cups fat-free cottage cheese
½ cup part-skim mozzarella cheese

Melt the butter in a heavy medium saucepan over medium heat. Add the onion and cook, stirring occasionally, 3 minutes. Add the mushrooms, salt, and pepper and sauté over medium-high heat, stirring often, 3 minutes. Stir in the flour, and cook over low heat, stirring constantly, 1 minute. Remove from heat. Stir in the milk, scraping the bottom of the pan to thoroughly blend. Cook over medium-high heat, stirring constantly, until the sauce thickens and comes to a boil. Add a pinch of salt, pepper, and nutmeg. Simmer over low heat, stirring often, 5 minutes. Add cayenne pepper to taste.

Preheat the oven to 375°F. Cook the frozen vegetables and noodles uncovered in a large pot of boiling salted water over high heat, stirring occasionally, about 5 minutes or until the noodles are nearly tender but a little firmer than usual. Drain, rinse with cold water, and drain well. Transfer to a large bowl.

Lightly butter a 2-quart baking dish. Add the sauce to the noodles and stir. Add the cottage cheese and mix well. Taste and adjust seasoning. Spoon into baking dish and sprinkle with mozzarella cheese. Bake 20 to 30 minutes or until bubbling. Brown under broiler, about 1 to 2 minutes. Serve from baking dish.

. . . .

Makes 8 servings
Nutritional information per serving: 378 calories; 10.5 g fat—24.5% calories from fat;
5.5 g saturated fat; 73 mg cholesterol

Low-Fat Macaroni and Cheese
{ d a i r y }

A rich-tasting casserole of this ever-popular dish with a buttery cream sauce can be low in fat. I like to add sautéed onion, hot pepper, and freshly grated nutmeg for extra zip.

In kosher markets and some supermarkets, you will find a variety of tasty kosher cheeses from Israel in addition to those made in America; choose any firm cheese that can be grated. If your market carries mostly sliced cheese, crumble the slices instead of trying to grate them. The casserole will be lowest in fat if you choose a part-skim mozzarella or another reduced-fat cheese.

3 tablespoons butter or margarine
¼ cup minced onion
1 fresh jalapeño pepper, seeded and minced (optional)
¼ cup all-purpose flour
2¼ cups skim milk

Salt and ground white pepper
Freshly grated nutmeg
2½ cups elbow macaroni
¾ cup shredded part-skim mozzarella or Swiss cheese
Paprika

Melt the butter in a heavy medium saucepan over low heat. Add the onion and jalapeño pepper if desired and cook, stirring occasionally, 5 minutes. Remove from the heat and stir in the flour. Cook over low heat, stirring constantly, 2 minutes. Remove from heat. Whisk in the milk. Cook over medium-high heat, whisking constantly, until the sauce thickens and comes to a boil. Add a pinch of salt, white pepper, and nutmeg to taste. Simmer over low heat, whisking often, 7 minutes. Taste and adjust seasoning.

Preheat the oven to 375°F. Cook the macaroni uncovered in a large pot of boiling salted water over high heat, stirring occasionally, about 6 minutes or until nearly tender but a little firmer than usual. Drain, rinse with cold water, and drain well. Transfer to a large bowl.

Lightly butter a 6- to 7-cup baking dish. Add the sauce to the macaroni and stir. Add all but 2 tablespoons cheese. Taste the mixture and adjust the seasoning. Spoon into baking dish, and sprinkle with the remaining cheese and with paprika.

Bake 20 to 30 minutes or until bubbling. Brown under broiler, about 1 to 2 minutes. Serve from the baking dish.

. . . .

Makes 4 to 6 servings
Nutritional information per serving: 308 calories; 9.1 g fat—26.7% calories from fat;
5.3 g saturated fat; 25 mg cholesterol

Fettuccine with Parmesan, Porcini, and Peas

{ d a i r y }

A combination of nonfat sour cream, grated Parmesan, and a touch of butter make this dish rich tasting and creamy. You can even pass a bowl of grated Parmesan separately for sprinkling lightly on each portion—up to 1 tablespoon per plate—and the pasta will still be low in fat. Diced yellow squash, thyme-scented tomatoes, and peas contribute color, flavor, and nutrients to this pasta entree.

1 ounce dried porcini mushrooms

1 28-ounce can tomatoes, drained and chopped

3 tablespoons butter

Salt and freshly ground black pepper

2 teaspoons chopped fresh thyme, or $\frac{1}{2}$ teaspoon dried

1 cup cooked peas

1 small yellow or green zucchini or crookneck squash, halved and cut crosswise into $\frac{1}{4}$-inch slices

8 ounces dried fettuccine or homemade Tomato Pasta (page 263)

$\frac{1}{3}$ cup nonfat sour cream, at room temperature

3 tablespoons grated Parmesan cheese

Grated Parmesan cheese, for serving

Soak the porcini in enough hot water to cover about 30 minutes or until tender; drain well. Remove the porcini, rinse, and discard any hard parts. Chop the porcini. Put the chopped tomatoes in a strainer to drain while preparing the remaining ingredients.

Melt 1 tablespoon butter in a medium skillet over medium heat. Add the porcini and stir. Add the tomatoes and salt and pepper to taste and cook, stirring often, 10 to 12 minutes or until mixture is thick. Stir in the thyme and peas. Heat 1 to 2 minutes. Taste and adjust seasoning. Keep warm over low heat.

Melt the remaining 2 tablespoons butter in a medium skillet. Add the zucchini and sauté over medium heat about 2 minutes or until just tender. Remove the zucchini with its cooking butter to a bowl, cover, and keep warm.

Cook the pasta uncovered in a large pot of boiling salted water over high heat, separating the strands occasionally with a fork, 1 to 2 minutes for fresh or 2 to 5 minutes for dried or until tender but firm to the bite. Drain well and transfer to a large, deep, heated serving dish.

Add the squash to the pasta and toss. Add the sour cream and toss. Sprinkle with 2 tablespoons cheese and spoon the tomato mixture on top. Sprinkle with the remaining tablespoon cheese. Toss at the table. Serve on hot plates, with additional cheese.

. . . .

Makes 3 main-course servings

Nutritional information per serving: 574 calories; 16.6 g fat—26.3% calories from fat;
9.3 g saturated fat; 39 mg cholesterol

Spinach and Rice Gratin

{ d a i r y }

*L*ayers of rice and spinach are topped here with a creamy sauce, crowned with grated cheese and
browned in the oven. This gratin makes a good dish for Shavuot. You can make it with cooked
white or brown rice. Accompany it with a selection of light vegetable salads, such as Israeli salad,
tomato salad, beet salad, and green salad.

2 tablespoons butter or margarine

3 tablespoons all-purpose flour

1 ½ cups skim milk

Salt and ground white pepper

Freshly grated nutmeg

Pinch of cayenne pepper

1 ½ tablespoons vegetable oil

1 large onion, chopped

3 cups cooked rice

1 ½ pounds fresh spinach, or 1
    10-ounce package cleaned spinach
    leaves (see Note opposite)

¼ cup grated Swiss cheese

In a heavy, medium saucepan, melt the butter over low heat, add the flour, and cook,
whisking constantly, about 2 minutes or until foaming but not browned. Remove
from heat. Gradually whisk in the milk. Bring to a boil over medium-high heat,
whisking. Add salt, white pepper, and nutmeg. Reduce the heat to low and cook,
whisking often, for 3 minutes. Remove from the heat and add the cayenne pepper.
Taste and adjust seasoning.

Heat the vegetable oil in a large nonstick skillet. Add the onion and sauté over
medium heat, stirring often, about 7 minutes or until softened. Mix with rice. Season
to taste with salt and pepper.

Preheat the oven to 400°F. If using fresh spinach bunches, pull off and discard
stems and rinse leaves thoroughly. Put the spinach leaves in a large saucepan of boiling salted water. Boil uncovered about 2 minutes or until just tender and wilted.
Drain, rinse with cold water, and drain well. Squeeze the spinach by handfuls to
remove as much water as possible. Coarsely chop with a knife.

Butter a heavy 2-quart gratin dish or other shallow baking dish. Spoon the rice
into the dish. Spoon ¼ cup sauce over rice and top with spinach. Spoon the remaining sauce carefully over the spinach to coat completely. Sprinkle evenly with cheese.

Bake until the sauce begins to bubble, about 10 minutes if sauce was still hot, or about 15 minutes if ingredients were at room temperature. If the top is not brown, transfer the dish to the broiler and broil just until cheese is lightly browned, about 1 minute, checking often and turning dish if necessary to brown it evenly. Serve hot.

Makes 4 servings

Nutritional information per serving: 418 calories; 14 g fat—29.7% calories from fat; 5.7 g saturated fat; 23 mg cholesterol

N O T E : You can substitute a 10-ounce package of frozen spinach. Let it thaw, squeeze out the excess liquid, and chop it coarsely.

Kosher Mushroom-Tomato Pizza

{ d a i r y }

*V*egetable pizzas are my favorite kind. Instead of the mushrooms in this pizza, you can use broiled eggplant (see Broiled Eggplant Slices with Fresh Tomato Salsa, page 125) or grilled peppers (page 157). Use kosher Parmesan or any kosher grating cheese available in your market. The dough is easy to make in the food processor.

PIZZA DOUGH
1 envelope (¼ ounce) active dry
   yeast, or 1 cake fresh yeast
½ cup lukewarm water
1½ cups all-purpose flour
2½ teaspoons olive oil
¾ teaspoon salt

TOPPING
¾ pound ripe tomatoes, peeled,
   seeded, and coarsely chopped (see
   Note opposite)

2 garlic cloves, finely chopped
1 teaspoon dried thyme
Salt and freshly ground black pepper
¼ teaspoon hot red pepper flakes, or
   to taste
½ pound mushrooms, thinly sliced
3 tablespoons grated Parmesan
   cheese
1 tablespoon plus 1 teaspoon extra-
   virgin olive oil

To make the dough in a food processor (or see Note opposite), sprinkle the dry yeast or crumble the fresh yeast over ¼ cup of the lukewarm water in a cup or small bowl and let stand for 10 minutes. Stir until smooth. In a food processor fitted with a dough blade or metal blade, process the flour and salt briefly to mix them. Add the remaining ¼ cup water and the olive oil to the yeast mixture. With the blades of the processor turning, gradually pour in the yeast mixture. If the dough is too dry to come together, add 1 tablespoon water and process again. Process for 1 minute to knead dough.

Transfer the dough to a clean bowl and sprinkle it with a little flour. Cover with a damp towel and leave to rise 45 to 60 minutes or until doubled in volume.

To make the topping, put the tomatoes in a colander or strainer, so their excess liquid can drain off.

Oil a baking sheet. Knead the dough again briefly and put it on a baking sheet. With oiled hands, pat the dough out to a 9- or 10-inch circle, with a rim slightly higher than center. Mix the tomatoes with the garlic, thyme, salt, pepper, and red pepper flakes. Spread the tomato mixture over the dough. Arrange the mushroom slices on top and sprinkle them lightly with Parmesan cheese and hot pepper flakes. Drizzle olive oil evenly over all, making sure that the rim of the dough is moistened with oil as well. Preheat the oven to 400°F. Let the dough rise for about 15 minutes.

Bake the pizza for 25 to 30 minutes or until the dough is golden brown and firm but not hard. Serve hot.

· ·

Makes 3 or 4 servings

Nutritional information per serving: 297 calories; 9.6 g fat—28.6% calories from fat;
1.9 g saturated fat; 3 mg cholesterol

N O T E : If you don't have ripe tomatoes for the topping, use a 14½-ounce can of tomatoes, drain off the liquid, and chop the tomatoes.

To make the dough by hand instead of in a food processor, sift the flour into a bowl and make a well in the center. Sprinkle the dry yeast or crumble the fresh yeast into the well. Pour ¼ cup lukewarm water over yeast and let stand for 10 minutes. Stir until smooth. Add the remaining ¼ cup water, the oil, and salt and mix with the ingredients in the middle of the well. Stir in the flour and mix well to obtain a fairly soft dough. If the dough is dry, add 1 tablespoon water. Knead the dough vigorously, slapping it on a lightly floured working surface until it is smooth and elastic. If it is very sticky, flour it occasionally while kneading.

Country Vegetable Tart

{ d a i r y }

This tart contains a medley of colorful vegetables embedded in a creamy filling. Savory tarts made with a yeast pastry crust are time-honored favorites in Europe and deserve to be better known in this country. Using this type of crust rather than pie dough is a good way to prepare a quiche-like tart with less fat.

YEAST PASTRY CRUST

1½ cups all-purpose flour

1 envelope (¼ ounce) active dry yeast, or 1 cake fresh yeast

6 tablespoons lukewarm water

1 extra-large egg

1½ teaspoons vegetable oil

¾ teaspoon salt

VEGETABLE FILLING

3 medium carrots, peeled

White and light green part of 2 large leeks, cleaned

2 small yellow crookneck squash or yellow zucchini

2½ tablespoons butter, margarine, or vegetable oil

Salt and freshly ground black pepper

½ cup frozen peas, thawed

6 ounces mushrooms, halved and thinly sliced

2 large eggs

½ cup 1 percent milk

White pepper

Freshly grated nutmeg

To make the yeast pastry (see Note opposite), sift the flour into a bowl and make a well in the center. Sprinkle the dry yeast or crumble the fresh yeast into the well. Pour 4 tablespoons lukewarm water over the yeast and let stand for 10 minutes. Stir until smooth. Add the remaining 2 tablespoons water, the egg, vegetable oil, and salt and mix with the ingredients in the middle of the well. Stir in the flour and mix well to obtain a fairly soft dough. If the dough is dry, add 1 tablespoon water. Knead the dough vigorously, slapping it on a working surface, until it is smooth and elastic. If it is very sticky, flour it occasionally while kneading.

Transfer the dough to a clean bowl and sprinkle it with a little flour. Cover with a damp towel and leave to rise 45 to 60 minutes or until doubled in volume.

To make the filling, cut the carrots, leeks, and squash in pieces about 1½ inches long. Cut these pieces in thin lengthwise slices, and each slice in thin lengthwise strips.

In a large skillet, melt 1½ tablespoons butter over low heat. Add the carrots, leeks, salt, and pepper. Cover and cook, stirring often, 15 minutes; if the mixture becomes dry, add 1 or 2 tablespoons water. Add the squash and cook, uncovered, about 3 minutes, or until all vegetables are tender. Taste and adjust seasoning. Add peas.

In a medium skillet, melt the remaining tablespoon butter over medium heat. Add the mushrooms and salt and pepper to taste, and sauté, stirring often, about 3 minutes or until tender.

Whisk the eggs and milk in a bowl until blended. Add salt, white pepper, and nutmeg.

Position a rack in the center of the oven and preheat to 400°F. Butter a 9- or 10-inch round fluted tart pan with removable bottom. Knead the dough lightly in bowl. Transfer the dough to the tart pan with aid of rubber spatula. With oiled knuckles, push dough outward from center toward rim, to line pan. Push the dough against rim of pan with oiled fingers, so tart has border about ½ inch thick at top edge. Set tart pan on a baking sheet.

Scatter the mushrooms over the dough and top evenly with vegetable mixture. Ladle the milk mixture carefully over the vegetables. Let rise in a warm, draft-free area 10 minutes.

Bake about 40 to 45 minutes or until dough browns and filling sets. Let cool on a rack for 15 minutes, then remove tart pan rim by setting pan on an overturned bowl. (Tart can be baked up to 4 hours ahead and kept at room temperature; it can also be frozen. Heat in 300°F. oven before serving.) Serve tart warm or at room temperature.

. . . .

Makes 6 servings

Nutritional information per serving: 283 calories; 9.5 g fat—29.5% calories from fat;
4.1 g saturated fat; 120 mg cholesterol

N O T E : If you wish to make the dough in a food processor, sprinkle the dry yeast or crumble the fresh yeast over 4 tablespoons lukewarm water in a cup or small bowl and let stand for 10 minutes. Stir until smooth. In a food processor fitted with the dough blade or metal blade, process the flour and salt briefly to mix. Add the remaining water, oil, and egg to the yeast mixture. With the blades of the processor turning, gradually pour in the yeast mixture. If the dough is too dry to come together, add 1 tablespoon water and process again. Process for 1 minute to knead dough. Transfer to a bowl and let rise as directed.

Cauliflower and Corn Soufflé

{ d a i r y }

As every good chef knows, a soufflé needs more egg whites than yolks so it rises high. I omit the yolks entirely for this soufflé, and with the fat saved I flavor it with a bit of Parmesan cheese. The result is a deliciously creamy yet low-fat soufflé, with corn kernels adding a pleasant texture and taste.

Serve this light, elegant dish as a first course, followed by a fish dish or a hearty vegetarian pasta or bean dish.

1 1-pound cauliflower, divided into
medium florets
2 tablespoons butter or margarine
4 tablespoons all-purpose flour
1 cup skim milk
Salt and freshly ground black pepper
Freshly grated nutmeg

1 1/2 cups frozen corn kernels, cooked
and drained
3 tablespoons grated Parmesan
cheese
1/4 cup nonfat sour cream
5 large egg whites

Butter five 1 1/4-cup soufflé dishes. Position the rack in the lower third of the oven and preheat to 425°F.

Place the cauliflower in a large pan of boiling salted water. Return to a boil and cook uncovered over high heat about 7 minutes or until very tender. Drain, rinse with cold water, and drain well. Puree in a food processor until very smooth. You will need 1 cup puree. Return the puree to the saucepan and cook over medium heat, stirring often, about 3 minutes to dry.

In a small, heavy saucepan, melt the butter over low heat, add the flour, and cook, whisking constantly, 2 minutes. Remove from the heat. Gradually whisk in the milk, thoroughly whisking in flour from sides of pan. Bring to a boil over medium-high heat, whisking. Reduce the heat to low, and cook, whisking often, 3 minutes. Remove from the heat and whisk in the cauliflower puree. Season with salt, pepper, and nutmeg. Stir in the corn. Bring to a boil, stirring.

With the pan off the heat, whisk 2 tablespoons cheese into the hot soufflé mixture, followed by the sour cream. Taste and add more salt, pepper, and nutmeg if needed. (Mixture can be prepared ahead to this point and refrigerated, covered.)

Have 5 plates ready near oven. If the soufflé mixture was cold, heat it in a small saucepan over low heat, stirring, until just warm. Remove from heat.

In a large bowl, beat the egg whites at medium speed until soft peaks form. Continue beating at high speed until whites are stiff but not dry. Quickly fold about one-quarter of the whites into the cauliflower mixture. Spoon this mixture over the remaining whites and fold in lightly but quickly, just until mixture is blended.

Divide the mixture among the prepared soufflé dishes. Sprinkle with remaining tablespoon cheese. Bake about 15 minutes, or until puffed and browned; when you gently move the oven rack, the soufflés should shake very slightly in center. Do not overbake or soufflés may burn on top and may shrink. Set the soufflé dishes on plates and serve immediately.

. . . .

Makes 5 servings

Nutritional information per serving: 184 calories; 6.2 g fat—29.6% calories from fat; 3.6 g saturated fat; 15 mg cholesterol

Poached Eggs with Zucchini, Tomatoes, and Mushrooms

{ p a r e v e }

Eggs poached directly in a tomato sauce make a quick and easy brunch entree or a casual supper dish for after Shabbat. Some Middle Eastern restaurants in Israel serve this type of dish and call it shakshuka. It can be made with a variety of vegetables. For example, if you have some leftover green beans or cauliflower, dice them and heat them in the sauce before adding the eggs.

1 1/2 teaspoons vegetable oil

1 small onion, chopped

2 small zucchini, cut into small cubes

4 ounces mushrooms, diced

1 14 1/2-ounce can tomatoes, drained and chopped

Salt and freshly ground black pepper

1/4 teaspoon chili powder, or to taste

2 large eggs

4 slices toast, for serving

Heat the vegetable oil in a heavy nonstick skillet. Add the onion and sauté over medium heat, stirring often for 3 minutes. Add the zucchini and mushrooms and sauté 2 minutes. Add the tomatoes, salt, pepper, and chili powder. Bring to a boil, cover, and cook 5 minutes. Carefully break each whole egg into a cup, then slide into the sauce. Cover and cook over low heat about 3 minutes or until eggs set. Serve with toast.

. . . .

Makes 2 servings

Nutritional information per serving: 327 calories; 11.3 g fat—29.9% calories from fat; 2.5 g saturated fat; 213 mg cholesterol

Scrambled Eggs with Green Onions and Tomatoes

{ p a r e v e }

*A*dding vegetables to scrambled eggs is a common technique in Sephardic homes in Israel. The favorites are leeks and other onion family members, tomatoes, peppers, and cauliflower. To cut the fat and cholesterol, I use a mixture of whole eggs and egg whites. Serve the eggs for supper or brunch with a cucumber or a pepper salad.

1 tablespoon vegetable oil
½ cup chopped green onion
　(scallion)
6 ripe plum tomatoes, diced
2 large eggs
2 large egg whites

Salt and freshly ground black pepper
Cayenne pepper
2 tablespoons chopped cilantro or
　parsley (optional)
2 fresh pita breads, halved, for
　serving

Heat the vegetable oil in a medium nonstick skillet over medium heat. Add the green onion and tomatoes and sauté about 2 minutes. Beat the eggs with the egg whites, salt, pepper, and cayenne pepper to taste. Add the egg mixture and cilantro to the skillet and scramble over low heat until set. Serve immediately with pita breads.

Makes 2 servings

Nutritional information per serving: 407 calories; 13.9 g fat—29.9% calories from fat;
2.6 g saturated fat; 213 mg cholesterol

13

The Fish Course

Sea Bass with Saffron, Basil, and Tomatoes

Steamed Sole with Mushrooms, Peppers, and Sage Vinaigrette

Broiled Halibut with Moroccan Marinade

Baked Fish with Tomato-Garlic Sauce

Fish and Rice Casserole with Green Beans and Onions

Haddock with Leeks and Olives

Steamed Bass with Green Onions and Ginger

Caper-Accented Tuna-Rice Salad in Tomato Cups

Sole with Tarragon-Scented Mushroom Sauce

Mediterranean Fish Soup with Linguine

FISH HAS A UNIQUE PLACE in the kosher kitchen because it can be served at meals that are either meat or dairy. Often it plays the role of first course. This is especially true of Rosh Hashanah and Shabbat meals, where fish is a traditional delicacy that is cooked ahead and usually served cold.

The most familiar fish appetizer in the Ashkenazic kitchen is gefilte fish (page 88). These poached balls of ground fish are made in many regional variations, some based on carp, some on whitefish, others on a mixture of fish. They might be delicately flavored or they might be sweet. Gefilte fish is easy to find in jars at the store, but it tastes so much better when made at home and is perfect for low-fat menus.

Many other tasty fish dishes can make terrific holiday starters. Sea bass cooked in the Sephardic style, with saffron, basil, and tomatoes (opposite), is wonderful served hot or cold. So are Haddock with Leeks and Olives (page 200) and Baked Fish with Tomato-Garlic Sauce (page 198).

For healthy cooking, fish is most valuable, as it is much lower in fat than meat. Fresh fish that is properly cooked can make an elegant, delicious main course. For example, sole fillets poached with white wine, fish broth, and shallots and served in a tarragon-scented mushroom sauce (page 204) is worthy of the best occasions. Serve it with aromatic basmati rice and freshly cooked asparagus.

Unlike meat, fish does not have to be salted and requires no special preparation to be kosher. Since fish cooks quickly, it is convenient for serving often for family meals.

When you're preparing low-fat menus, avoid fried fish and opt for baked, broiled, grilled, braised, or poached fish. A good-quality fish needs little embellishment; I love to prepare broiled Chilean sea bass or salmon steaks, sprinkled with thyme, paprika, salt, pepper, and olive oil before they are put on the broiler or grill.

Steaming is also a useful, healthful technique for cooking fish. You can steam fish in the Chinese manner, sprinkled with a little soy sauce, ginger, and green onion (page 202). Or you might like to try the French way of steaming fish, first seasoning with salt, pepper, and herbs, then serving it on fresh lettuce with a light sprinkling of vinaigrette dressing (page 196).

Other Fish Dishes

Baked Fish Steaks with Pistou (page 13) · Sephardic Sea Bass with Sweet Peppers and Garlic (page 45) · Roasted Salmon with Asparagus (page 91) · Sea Bass in Tomato Sauce with Bell Peppers and Garlic (page 129)

Sea Bass with Saffron, Basil, and Tomatoes

{ p a r e v e }

This dish boasts the flavors of bouillabaisse, the gem of Provençal cuisine. When you have good ingredients, like fresh Chilean sea bass, ripe tomatoes, and garden-fresh basil, this easy-to-make dish becomes an elegant creation. Serve it as a main course with basmati rice or fine-quality pasta. If served cold, it also makes a tasty first course for Rosh Hashanah or Shabbat.

1 tablespoon extra-virgin olive oil

1 large garlic clove, chopped

1 pound ripe tomatoes, peeled, seeded, and chopped, or 1 28-ounce can tomatoes, drained and chopped

Salt and freshly ground black pepper

¼ teaspoon saffron threads

1 tablespoon chopped fresh basil, or 1 teaspoon dried

1½ pounds sea bass steaks or fillets, about 1 inch thick

Preheat the oven to 400°F. Heat the olive oil in a large skillet. Stir in the garlic, then the tomatoes, salt, pepper, and saffron and cook over medium heat 10 minutes or until thick. Add dried (but not fresh) basil.

Put the fish in a baking dish and sprinkle lightly with salt and pepper. Top with the sauce. Cover and bake 18 minutes. Uncover and bake 5 minutes or until fish can just be flaked but is not falling apart. Add fresh basil to sauce if using. Taste and adjust seasoning. Serve fish hot, warm, or cold.

. . . .

Makes 4 servings

Nutritional information per serving: 220 calories; 7.2 g fat—29.9% calories from fat; 1.3 g saturated fat; 70 mg cholesterol

Steamed Sole with Mushrooms, Peppers, and Sage Vinaigrette

{ p a r e v e }

Prepare this light, colorful fish entree when you have fresh sage. You can make it with flounder or any members of the sole family. If possible, use extra-virgin olive oil for the dressing. The fish is good hot or cold, but the accompanying potatoes really should be hot. If you wish to serve it as a first course, it will make 6 to 8 servings.

6 ounces small mushrooms
2½ tablespoons olive oil
1 medium red bell pepper, cored, seeded, and diced
1 small green bell pepper, cored, seeded, and diced
Salt and freshly ground black pepper
1 tablespoon white wine vinegar or herb vinegar

½ tablespoon water
3 tablespoons minced fresh sage leaves
1¼ pounds sole fillets
¼ cup chopped green onions (scallions)
2 large garlic cloves, minced
8 small red potatoes, boiled, for serving

Stem the mushrooms. Halve the mushroom caps and cut them into thin slices; reserve stems for other uses. In a large, heavy skillet, heat 1 tablespoon of the olive oil over medium-high heat. Add the mushrooms, diced peppers, salt, and pepper and sauté about 7 minutes or until vegetables are just tender and any excess liquid evaporates; cover and reduce heat if the vegetables begin to brown. Set aside.

In a small bowl, combine the remaining 1½ tablespoons olive oil with the vinegar, water, and 2 tablespoons minced sage. Whisk until blended. Season to taste with salt and pepper.

Run your fingers over the fillets to check for bones; pull out any bones using tweezers or a sharp paring knife. Sprinkle the sole on both sides with salt and pepper. Sprinkle lightly with about ½ tablespoon sage and fold each fillet in half. Sprinkle top with remaining sage. Set the sole on the top portion of a steamer over boiling water, cover, and cook over high heat about 2 or 3 minutes or until fillets become opaque. Transfer them to a platter and keep warm.

Reheat the vegetables over medium heat. Stir in the green onions and garlic and cook 1 minute. Transfer the fish to plates, discarding liquid from their platter. Scatter the vegetables over and around the fish. Whisk the vinaigrette, spoon it over fish, and serve with boiled potatoes.

· ·
Makes 4 main-course or 6 to 8 first-course servings
Nutritional information per serving: 288 calories; 9.7 g fat—29.8% calories from fat;
1.3 g saturated fat; 0 mg cholesterol

Broiled Halibut with Moroccan Marinade
{ p a r e v e }

*F*ish *needs to be marinated only about 30 minutes to absorb flavors, so a marinated fish is much quicker to prepare than meat. This marinade, called* chermoula, *is a classic North African seasoning for fish. I find it to be a fine marinade for chicken breasts too before they are broiled or grilled.*

Serve the fish with potatoes, rice, or couscous. Broccoli florets or roasted red bell peppers make good vegetable accompaniments.

1 tablespoon chopped cilantro	2½ teaspoons olive oil
1 medium garlic clove, minced	Pinch of salt
1 teaspoon ground cumin	1½ pounds halibut steaks
1 teaspoon paprika	Lemon wedges, for serving
Pinch of cayenne pepper	

Mix the cilantro, garlic, cumin, paprika, cayenne pepper, olive oil, and salt in a small bowl. Drizzle over the halibut steaks and turn to coat both sides. Marinate 30 minutes.

Line a broiler rack with foil if desired. Preheat the broiler with the rack about 4 inches from the heat source. Lightly oil the broiler rack or foil.

Set the fish on the broiler rack and broil 4 minutes. Turn over and broil 4 to 5 more minutes. To check whether fish is done, make a small cut with a sharp knife near the bone; the flesh should have become opaque white all the way through. Serve hot, with lemon wedges.

· ·
Makes 4 servings
Nutritional information per serving: 224.5 calories; 7 g fat—28.1% calories from fat;
1 g saturated fat; 54 mg cholesterol

Baked Fish with Tomato-Garlic Sauce

{ p a r e v e }

*S*ea bass, cod, scrod, haddock, halibut, or Pacific snapper can be used in this piquant entree. *Sautéed or steamed zucchini sticks and pasta shells make good accompaniments.*

1 tablespoon olive oil

2 28-ounce cans whole tomatoes, drained and chopped

Salt and freshly ground black pepper

½ teaspoon dried thyme

1 ½ pounds fish steaks or fillets, about 1 inch thick

2 tablespoons dry white wine

½ to ⅔ cup fish or vegetable broth

3 large garlic cloves, minced

Preheat the oven to 425° F. Heat the olive oil in a large sauté pan over medium heat. Stir in the tomatoes, salt, pepper, and thyme. Bring to a boil. Cook uncovered, stirring occasionally, until sauce is thick, about 15 minutes.

Lightly oil a 10-cup oval gratin dish or other heavy, shallow baking dish. Cut a piece of parchment paper or foil to the size of the dish; lightly oil the paper or foil. If using fish fillets, run your fingers over them and carefully pull out any bones with tweezers or sharp paring knife.

Arrange the fish pieces in the dish in one layer. Pour the wine over them. Sprinkle the fish lightly with salt and pepper. Bring ½ cup broth to a simmer in a small saucepan and pour it over the fish. If the liquid doesn't cover the base of the dish, add more broth. Set the oiled paper directly on the fish. Bake about 10 minutes. When tested with a fork at its thickest point, the fish should be opaque and should just flake.

Remove the fish carefully to a platter with 2 wide slotted spatulas, reserving the cooking liquid. Cover the fish with its oiled paper and keep warm.

Pour the fish cooking liquid from the baking dish into the tomato sauce. Add the garlic. Boil the sauce, stirring often, until it thickens, about 2 minutes. Taste and adjust seasoning. Discard any liquid from the fish platter. Coat the fish with sauce and serve hot or cold.

Makes 4 servings

Nutritional information per serving: 271 calories; 6.3 g fat—21.1% calories from fat; 1.2 g saturated fat; 75 mg cholesterol

Fish and Rice Casserole with Green Beans and Onions

{ p a r e v e }

Casseroles do not necessarily have a white sauce. In this one, seasoned in the Indian manner, golden rice is flavored with cilantro and layered with green beans and fish. It's an excellent way to make use of extra cooked fish and is easy to prepare. The green beans and rice are parboiled together, then finish cooking with the fish and sautéed onions in a casserole in the oven.

3 tablespoons vegetable oil

2 medium onions, sliced

6 cups water

Salt and freshly ground black pepper

1⅓ cups long-grain rice

¾ pound green beans, ends removed, cut into 1-inch pieces

½ teaspoon turmeric

2 cups flaked cooked fish, preferably salmon

⅓ cup coarsely chopped cilantro

Preheat the oven to 350°F. Heat 2 tablespoons of the vegetable oil in large saucepan, add the onions, and sauté over medium heat, stirring often, about 7 minutes or until beginning to brown. Remove from pan.

In the same pan, bring the water to a boil with a pinch of salt. Add the rice and boil uncovered 5 minutes. Add the green beans and boil uncovered 5 minutes. Drain the rice and beans, rinse with cold water, and drain well. The rice will be partially cooked, beans nearly cooked.

In a bowl, mix the rice and beans with the turmeric and with salt and pepper to taste. Lightly mix in the fish.

Spoon half the onions into a 2-quart casserole. Top with half the rice and half the cilantro. Repeat the layers. Drizzle the remaining tablespoon of oil over top. Pour ½ cup hot water around edge of casserole. Cover and bake 45 minutes or until the rice is tender and the water is absorbed.

. . . .

Makes 4 servings

Nutritional information per serving: 440 calories; 14.7 g fat—30% calories from fat; 1.9 g saturated fat; 62 mg cholesterol

Haddock with Leeks and Olives

{ p a r e v e }

This festive dish is based on a fish entree I learned from master chef Fernand Chambrette in Paris. The fish cooks in a garlic-scented tomato sauce enhanced with leeks, then is embellished with black and green olives. It makes a delicious cold fish course for Shabbat, or a hot main course with rice.

2 medium leeks, white and light green parts only, halved lengthwise and rinsed well

1 tablespoon plus 2 teaspoons olive oil

1 small onion, chopped

1 small carrot, peeled and finely diced

3 large garlic cloves, coarsely chopped

1 ½ pounds ripe tomatoes, cut into chunks, or 1 28-ounce and 1 14-ounce can whole tomatoes, drained and quartered

1 cup Quick Fish Broth (page 171)

Salt and freshly ground black pepper

1 bay leaf

1 large sprig fresh thyme, or ½ teaspoon dried, crumbled

1 ½ pounds haddock or cod fillet, cut into 4 or 6 pieces

1 tablespoon tomato paste

¼ cup pitted green olives, drained well

¼ cup pitted black olives, drained well

Cut the leeks in 3 × ⅛-inch strips and set aside. Heat 1 tablespoon of the olive oil in a large, deep skillet over medium heat. Add the onion, carrot, and garlic. Cook over low heat 3 minutes; do not let vegetables brown. Add the tomatoes, broth, salt, bay leaf, and thyme. Bring to a boil. Cover and cook over low heat 10 minutes. Add the fish pieces. Cover and poach over low heat about 10 minutes or until fish can just be flaked with a fork. With a slotted spatula, carefully remove the fish pieces.

Crush the tomato pieces in the skillet lightly with a spoon. Simmer the sauce uncovered over medium heat, stirring often, until the tomatoes are very soft, about 10 minutes. Strain the sauce, pressing firmly on the vegetables in a strainer to extract as much juice as possible. Return strained sauce to skillet.

Heat the remaining 2 teaspoons olive oil in another large skillet over low heat. Add the leeks and mix well. Cover and cook, stirring often, until tender, about 7 minutes.

Boil the tomato sauce, stirring, until thick enough to coat a spoon, about 5 minutes. Stir the tomato paste into the sauce until well blended. Stir in the leeks and green olives and simmer 1 minute. Remove from the heat. Taste and adjust seasoning.

Discard any vegetable dice attached to the fish. To serve hot, return the fish to the sauce in the skillet, cover, and reheat briefly. Transfer to a platter. Spoon the sauce, olives, and leeks around the fish. Garnish fish with a few black olives. Serve hot or cold.

. . . .

Makes 4 main-course or 6 first-course servings

Nutritional information per serving: 225 calories; 7.3 g fat—29.6% calories from fat; 1.4 g saturated fat; 67 mg cholesterol

Steamed Bass with Green Onions and Ginger

{ p a r e v e }

The Chinese technique for steaming whole fish keeps them moist and produces delectable results. Serve the fish with steamed rice and with a colorful vegetable accompaniment, such as Snow Peas with Baby Corn and Chinese Mushrooms (page 301).

1 1½-pound whole bass or other whole fish

Salt and freshly ground black pepper

2 tablespoons dry sherry

1½ tablespoons soy sauce

½ teaspoon sugar

Pinch of cayenne pepper

1½ tablespoons water

2 teaspoons vegetable oil

1 tablespoon minced, peeled fresh ginger

2 tablespoons minced green onion (scallion)

2 large garlic cloves, minced

3 tablespoons very thin strips of green onion (scallion), about 1½ inches long

Snip the fins and trim the tail of the fish straight, using sturdy scissors. Rinse the fish inside and out, removing any scales, and pat dry. Bring at least 1 inch of water to a boil in the base of a steamer. The water should not reach holes in top of steamer.

Make 3 diagonal slashes on each side of the fish. Rub the fish inside and out with salt, pepper, and 1 teaspoon sherry. Set the fish on a heatproof deep plate that can fit easily in steamer top. In a small cup, mix the remaining sherry with the soy sauce, sugar, cayenne pepper, and water.

Heat the vegetable oil in a small, heavy saucepan over medium-high heat. Add the ginger, minced green onion, and garlic and sauté, stirring, for ½ minute. Add the soy sauce mixture and bring to a simmer. Pour mixture over fish.

Set the fish on its plate in the steamer top above boiling water and cover tightly. Steam the fish over high heat about 10 minutes or until a cake tester or thin skewer inserted into the thickest part of the fish comes out hot to your touch. Remove the fish from the steamer and scatter the green onion strips over it. Serve fish on its plate.

. . . .

Makes 2 servings

Nutritional information per serving: 409 calories; 12.6 g fat—29.9% calories from fat;
2.3 g saturated fat; 272 mg cholesterol

Caper-Accented Tuna-Rice Salad
in Tomato Cups
{ p a r e v e }

Tomato halves filled with a savory salad are a welcome summer entree or appetizer. You can serve this salad for a Shavuot buffet together with Cucumber Salad with Yogurt Dill Dressing (page 31), grilled marinated peppers (page 145), Creamy Broccoli-Noodle Kugel (page 111), and homemade cheesecake (page 117) with fresh strawberries for dessert.

1 ¼ cups long-grain white rice
12 ounces water-packed canned
   tuna, drained
¼ cup chopped red onion
3 tablespoons chopped fresh basil or
   parsley

2 teaspoons drained capers
1 ½ tablespoons white wine vinegar
3 tablespoons olive oil
Salt and freshly ground black pepper
6 large firm tomatoes
6 black olives, halved, for garnish

In a large saucepan, bring about 2 quarts water to a boil and add a pinch of salt. Add the rice and boil uncovered about 12 to 14 minutes or until just tender but still firm; check by tasting. Drain, rinse with cold water, and drain well. Mix the rice with the tuna, onion, basil, and capers in a large bowl.

Make a vinaigrette dressing by combining the vinegar, olive oil, salt, and pepper to taste in small bowl; whisk thoroughly. Add to the rice mixture; mix gently. Taste and adjust the seasoning; add more oil and vinegar if desired. Cover and refrigerate 30 minutes or up to 2 days.

Halve the tomatoes horizontally. Remove the interior with a teaspoon, leaving a layer of pulp attached to the skin to form a shell. Turn the tomatoes over on a plate and leave to drain about 30 minutes.

Fill the tomato halves with the salad, mounding filling. Garnish each with half a black olive. Serve within 1 hour.

Makes 12 appetizer or 6 light main-course servings
Nutritional information per serving: 262 calories; 8.1 g fat—27.8% calories from fat; 1.2 g saturated fat; 17 mg cholesterol

Sole with Tarragon-Scented Mushroom Sauce

{ d a i r y }

For an elegant entree, poach sole fillets the classic European way in white wine and fish broth flavored with shallots, then thicken the poaching liquid to turn it into a luscious sauce. Steamed new potatoes are the sole's classic partner. You can substitute flounder fillets for the sole.

½ pound mushrooms, cut into thin slices
1 teaspoon lemon juice
Salt and ground white pepper
2 pounds sole fillets
⅓ cup dry white wine

2 cups Quick Fish Broth (page 171)
3 shallots, finely chopped
2 tablespoons butter or margarine
2½ tablespoons all-purpose flour
½ cup skim milk
1 tablespoon chopped fresh tarragon

Combine the mushrooms, lemon juice, salt, and white pepper in a medium saucepan. Cover and bring to a boil. Cook over medium-high heat about 3 minutes or until tender. Drain the mushrooms, reserving the liquid.

Fold the sole fillets in half, with the whiter side outward. Combine the white wine, broth, and shallots in a sauté pan or large saucepan. Bring to a simmer. Add the folded fillets and sprinkle them with salt and white pepper. Return to a simmer. Cover, reduce heat to low, and cook about 8 minutes or until the fish is opaque and a cake tester or thin skewer inserted into thickest part of the fish comes out hot to the touch. Carefully remove the fish from the liquid, using 2 slotted spatulas, and set on paper towels. Transfer carefully to a platter, cover, and keep warm. Strain the cooking liquid and reserve.

Pour the mushroom liquid into a measuring cup. Add enough of the cooking liquid to make 1½ cups. (Reserve remaining liquid as fish broth for other recipes.)

Melt the butter in a heavy, medium saucepan over low heat. Whisk in the flour. Cook, whisking constantly, about 2 minutes or until the mixture turns light beige. Remove from the heat and let cool slightly. Gradually whisk in the measured liquid. Bring to a boil over medium-high heat, whisking. Reduce heat to medium-low and simmer, uncovered, whisking often, for 5 minutes. Whisk in the milk and bring to a boil. Simmer, whisking often, about 3 minutes or until the sauce is thick enough to coat a spoon.

Add the mushrooms to the sauce and warm over low heat. Remove from the heat and stir in the tarragon. Taste, and add salt and white pepper if needed. Spoon the sauce and mushrooms over the sole and serve immediately.

. . . .

Makes 4 servings

*Nutritional information per serving: 315 calories; 9.4 g fat—29.6% calories from fat;
5 g saturated fat; 22 mg cholesterol*

Mediterranean Fish Soup with Linguine

{ p a r e v e }

Sea bass and linguine in a tomato, garlic, and saffron broth makes a light, elegant main course. You might like to present it as the center of a Shavuot meal, followed by a salad, then cheesecake for dessert. This fish soup is also perfect for Succot; bring it to the Succah in a beautiful soup tureen.

To vary this recipe, omit the linguine and serve each portion topped with a heaped spoonful of rice; or simply serve the soup with crusty bread. If you don't have leeks, you can add another onion.

1 tablespoon plus 1 teaspoon olive oil

2 medium onions, halved and thinly sliced

2 medium leeks, white part only, split, rinsed well, and sliced

3 celery stalks, sliced

1¼ pounds ripe tomatoes, peeled, seeded, and chopped

4 large garlic cloves, chopped

4½ cups Quick Fish Broth (page 171)

1 bay leaf

¼ teaspoon lightly crushed saffron threads

Salt and freshly ground black pepper

2 tablespoons tomato paste

4 ounces dried linguine

1 pound sea bass or halibut fillet, cut into ¾-inch dice

3 tablespoons chopped parsley

1½ teaspoons chopped fresh thyme leaves, or ½ teaspoon dried

Heat the olive oil in a large, wide casserole over medium-low heat. Add the onions, leeks, and celery and cook about 5 minutes or until soft but not brown. Add the tomatoes and garlic and cook 1 minute. Add the broth, bay leaf, saffron, and salt and pepper to taste. Bring to a boil. Cook uncovered over low heat 20 minutes. Add the tomato paste and cook 1 minute.

Cook the linguine uncovered in a large pan of boiling salted water over high heat about 8 minutes or until tender but firm to the bite. Drain, rinse, and drain well.

Bring the soup to a simmer. Add the sea bass and simmer uncovered 5 minutes or until it is just tender. Add the linguine, parsley, and thyme and heat through. Taste and adjust seasoning. Serve hot.

. . . .

Makes 4 main-course or 6 first-course servings

Nutritional information per serving: 317 calories; 9.8 g fat—30% calories from fat; 3.7 g saturated fat; 43 mg cholesterol

14

Chicken and Turkey Dishes

Moroccan Chicken with Mushrooms, Olives, and Cilantro

Kosher Coq au Vin

Tandoori Chicken with Basmati Rice

Baked Chicken Legs with Orange and Soy Marinade

Sweet and Sour Chicken Breasts with Ginger

Jewish Jambalaya

Chicken Chili with Beans

Chicken with Forty Cloves of Garlic

Broiled Chicken with Easy Mushroom Sauce

Rice with Chicken and Green Onions

Chicken Stew with Green Peas and Baby Onions

Cornish Hens with Couscous and Figs

Spicy Turkey Burgers with Cumin, Coriander, and Cilantro

Rice Pilaf with Turkey Sausages and Black Olives

Turkey Salad with Red Beans and Rice

Turkey, Mango, and Brown Rice Salad

IF WE WERE TO JUDGE foods according to their importance in traditional kosher menus, chicken would be king. In many homes, a roasted, golden brown chicken is an eagerly anticipated main course for Shabbat and most festivals.

Today there are so many more kosher poultry products widely available than there were thirty years ago. In addition to whole chickens, turkeys, and Cornish hens, you can buy chicken and turkey parts, such as boneless and skinless breasts, a boon to low-fat cooking. Some markets carry kosher ducks and geese, but these birds will not make frequent appearances on your table if you're sticking to a low-fat eating program. Many supermarkets now carry both fresh and frozen kosher poultry. You can also find ready-cooked kosher poultry items, such as roasted and barbecued chicken, smoked turkey and chicken and turkey frankfurters.

Chicken breasts contain the least amount of fat, but you can use the dark meat in low-fat meals as long as you don't eat the skin, which contains most of the fat. Cook the chicken with or without its skin, but remove the skin before eating the chicken. Skim the cooking liquid or braising sauce as thoroughly as possible before it is served.

For low-fat cooking, baking a chicken with sauce or liquid is a useful technique. The liquid will help keep skinless meat from drying out. In actually roasting poultry, the skin is needed so the meat will not become dry. Another convenient cooking method is braising in a flavorful liquid. The sauce acquires a depth of flavor from cooking with the chicken, and is perfect for moistening couscous or rice.

Gentle poaching is a traditional, low-fat method for cooking chicken and has the benefit of producing a rich, delicious broth. One advantage is that it's easy to add a variety of seasonal vegetables while the chicken cooks, so you have a nutritious meal in one pot.

Other Chicken and Turkey Dishes

Baked Chicken in Spicy Tomato and Grilled Pepper Sauce (page 14) · Turkey Tsimmes with Apricots and Red Wine (page 16) · Chicken in the Pot with Fresh Herbs (page 27) Stuffed Tomatoes with Chicken, Rice, and Ginger (page 39) · Sweet and Sour Cabbage Rolls with Turkey Stuffing (page 40) · Eggplant Stuffed with Chicken, Cilantro and Sun-Dried Tomatoes (page 42) · Stuffed Peppers, Latin American Style (page 44) · Chicken Chasseur (page 48) · Easy Chicken Breast Paella (page 65) Turkey Breast with Mushrooms and Red Wine (page 76) · Roast Turkey Breast with Potatoes and Rosemary (page 92) · Baked Chicken with Garlic, Cumin, and Tomatoes (page 94) · Lighter Chopped Liver (page 121) · Golden Roast Chicken with Corn and Cilantro Stuffing (page 130) · Yemenite Chicken Cholent (page 132)

Moroccan Chicken with Mushrooms, Olives, and Cilantro

{ m e a t }

*C*hicken imparts a rich flavor to the tomato-mushroom sauce in which it simmers for this entree. Since it can be made ahead, it's convenient for Shabbat and in fact for any holiday. If you're serving it for Passover, accompany it with boiled or baked potatoes instead of couscous.

2½ pounds chicken pieces

1 tablespoon olive oil

Salt and freshly ground black pepper

½ pound mushrooms, quartered

4 large garlic cloves, minced

2 pounds ripe tomatoes, peeled, seeded, and chopped, or 2 28-ounce cans tomatoes, drained and chopped

½ cup chicken broth or water

½ cup pitted green olives

Pinch of cayenne pepper

½ teaspoon fresh lemon juice

3 tablespoons chopped cilantro or Italian parsley

4 cups hot cooked couscous or rice, for serving

Pat the chicken pieces dry. In a large skillet, heat the olive oil over medium-high heat. Sprinkle the chicken with salt and pepper on both sides and brown it in batches in oil; transfer browned pieces to a plate. Discard all but 1 tablespoon fat from the skillet. Add the mushrooms and salt and pepper to taste, and sauté over medium-high heat until lightly browned. Remove from skillet.

Add the garlic to the skillet and sauté a few seconds. Stir in the tomatoes and broth. Return the chicken to the skillet with any juices on the plate and bring to a boil. Cover and simmer over low heat about 35 minutes or until the breast pieces are tender and cooked through. Transfer them to a plate. Cook the remaining pieces about 10 minutes or until tender and cooked through. Skim fat from sauce.

If you prefer a thicker sauce, transfer the remaining chicken to a plate and boil the sauce about 5 minutes, stirring. Return the chicken and mushrooms to the skillet and add the olives, cayenne pepper, and lemon juice. Cover and warm over low heat 3 minutes. Add the cilantro and adjust seasoning. Serve with couscous or rice.

Makes 4 servings

Nutritional information per serving: 690 calories; 21.9 g fat—28.6% calories from fat; 5 g saturated fat; 155 mg cholesterol

Kosher Coq au Vin

{ m e a t }

Dry red wine, pearl onions, and mushrooms are the stars in this rendition of the favorite French poultry specialty. Traditional accompaniments are potatoes (as below), rice, or crusty baguette to soak up the savory sauce.

20 baby onions (pearl onions)	1 cup dry red wine
1 tablespoon plus 2 teaspoons vegetable oil	1 tablespoon all-purpose flour
½ pound mushrooms, quartered	1 garlic clove, minced
Salt and freshly ground black pepper	⅔ cup chicken broth
2½ pounds chicken pieces	Pinch of sugar (optional)
	8 small boiled potatoes, for serving

Put the baby onions in a small saucepan, cover with water, and bring to a boil. Boil 1 minute. Drain, rinse under cold water, and drain well. Peel onions with the aid of a paring knife.

Heat 1 tablespoon vegetable oil in large, heavy nonstick skillet over medium-low heat. Add the baby onions and sauté over medium-high heat, shaking the pan often and turning them over carefully, until browned on all sides. Transfer to a bowl with a slotted spoon. Reheat the pan. Add the mushrooms, salt, and pepper and brown lightly. Transfer to a bowl.

Pat the chicken pieces dry. Sprinkle lightly with pepper on all sides. Add remaining 2 teaspoons oil to the skillet and heat over medium heat. Add the chicken leg and thigh pieces and brown lightly on all sides. Set on a plate, using a slotted spoon. Add the breast and wing pieces to the skillet and brown them lightly. Return the leg and thigh pieces, with juices from the plate, and baby onions to skillet. Scatter the mushrooms over them and arrange the breast and wing pieces on top. Add ½ cup wine. Cover and cook over low heat about 30 minutes or until the breast pieces are tender when pierced with a knife and cooked through.

Meanwhile, in a small cup, whisk 2 tablespoons of the wine into the flour until the mixture is smooth.

Transfer the chicken breast pieces to a platter; cover and keep warm. Cook the remaining chicken pieces and vegetables about 10 minutes more or until all are tender and cooked through. Add the leg and thigh pieces to platter. With a slotted spoon, transfer the mushrooms and baby onions to a bowl.

Skim as much fat as possible from the chicken cooking liquid. Reheat the liquid until very hot. Add the garlic and remaining wine and bring to a boil, stirring. Add the broth and boil, stirring and skimming fat often, until mixture is reduced to about 1 cup. Gradually whisk the flour mixture into the simmering sauce. Bring to a boil, whisking.

Return the mushrooms and onions to the sauce and heat 2 minutes over low heat. Taste sauce for seasoning; if the flavor is too acid, add a pinch of sugar. Spoon the sauce and vegetable mixture over the chicken and serve, accompanied by boiled potatoes.

Makes 4 servings

Nutritional information per serving: 782 calories; 22.3 g fat—26.8% calories from fat; 5 g saturated fat; 155 mg cholesterol

Tandoori Chicken with Basmati Rice

{ m e a t }

Tandoori chicken may be the best-known dish in Indian cuisine. This tasty roast chicken is aromatic from the medley of spices used in its marinade, but it is not hot. In addition to spices, the marinade contains chopped onion, garlic, and fresh ginger. This famous dish is perfect for low-fat cooking because the chicken traditionally is cooked without the skin.

Jews from India have developed a kosher version of tandoori chicken marinade. They mix the spices with lemon juice and oil instead of the customary yogurt. Some also add a small amount of mayonnaise.

Serve the chicken and its fragrant basmati rice with cooked cauliflower, peas, green beans, or mushrooms.

½ small onion, diced

3 large garlic cloves, peeled

1 tablespoon coarsely chopped, peeled fresh ginger

2 tablespoons fresh lemon juice

2 tablespoons vegetable oil

1 tablespoon mayonnaise (optional)

1½ teaspoons ground coriander

1½ teaspoons ground cumin

½ teaspoon turmeric

¼ teaspoon ground allspice

¼ teaspoon ground cinnamon

Pinch of cloves

¼ teaspoon ground black pepper

¼ teaspoon cayenne pepper

2½ pounds chicken thighs

2 cups basmati rice

3½ cups water

Pinch of salt

Lemon wedges, for serving

In a food processor, combine the onion, garlic, and ginger and process until finely chopped. Add the lemon juice and 1 tablespoon vegetable oil and process to blend. Transfer to a bowl and stir in the mayonnaise if desired, coriander, cumin, turmeric, allspice, cinnamon, cloves, pepper, and cayenne pepper.

Remove skin and trim excess fat from the chicken thighs. Make 2 or 3 small slits in each chicken piece so the marinade will penetrate better. Put in a shallow dish. Add the marinade and rub it all over chicken. Cover and refrigerate 2 hours to overnight.

Preheat the oven to 400°F. Set the chicken in a single layer on a rack in a roasting pan. Roast until juices come out clear when meat is pricked in thickest part with a thin knife, about 45 minutes. If the juices are pink, roast a few more minutes.

Meanwhile, rinse the rice well. In a large pan, combine the rice with the remaining tablespoon oil, water, and a pinch of salt. Bring to a boil. Cover and cook over very low heat about 20 minutes or until just tender. Let stand 10 minutes, covered. Fluff lightly with a fork.

Serve chicken with lemon wedges and rice.

. . . .

Makes 4 servings

Nutritional information per serving: 682 calories; 16.3 g fat—22% calories from fat; 3 g saturated fat; 186 mg cholesterol

Baked Chicken Legs with Orange and Soy Marinade

{ m e a t }

*C*hicken drumsticks and thighs can fit into low-fat meals if you remove the skin. In this recipe, the easy-to-make marinade keeps the chicken moist and adds a delightful sweet, spicy, and tangy flavor. Serve the chicken with rice and with green beans, zucchini, or broccoli. You might like to garnish each plate with slices of fresh orange.

2¾ pounds chicken legs	1 teaspoon grated orange rind
¼ cup orange juice	1 medium shallot, minced
2 tablespoons soy sauce	1 teaspoon ground ginger
2 tablespoons fresh lemon juice	¼ teaspoon ground cloves
1½ tablespoons vegetable oil	Pinch of freshly ground black pepper
1 tablespoon honey	6 cups hot cooked rice, for serving

Remove the skin from the chicken. In a shallow dish, mix the orange juice, soy sauce, lemon juice, vegetable oil, honey, orange rind, shallot, ginger, cloves, and pepper. Add the chicken pieces and turn them over in mixture. Rub the mixture thoroughly into the chicken. Cover and refrigerate chicken for 2 hours or up to 24 hours, turning occasionally.

Preheat the oven to 400°F. Lightly oil a roasting pan. Put the chicken in pan in a single layer. Cover with foil and bake 30 minutes. Uncover and bake, basting occasionally, 25 to 30 minutes or until tender; juices should no longer be pink when thickest part of thigh is pierced.

Serve hot, with rice.

. . . .

Makes 4 servings

Nutritional information per serving: 749 calories; 14.7 g fat—18.2% calories from fat; 3.1 g saturated fat; 182 mg cholesterol

Sweet and Sour Chicken Breasts with Ginger

{ m e a t }

This easy, Chinese-style dish is good for a weekday supper, but it's suitable for holiday meals, too. For Succot, you can serve it with rice and baked sweet potatoes or winter squash, to highlight the holiday's harvest theme. For Hanukkah, Potato Latke "Muffins" (page 57) are delicious with this dish. If you're preparing the chicken in spring or summer, sugar snap peas or snow peas make a colorful, tasty accompaniment.

1 ¼ pounds boneless and skinless chicken breasts

1 tablespoon vegetable oil

1 tablespoon minced, peeled fresh ginger

1 large garlic clove, minced

¼ cup sugar

¼ cup wine vinegar

¼ cup ketchup

2 tablespoons soy sauce

2 tablespoons chicken broth or water

¼ teaspoon hot sauce, or to taste

1 ¼ teaspoons cornstarch

1 tablespoon water

1 small green onion (scallion), chopped

Trim all visible fat from the chicken and cut meat into 1-inch cubes. Heat the vegetable oil in a heavy sauté pan or wok. Add the chicken and sauté over medium heat, stirring, 1 minute. Cover and sauté 3 minutes, stirring once or twice. Add the ginger and garlic and sauté 1 minute.

Meanwhile, thoroughly mix the sugar, vinegar, ketchup, soy sauce, broth, and hot sauce. Add to the pan of chicken and mix well. Bring to a simmer. Cover and cook over low heat 5 minutes or until chicken is tender. Chicken is done when the color is no longer pink; cut into a thick piece to check.

In small cup, blend the cornstarch and water. Add to the center of the simmering sauce, then quickly stir into remaining sauce. Heat until bubbling. Stir in half the chopped green onion. Serve hot, sprinkled with remaining green onion.

· ·

Makes 4 servings

Nutritional information per serving: 282 calories; 6 g fat—19.2% calories from fat;
1.1 g saturated fat; 82 mg cholesterol

Jewish Jambalaya

{ m e a t }

The spicy Cajun rice stew, jambalaya, usually contains nonkosher meats or seafood, and plenty of fat. For this healthy kosher version, I use chicken pieces and turkey frankfurters. Together with aromatic vegetables, hot peppers, and cayenne pepper, they give the rice a fabulous flavor. This is a meal in one dish, great for Succot as it's very portable.

Serve the jambalaya with a bottle of hot sauce, in case anyone wants it more fiery.

1 2½-pound chicken, cut into small pieces

1½ tablespoons vegetable oil

1 large onion, chopped

1 medium green bell pepper, cored, seeded, and chopped

½ cup chopped celery

4 large garlic cloves, chopped

2 jalapeño peppers, seeded and chopped

1 cup tomato sauce

1 teaspoon dried oregano

1 bay leaf

3 cups chicken broth

2 cups long- or medium-grain white rice

6 ounces turkey frankfurters or sausage, cut into chunks

Salt and black pepper

½ teaspoon cayenne pepper, or to taste

⅓ cup chopped parsley

Pat the chicken dry. Heat the vegetable oil in a large, deep skillet over medium-high heat. Add the chicken pieces in batches, brown them well on all sides, and remove. Add the onion, bell pepper, and celery and sauté over medium heat, stirring, 7 minutes. Add the garlic, jalapeño peppers, tomato sauce, oregano, bay leaf, and broth. Bring to a boil. Cover and cook 10 minutes.

Bring the mixture to a boil and stir in the rice. Return the chicken to the skillet. Add the frankfurter pieces, salt, pepper, cayenne, and 3 tablespoons parsley. Cover and cook over low heat 30 to 40 minutes or until chicken and rice are tender. Do not stir often, to avoid crushing rice. Remove the bay leaf. Sprinkle with remaining parsley and serve.

. . . .

Makes 6 servings

Nutritional information per serving: 612 calories; 19.8 g fat—29.7% calories from fat; 5.1 g saturated fat; 133 mg cholesterol

Chicken Chili with Beans

{ m e a t }

Serve this chili with country bread or pita bread, or over rice or spaghetti. If you don't like hot food, use only ½ teaspoon hot pepper flakes. You can add 1 diced red or green bell pepper to the chili with the onion, for extra flavor and nutrients.

Accompany the chicken chili with sliced or diced avocado, *Sephardic Hot Salsa* (page 59), diced tomato, bottled hot sauce, cilantro sprigs, and chopped or thinly sliced onion—white, red, or green.

Use a sauté pan rather than a saucepan to cook the chili so it thickens faster.

1 tablespoon olive or vegetable oil
1 large onion, chopped
1 pound ground chicken
4 large garlic cloves, minced
1 tablespoon chili powder
1 tablespoon ground cumin
1 tablespoon dried oregano, crumbled

1 teaspoon hot red pepper flakes, or to taste
Salt and freshly ground black pepper
1 28-ounce can whole tomatoes, with their juice
1 15- or 16-ounce can pinto beans or red beans, drained and rinsed

Heat the oil in a sauté pan. Add the onion and cook over medium heat, stirring often, 5 minutes. Add the chicken and cook, stirring, until it changes color, about 5 minutes. Add the garlic, chili powder, cumin, oregano, red pepper flakes, and salt and pepper to taste. Stir over low heat for 1 minute to coat meat with spices.

Add the tomatoes and bring to a boil, breaking them apart with a wooden spoon. Cook uncovered over medium-low heat 8 minutes. Add the beans and simmer 10 to 15 minutes or until mixture is thick. Taste and adjust seasoning. Serve hot.

. . . .

Makes 4 to 6 servings

Nutritional information per serving: 310 calories; 10.3 g fat—29.6% calories from fat; 2.3 g saturated fat; 71 mg cholesterol

Chicken with Forty Cloves of Garlic

{ m e a t }

People hearing the name of this dish for the first time often worry about having an overly aggressive-flavored entree. The garlic cloves slowly bake with the chicken, become mellow, and lend a wonderful aroma and taste to the dish. Chicken prepared this way is a specialty of southern France and a popular item in my California cooking classes. It's suitable for low-fat cooking because you can bake the chicken without its skin and still obtain moist meat.

A special technique is used to ensure that the chicken remains succulent and tender. First, you put the chicken and the remaining ingredients in a deep, heavy casserole and cover it. Then you make a paste of flour and water and smear it around the lid of the casserole to be sure it is sealed. A short time before serving, you remove the paste, which has baked to a dough, and enjoy the wonderful aroma of the chicken and garlic when you lift the lid.

The garlic cloves are baked in their peels. You can remove them, squeeze the pulp out of each clove, and spread it on toast to accompany the chicken. Or add a few whole garlic cloves to each plate and each diner can squeeze and crush his or her own garlic.

About 2½ pounds chicken pieces,
   skin removed
Salt and freshly ground black pepper
2 tablespoons plus 1 teaspoon olive
   oil
2 celery stalks, cut into thin slices
3 fresh thyme sprigs, or
   1¼ teaspoons dried
1 bay leaf

2 tablespoons chopped parsley
40 medium cloves garlic, unpeeled
¼ cup brandy
6 tablespoons all-purpose flour
3½ tablespoons water
8 thin slices of large French bread
   (3 to 4 inches in diameter),
   halved, or 16 thin slices baguette

Preheat the oven to 350°F. Sprinkle the chicken pieces with pepper. In a deep, heavy casserole with a tight-fitting cover, mix 2 tablespoons of the olive oil with the celery, thyme, bay leaf, 1 tablespoon parsley, and a pinch of salt. Add the chicken pieces to the casserole and stir well to coat them with oil.

Separate the garlic cloves from the heads and remove any loose skin. Add the garlic and brandy to the casserole. Cover tightly. In a small cup, stir the flour with the water to make a paste. Smear the paste at the edge of the lid to seal the casserole closed. Bake the chicken for 1¼ hours. Keep it warm, covered.

Raise the oven temperature to 425°F. Arrange the bread on a lightly oiled baking sheet and brush it lightly with olive oil, using a total of about 1 teaspoon. Toast the bread lightly in the oven on both sides.

Break the seal of hardened "dough" around the lid. Remove the garlic, squeeze out the pulp from skin, and crush each clove with a fork. Spread the garlic pulp on toasted bread.

To serve, transfer the chicken to a platter. Discard the bay leaf and thyme sprigs, taste juices for seasoning, and pour them over chicken. Sprinkle chicken with remaining tablespoon parsley. Arrange the garlic toast around chicken or serve it separately.

. . . .

Makes 4 servings

Nutritional information per serving: 547.5 calories; 15.4 g fat—27.5% calories from fat; 2.9 g saturated fat; 159 mg cholesterol

Broiled Chicken with Easy Mushroom Sauce

{ m e a t }

*W*ine and chicken broth are simmered with the French chopped mushroom preparation called *duxelles to quickly produce a flavorful sauce. This sauce is also good with roasted or poached chicken, veal chops, and such vegetables as cauliflower, zucchini, and potatoes.*

½ pound mushrooms, rinsed and
    patted dry
About 3½ teaspoons vegetable oil or
    margarine
1 small shallot or green onion
    (scallion), minced
Salt and freshly ground black pepper
¼ cup dry white wine
4 teaspoons tomato paste

1½ cups chicken broth
1 teaspoon dried leaf thyme,
    crumbled
1 tablespoon cornstarch, dissolved in
    2 tablespoons water
2 tablespoons chopped parsley
4 boneless and skinless chicken
    breast halves (1¼ to 1½ pounds
    total)

To make duxelles, pulse the mushrooms in a food processor so they are chopped in fine pieces but are not pureed. In a medium skillet, heat 1½ teaspoons vegetable oil over low heat, add the shallot, and sauté about 30 seconds until soft. Add the mushrooms and sprinkle with salt and pepper. Cook over high heat, stirring, 3 to 5 minutes or until mixture is dry. (Duxelles can be kept, covered, 2 days in refrigerator.)

In a medium saucepan, mix the duxelles with the wine, tomato paste, broth, and thyme. Bring to a boil, then reduce heat to medium low. Add the dissolved cornstarch, stirring. Return to a boil and add the parsley. Season to taste with salt and pepper.

Heat a broiler with the rack about 4 inches from the heat source; or heat a ridged stove-top grill pan over medium-high heat. Rub the chicken with the remaining 2 teaspoons oil. Sprinkle with pepper on both sides. Grill or broil the chicken until done, about 5 to 7 minutes per side. Spoon hot sauce over chicken and serve.

Makes 4 servings

Nutritional information per serving: 273 calories; 7.7 g fat—26.6% calories from fat; 1.4 g saturated fat; 83 mg cholesterol

Rice with Chicken and Green Onions

{ m e a t }

Many of us roast an extra chicken for Shabbat in order to have the basis for an easy-to-cook main course during the week. This recipe provides a quick, tasty way to stretch a small amount of cooked chicken or turkey. If you haven't cooked extra chicken and don't have homemade chicken broth, you can use prepared kosher frozen roasted chicken and canned chicken soup, which are available in many markets.

2 tablespoons vegetable oil

1 medium onion, finely chopped

1½ cups long-grain white rice

3 cups hot chicken broth

Salt and freshly ground black pepper

½ teaspoon dried thyme

2 to 3 cups diced cooked chicken or turkey

3 green onions (scallions), green and white parts

Heat 1 tablespoon vegetable oil in a large sauté pan or wide casserole. Add the onion and cook over low heat, stirring, about 7 minutes or until soft but not brown. Add the rice and sauté, stirring, about 2 minutes or until the grains turn milky white.

Add the broth, salt, pepper, and thyme. Stir once with a fork and cover. Cook over low heat, without stirring, for 20 minutes. Taste the rice; if not yet tender, simmer 2 more minutes.

Heat the remaining tablespoon oil in a skillet, add the chicken and green onions, and sauté over medium heat, stirring, 1 to 2 minutes or until chicken is hot. Spoon evenly over rice. Cover and let stand for 10 minutes. Gently fluff with a fork. Serve hot.

. . . .

Makes 4 servings

Nutritional information per serving: 508 calories; 11.7 g fat—21.1% calories from fat; 2.2 g saturated fat; 59 mg cholesterol

Chicken Stew with Green Peas and Baby Onions

{ meat }

A tomato sauce accented with white wine and herbs makes a delicious cooking liquid for the chicken and its colorful vegetable medley. Serve this chicken for Shabbat, Succot, Hanukkah, or any other festive occasion. White or brown rice or couscous is a good accompaniment.

3 large fresh thyme sprigs, or
  1 teaspoon dried
1 bay leaf
2 fresh marjoram sprigs, or ½
  teaspoon dried
1 tablespoon olive oil
2½ pounds chicken pieces
1 medium onion, minced
4 large garlic cloves, minced
2 pounds ripe tomatoes, peeled,
  seeded, and chopped, or 2
  28-ounce cans whole tomatoes,
  drained and chopped

½ cup dry white wine
Salt and freshly ground black pepper
½ pound fresh or frozen baby onions
  (optional)
¼ pound baby carrots or large
  peeled carrots (optional)
1½ pounds fresh peas, shelled, or
  1½ cups frozen
½ cup chicken broth
Pinch of cayenne pepper

If using all fresh herbs, tie the thyme sprigs, bay leaf, and marjoram sprigs together with string or in cheesecloth.

Heat the olive oil in a large nonstick sauté pan or deep skillet over medium-high heat. Add the chicken pieces in batches and brown them lightly. Reduce the heat to medium if necessary. Remove the pieces. Pour off the fat into a bowl.

Return 1 tablespoon fat to the pan and heat over medium-low heat. Add the minced onion and cook, stirring occasionally, about 5 minutes or until softened. Add the garlic, then the tomatoes and herb bundle or dried herbs and bring to a boil. Return the chicken to the pan; add the wine, salt, and pepper and bring to a simmer. Cover and simmer over low heat, turning pieces occasionally, until tender and cooked through when pierced with a knife, about 25 minutes for breast pieces and about 35 minutes for legs. Remove the chicken.

Put the fresh baby onions if using in a small saucepan, cover with water, and bring to a boil. Boil 1 minute; drain, rinse with cold water, and drain well. Peel with the aid of a paring knife. If using large carrots, cut them into 1½-inch lengths, then quarter each lengthwise. Cook the peas in a medium saucepan of boiling salted water about 2 minutes or until just tender. Drain, rinse with cold water, and drain well.

Add the fresh baby onions (but not frozen), carrots, and broth to the skillet. Cover and simmer 20 minutes or until vegetables are tender; add frozen baby onions for last 5 minutes. Discard the tied herbs. If necessary, cook the sauce uncovered a few more minutes or until it is thick. Skim fat from sauce, then add cayenne pepper. Taste and adjust seasoning.

Remove the skin from the chicken pieces. Return pieces to sauce and reheat gently before serving. Add the peas and heat through. Taste again and serve.

. . . .

Makes 4 servings

Nutritional information per serving: 644 calories; 20.3 g fat—29.2% calories from fat; 4.9 g saturated fat; 155 mg cholesterol

Cornish Hens with Couscous and Figs

{ m e a t }

*L*emon zest, figs, and couscous give the stuffing in these Cornish hens a distinctly Mediterranean *flavor. The stuffing is delicious with the rich, juicy meat of the birds and is one of the quickest, easiest stuffings to make.*

2¼ cups chicken broth

1⅔ cups couscous (1 10-ounce package)

1 cup dried figs, preferably dark ones such as Mission figs, diced

1½ teaspoons grated lemon rind

3 green onions (scallions), chopped

Salt and freshly ground black pepper

2 Cornish hens, each about 1½ pounds

½ teaspoon ground black pepper

Bring the broth to a boil in a small saucepan. Stir in the couscous and figs. Cover the pan, remove from the heat, and let stand 5 minutes. Fluff the couscous with a fork. Add the lemon rind and green onions and stir with a fork. Season to taste with salt and pepper. Let stuffing cool completely.

Preheat the oven to 400° F. Discard excess fat from the hens. Rub hens with pepper, then spoon ⅓ to ½ cup stuffing into each hen, packing it in gently. Reserve remaining stuffing mixture at room temperature.

Set the hens in a small roasting pan or shallow baking dish just large enough to contain them. Roast the hens, basting 2 or 3 times, for 45 minutes or until the thickest part of a drumstick is tender when pierced with a skewer and juices that run from drumstick are clear; if juices are pink, roast hens for a few more minutes and check again. During roasting, add 2 tablespoons hot water to pan juices if they brown.

To serve, spoon the stuffing from the hens onto a platter. Cut each hen in half lengthwise with poultry shears. Arrange the pieces over stuffing on platter or plates. Cover and keep warm.

Heat the remaining stuffing mixture in a medium skillet over low heat, stirring gently with a fork, about 2 minutes; or heat it in a covered dish in the microwave. Serve in a separate heated dish.

. . . .

Makes 4 servings

Nutritional information per serving: 1,134 calories; 37.4 g fat—29.7% calories from fat; 10.3 g saturated fat; 225 mg cholesterol

Spicy Turkey Burgers with Cumin, Coriander, and Cilantro

{ m e a t }

The spices make these burgers taste like falafel, Israel's most popular street food. In fact, you can serve them like falafel in a pita with diced tomatoes and cucumbers and a few drops of hot sauce. Or serve them in hamburger rolls with sliced red onion, sliced tomato, pickles, ketchup, and mustard.

4 garlic cloves, minced
½ teaspoon ground black pepper
2 teaspoons ground coriander
1 teaspoon ground cumin
½ teaspoon turmeric
½ teaspoon paprika

Pinch of cayenne pepper
3 tablespoons chopped cilantro or parsley
1¼ pounds ground turkey (about 2⅔ cups)
4 to 6 pita breads, for serving

Mix the garlic with the pepper, coriander, cumin, turmeric, paprika, and cayenne pepper. Add the spice mixture and cilantro to the turkey and mix lightly to blend. Shape into patties, each about 3 inches in diameter.

Lightly oil a broiler rack and position it about 4 inches from the heat source; or prepare a grill with the rack about 6 inches above glowing coals. Broil or grill the patties, turning once, about 8 minutes, or until they are springy when pressed and cooked through. Serve immediately on pita breads.

. . . .

Makes 4 to 6 servings

Nutritional information per serving: 259 calories; 8.5 g fat—30% calories from fat;
2.2 g saturated fat; 75 mg cholesterol

Rice Pilaf with Turkey Sausages and Black Olives

{ m e a t }

For this tasty Mediterranean pilaf, sausages add flavor to the rice as they cook together. I prefer light turkey or chicken sausages, but you can use any cooked low-fat kosher sausage you like. I usually add red peppers as well, for their color and lively flavor. A refreshing salad of diced cucumbers, tomatoes, and green onion is a perfect accompaniment.

1 ½ tablespoons olive oil
1 medium onion, halved and thinly sliced
1 red, yellow, or green bell pepper, diced
4 large garlic cloves, chopped
5 ounces turkey or chicken sausages, or frankfurters, preferably low-fat, sliced or diced

1 ½ cups long-grain white rice
3 cups chicken broth
1 teaspoon dried oregano
¼ teaspoon dried hot pepper flakes, or cayenne pepper to taste
¼ cup pitted black olives, sliced
Salt (optional) and freshly ground black pepper

Heat the olive oil in a medium nonstick sauté pan or deep skillet, add the onion and bell peppers, and sauté over medium heat about 5 minutes or until softened. Stir in the garlic, then add the sausages and rice and sauté together, stirring, 2 minutes, until the grains begin to turn white.

Add the broth, oregano, and pepper flakes. Stir and bring to a boil. Cover and cook over low heat, without stirring, for 15 minutes. Sprinkle the olives over top, cover, and cook 3 to 5 more minutes or until rice is tender. Add black pepper to taste; toss lightly with a fork to blend ingredients. Taste and adjust seasoning; salt may not be needed, depending on saltiness of the olives and sausages.

· ·

Makes 2 or 3 main-course servings

Nutritional information per serving: 513 calories; 13.8 g fat—25.9% calories from fat;
2.4 g saturated fat; 29 mg cholesterol

Turkey Salad with Red Beans and Rice

{ m e a t }

When I cook beans or rice, I find it practical to prepare enough for at least two meals, so I have plenty left for salad. Salads like this of turkey and rice are convenient for entertaining, since you can make them ahead and serve them buffet style. Preparing the salad a few hours earlier has another advantage: as the meat sits with the dressing, it gains in flavor. Refrigerate the salad if you make it early in the day. You can substitute cooked chicken for the turkey. If you would rather use brown rice, cook it for about 40 minutes. Serve this entree with a green salad and a tomato or bell pepper salad.

1 ¼ cups long-grain rice

1 cup cooked red beans, or 1 15- or 16-ounce can, drained and rinsed

3 cups diced cooked turkey

4 green onions (scallions), chopped

3 tablespoons extra-virgin olive oil

1 ½ tablespoons fresh lemon juice

Salt and freshly ground black pepper

1 teaspoon dried thyme

1 teaspoon dried oregano

2 tablespoons chopped parsley

Cook the rice in a large pan of about 2 quarts boiling salted water uncovered about 14 minutes or until just tender but still firm. Drain, rinse with cold water, and drain well. Mix the rice with the beans, turkey, and green onions.

In a small bowl, whisk the olive oil, lemon juice, salt, and pepper. Add to the salad. Sprinkle with thyme and oregano and fold in. Taste and adjust seasoning. Just before serving, fold in 1 tablespoon parsley. Sprinkle the remaining tablespoon parsley on top.

. . . .

Makes 4 servings

Nutritional information per serving: 530 calories; 16 g fat—26.9% calories from fat; 3.2 g saturated fat; 80 mg cholesterol

Turkey, Mango,
and Brown Rice Salad

{ m e a t }

With its ginger-scented orange dressing, diced mango, and crunchy water chestnuts, this salad makes a light and lively summer entree. It's also a delicious way to make use of extra turkey from Thanksgiving.

Be sure to choose good-quality mangoes that aren't stringy. If they are not available, substitute other fruit. Kiwifruit, papaya, pineapple, and orange segments make tasty additions to this salad, as do raisins or other dried fruit. If you like, serve the salad on a bed of mixed baby lettuces.

3 cups chicken broth

1 ½ cups long-grain brown rice

1 ½ tablespoons red wine vinegar

2 tablespoons orange juice

3 tablespoons vegetable oil

Salt and freshly ground black pepper

½ teaspoon ground ginger

½ teaspoon grated orange rind

3 cups cooked turkey or chicken,
  diced or cut into strips

⅓ cup chopped red onion

1 8-ounce can water chestnuts,
  drained and sliced

¼ cup chopped parsley

1 ripe mango, peeled and diced

In a large, heavy saucepan, bring the broth to a boil. Add the rice, cover, and cook over low heat 40 to 45 minutes or until just tender. Transfer to a large bowl, fluff with a fork, and cool.

While rice is cooking, whisk together the vinegar, orange juice, vegetable oil, salt, pepper, ginger, and orange rind. Add 3 tablespoons of this dressing to turkey. Add the onion and mix well.

Toss the turkey mixture with the rice and remaining dressing. Add the water chestnuts, parsley, and mango and mix lightly. Taste and adjust seasoning.

. . . .

Makes 3 or 4 main-course or 6 appetizer servings

Nutritional information per serving: 438 calories; 13.0 g fat—26.9% calories from fat; 2.6 g saturated fat; 54 mg cholesterol

15

Meat Main Courses

Boeuf Bourguignon

Italian Braised Beef with Porcini Mushrooms, Tomatoes, and Wine

Beef Stew with Ginger, Garlic, and Tomatoes

Veal Chops with Piperade

Veal Stew with Chickpeas and Rosemary

Veal Scallopini with Wild Mushroom Sauce and Sugar Snap Peas

Kosher Cassoulet

Tuscan Lamb with Peas

Moroccan Lamb Tajine with Prunes and Onions

Mediterranean Lamb Stew with White Beans

WHEN IT COMES TO COOKING MEAT, the kosher kitchen is best known for its braised dishes. Jewish women have known for ages that when meat, vegetables, and broth slowly cook together, a flavor exchange takes place among the ingredients, creating a delicious harmony of tastes. During the long, gentle cooking, braised meat remains moist and becomes fork-tender and succulent. This is true whether you are cooking beef, veal, or lamb.

There is another reason for the popularity of these moist-heat methods of cooking in kosher cuisine. These techniques are perfect for many kosher cuts of meat, which come from the fore quarter of the animal and most of which are more tender when cooked slowly and kept moist.

In addition to good taste, convenience is a great advantage of these "meals in one pot." Braised meats are ideal for Shabbat and holiday meals, as they can be kept warm over very low heat or can be cooked ahead and reheated. In fact, many taste even better when prepared a day or two ahead. Although the cooking time of beef stews and braised dishes is lengthy, they are easy to make, as they demand minimal attention while they simmer.

During braising, the meat is browned lightly, then simmered with aromatic vegetables, herbs, and liquid. Cuts of meat with some bone are best, as the bones' natural gelatin help to produce a wonderful sauce. The finest braising liquid is a rich home-made broth. It adds depth to the flavor of the sauce and an appealing color. The refreshing acidity of dry white and red wine and tomatoes makes those ingredients favorite additions, too. Sometimes wine and tomatoes can be used together, as in one of my favorite dishes, Italian Braised Beef with Porcini Mushrooms, Tomatoes, and Wine (page 234). When a liberal amount of spices or herbs is added, water can be used as the braising liquid instead of broth. The sauce will gain enough character from these flavorings and from the meat.

Over the years, several variations on the braising technique have been developed. Stewing is similar to braising, except that the meat is cut in smaller pieces. A Moroccan array of dishes known as *tajines* are basically stews, but the meat is not browned. This eliminates the fat used in browning and makes the tajine technique perfect for low-fat cooking. Tajines come in an enormous range of flavors, from hot and spicy with garlic and chiles to savory and sweet with saffron, cinnamon, and dried fruit.

Mediterranean seasonings, especially garlic and citrus rind and juice, are terrific for braised meats, as are fresh herbs, particularly thyme, rosemary, oregano, cilantro, and basil. Middle Eastern and Indian spices, notably cumin, coriander, turmeric, and hot pepper, also lend zest to these dishes.

Owing to their richness, braised meats pair well with sweet and sour combinations and with fresh and dried fruit. These dishes are especially popular for Rosh Hashanah.

Fresh, seasonal vegetables lend character and nutrients when simmered in the sauce alongside the meats. Two categories of vegetables are added: aromatic vegetables to flavor the sauce and accompanying vegetables to serve with the meat. Onions are the most frequently used aromatic vegetable and appear in most braised dishes and stews, with carrots, celery, and garlic close behind. Other good vegetable choices are asparagus, squash, potatoes, eggplant, leeks, artichoke hearts, corn, and all sorts of beans, both dried and fresh.

For low-fat cooking, it is best to serve more generous portions of the vegetables and smaller amounts of meat. If you treat the meat more as an accompaniment than as a main course, your meals will become healthier. Dried beans, especially, help provide protein and thus make the dish more satisfying with a smaller amount of meat, as in Veal Stew with Chickpeas and Rosemary (page 238).

The sauce for braised or stewed meats can be thickened with flour, cornstarch, or, for Passover, potato starch. During the simmering, the cooking liquid of braised meats also thickens naturally by reduction. The sauce is best if it's not thick and clinging, however, but just lightly coats a spoon.

Grains, pasta, and potatoes gain a tempting flavor when moistened with the rich braising sauce. In our family, rice is the favorite partner for braised and stewed meats, but we also love couscous, petite pasta shapes like orzo or shells, and boiled, steamed or mashed potatoes. (See page 297 for a recipe for fat-free mashed potatoes for *fleishig* meals.) If green vegetables are not already included in the recipe, try crisp-tender broccoli, snow peas, or green beans for their bright color and pleasing contrast in texture.

Kosher meats can also be cooked by the other common cooking techniques. Poaching beef or veal with vegetables in liquid produces a rich-tasting soup and a hearty meat entree for winter. Beef ribs and rack of lamb can be roasted. Steaks, veal cutlets, veal and lamb chops, and hamburgers can be broiled or pan-fried. Steaks and burgers are never served rare because blood is not kosher. For special occasions, ground beef, veal, or lamb is made into a stuffing for vegetables, for a delectable appetizer or entree.

Other Meat Dishes

Beef Stew with Dried Fruit (page 62) · Hearty Bean and Beef Soup (page 64)

Boeuf Bourguignon

{ m e a t }

Classic versions of this beef and red wine ragout call for baby onions, mushrooms, and herbs. Carrots are traditionally used only to flavor the sauce, and then are strained out. I like to serve carrots with the other vegetables in the stew, for their bright color and because their sweet flavor provides a pleasing balance to the red wine sauce. The stew is baked in the oven so it cooks very evenly. The technique of browning the beef with the flour in the oven gives the sauce a rich flavor.

1 ¾ pounds lean boneless beef chuck, fat trimmed, cut into 1 ¼-inch pieces
1 tablespoon vegetable oil
2 medium onions, chopped
4 medium garlic cloves, crushed
1 sprig fresh thyme, or ½ teaspoon dried
1 bay leaf
6 parsley stems, without leaves
1 tablespoon plus 1 teaspoon all-purpose flour

1 ½ cups dry red wine
1 ½ cups beef broth
¼ cup water
Salt and freshly ground black pepper
12 ounces thin carrots, peeled and cut into 1-inch chunks
6 ounces baby onions
1 pound mushrooms, quartered
2 tablespoons minced parsley
8 medium potatoes, boiled, for serving

Position a rack in the lower third of the oven and preheat to 450°F. Pat the beef dry. Heat the vegetable oil in 4- to 5-quart heavy flameproof casserole over medium-high heat. Add one-third to one-half of the beef, or enough so pieces do not touch each other. Brown the beef on all sides, taking 6 to 7 minutes. Using a slotted spatula, transfer it to a plate. Continue with the remaining beef.

Add the onions to the casserole and cook over low heat, stirring often, until softened, about 7 minutes. Meanwhile, put the garlic, thyme, bay leaf, and parsley stems on a piece of cheesecloth and tie in a bundle. Return the meat to the pan, reserving any juices on the plate, and sprinkle the meat with the flour. Toss lightly to coat meat with flour. Bake, uncovered, stirring once, 5 minutes. Remove the casserole and reduce the oven temperature to 325°F.

Pour the juices from the plate over the beef. Stir in the wine and broth. If necessary, add ¼ cup water or enough to barely cover beef. Add the cheesecloth bag, salt, and pepper and bring to a boil, stirring often and scraping any browned bits from the sides and bottom of the pan. If using dried herbs, just sprinkle them in. Cover and cook over low heat, stirring and turning beef cubes over occasionally, 45 minutes.

Add the carrots to the stew and push down into the liquid. Cover and continue baking, stirring occasionally, until beef and carrots are just tender when pierced with the tip of a knife, about 45 minutes to 1 hour. Discard the cheesecloth bag.

Add the baby onions to a medium saucepan of boiling water and boil 1 minute. Drain, rinse with cold water, and peel with the aid of a paring knife. Add the onions and mushrooms to the stew. Continue baking the stew 20 minutes or until beef and vegetables are tender.

Stir in the parsley. Taste and adjust seasoning. Serve the stew from the casserole or deep serving dish, accompanied by potatoes.

. . . .

Makes 4 servings

Nutritional information per serving: 683 calories; 21.5 g fat—29.9% calories from fat; 6.9 g saturated fat; 129 mg cholesterol

Italian Braised Beef with Porcini Mushrooms, Tomatoes, and Wine

{ m e a t }

When beef cooks gently with red wine, tomatoes, herbs, and dried mushrooms, the resulting sauce is just fabulous! Naturally, the perfect accompaniment is pasta. I like to serve the beef with broad noodles, but you can use shells, penne, orzo, or any pasta shape you like. If you wish to prepare the beef on Passover, serve it with boiled potatoes or with Passover noodles made of matzo meal.

1 tablespoon olive oil

1 2-pound piece lean boneless beef chuck roast, patted dry

1 large onion, diced

1 celery stalk, diced

1 small carrot, peeled and diced

2 medium garlic cloves, chopped

½ cup dry red wine

1 whole clove

4 large fresh thyme sprigs, or 1 teaspoon dried

1 bay leaf

1 pound ripe tomatoes, diced, or 1 28-ounce can diced tomatoes, diced

½ teaspoon dried leaf marjoram

About 2 cups beef broth

1 ounce dried porcini or other mushrooms

14 ounces broad noodles

3 tablespoons chopped parsley

In a heavy casserole that holds the meat snugly, heat the olive oil. Add the meat and brown it on all sides over medium heat. Remove from casserole. Add the onion, celery, and carrot and sauté, stirring often, about 5 minutes. Add the garlic and wine. Tie the clove, thyme sprigs, and bay leaf in a piece of cheesecloth and add. If using dried thyme, sprinkle it in. Bring to a boil and cook uncovered over medium heat, turning the meat from time to time, until the wine evaporates. Add the tomatoes, marjoram, and 1¼ cups broth. Bring to a simmer, cover, and cook over low heat, turning the meat over from time to time, about 1½ hours or until meat is very tender.

Soak the mushrooms in enough hot water to cover them for 30 minutes. Remove mushrooms, rinse, and coarsely chop. Combine them with the remaining ¾ cup broth in a very small saucepan. Cover and cook over low heat about 10 minutes or until tender.

When the meat is tender, remove it from the casserole. Cover it and keep warm.

Puree the sauce in a food processor or put it through a food mill. Return to the casserole. Add the mushrooms with their cooking liquid and heat through. If the sauce is too thin, simmer it uncovered about 5 minutes to thicken it.

In a large pot of boiling salted water, cook the noodles uncovered over high heat, stirring occasionally, 4 to 5 minutes or until tender but firm to the bite.

Meanwhile, cut the meat into thin slices for serving alongside the pasta. Drain the pasta well and transfer to a large heated bowl. Toss the pasta with 1½ cups sauce and 2 tablespoons parsley. Sprinkle with remaining tablespoon parsley. Serve remaining sauce separately for spooning over meat.

. . . .

Makes 4 main-course servings

Nutritional information per serving: 853 calories; 27.7 g fat—29% calories from fat; 8.8 g saturated fat; 242 mg cholesterol

Beef Stew with Ginger, Garlic, and Tomatoes

{ m e a t }

You might think of ginger, garlic, and cilantro as a Chinese seasoning formula, but here they add a fresh touch to Western-style meat and potatoes stewed in tomato sauce. Simple boiled broccoli, cauliflower, or green beans makes a good accompaniment.

2 pounds boneless lean beef chuck

1 tablespoon vegetable oil

1 large onion, chopped

1 tablespoon minced, peeled fresh ginger

4 large garlic cloves, minced

1 ½ pounds ripe tomatoes, peeled, seeded, and chopped, or 1 28-ounce can and 1 14-ounce can tomatoes, drained and chopped

1 ½ cups beef broth or water

Salt and freshly ground black pepper

¼ teaspoon hot red pepper flakes (optional)

2 pounds small or medium boiling potatoes

3 tablespoons minced cilantro or parsley

Trim the fat thoroughly and cut the beef into 1 ¼-inch cubes. Heat the vegetable oil in a large casserole, add the onion, and sauté about 5 minutes over medium-low heat. Add the beef and sauté about 5 minutes, stirring often. Stir in the ginger, garlic, tomatoes, and broth. Add the black pepper and hot pepper flakes if desired. Bring to a boil, stirring. Cover and cook over low heat, stirring occasionally, 2 hours.

Peel the potatoes and cut into chunks about 1 inch thick. Put in a saucepan, cover with water, and add a pinch of salt. Bring to a boil and simmer 10 minutes. Drain well.

Add the potatoes to the stew and sprinkle lightly with salt. Cover and cook about 20 minutes or until potatoes are tender. If the sauce is too thin, remove the beef and potatoes with a slotted spoon and simmer sauce to thicken it. If it is too thick, stir in a few tablespoons water.

Stir in 2 tablespoons cilantro. Taste and adjust seasoning. Sprinkle with remaining tablespoon cilantro and serve.

. . . .

Makes 4 servings

Nutritional information per serving: 711 calories; 23.8 g fat—30% calories from fat; 7.9 g saturated fat; 147 mg cholesterol

Veal Chops with Piperade

{ m e a t }

The Basque pepper sauce called piperade is popular on both sides of the French-Spanish border. Flavored with tomatoes, onion, and garlic, the sauce is a terrific complement for veal. You can grill the veal and serve the sauce separately, but I like to braise the veal directly in the sauce, which gains a meaty flavor. Rice is the customary partner for the veal, but it's also good with orzo or couscous.

4 veal chops, about 8 ounces each, ¾ to 1 inch thick
Salt and freshly ground black pepper
2 tablespoons vegetable or olive oil
1 large onion, chopped
3 large green bell peppers (about ¾ to 1 pound), cored, seeded, and diced
2 garlic cloves, chopped

1 28-ounce can diced tomatoes, drained
¼ teaspoon hot red pepper flakes, or to taste
1 tablespoon chopped parsley (optional)
4½ to 5 cups hot cooked rice, for serving

Trim all visible fat from the chops. Pat dry. Sprinkle the veal on both sides with salt and pepper. Heat the oil in large, heavy sauté pan or skillet over medium-high heat. Add the veal and brown it, in batches if necessary, taking about 2 minutes per side. Transfer to a plate.

Add the onion to the pan and sauté about 5 minutes over medium heat. Add the peppers and garlic and cook, stirring often, about 7 minutes or until peppers soften. Add the tomatoes, red pepper flakes, and a pinch of salt and pepper. Cook 2 minutes.

Add the veal to the sauce and bring to a simmer. Cover and cook over low heat 4 or 5 minutes per side or until veal is tender; meat should be white. Taste and adjust seasoning. Serve sprinkled with parsley if desired, with rice on the side.

. . . .

Makes 4 servings

Nutritional information per serving: 658 calories; 21.4 g fat—29.5% calories from fat; 6.7 g saturated fat; 115 mg cholesterol

Veal Stew with Chickpeas and Rosemary

{ m e a t }

Along with the fresh rosemary, hot pepper and garlic give this entree plenty of punch. I like to add part of the garlic at the end of the cooking time, to maximize its effect. My favorite vegetable additions are yellow crookneck squash and zucchini, but you can use only zucchini and double the amount.

This ragout reheats well and makes a good main course for Shabbat, Succot, Hanukkah, or Purim. Pasta bow ties sprinkled with chopped fresh parsley make a pretty accompaniment.

¾ cup dried chickpeas, rinsed and sorted

3 cups water

1 tablespoon vegetable oil

1 large onion, chopped

2 pounds veal shoulder, excess fat trimmed, cut into 1¼-inch pieces

1 tablespoon plus 1 teaspoon all-purpose flour

2 pounds ripe tomatoes, peeled, seeded, and chopped, or 2 28-ounce cans tomatoes, drained and chopped

2 cups chicken or veal broth or water

1 jalapeño pepper, seeded and minced

1 tablespoon minced fresh rosemary, or 1 teaspoon dried

6 large garlic cloves, minced

2 tablespoons tomato paste

½ pound yellow crookneck squash, cut into ½-inch cubes

½ pound zucchini, cut into ½-inch cubes

Salt and freshly ground black pepper

Soak the chickpeas in cold water to cover in a cool place for 8 hours or overnight. Drain the chickpeas and rinse. Put them in a medium saucepan and add the 3 cups water. Bring to a boil, cover, and simmer over low heat until tender, about 1 hour and 15 minutes.

Meanwhile, heat the vegetable oil in a large, heavy casserole. Add the onion and sauté over medium-low heat, stirring often, about 7 minutes. Add the veal to the pan, mix well with the onion, and sprinkle with the flour. Toss lightly to coat meat with flour. Cook over low heat, stirring, 2 minutes.

Stir in the tomatoes and 1¾ cups broth or enough to barely cover meat. Add the jalapeño pepper, rosemary, and half the garlic and bring to a boil, stirring often. Cover and cook over low heat, stirring occasionally, 1 hour. Stir in the tomato paste. Drain the chickpeas and add them to the stew. If the sauce is too thick, stir in a few tablespoons additional broth. Cook, stirring occasionally, about 15 minutes or until the veal is tender when pierced with a knife.

Add the squash and zucchini, cover, and simmer until nearly tender, about 4 minutes. Stir in the remaining garlic and simmer, uncovered, 30 seconds. Season to taste with salt and pepper. Serve hot.

. . . .

Makes 4 servings

Nutritional information per serving: 476 calories; 15.6 g fat—28.8% calories from fat;
4.2 g saturated fat; 142 mg cholesterol

Veal Scallopini with Wild Mushroom Sauce and Sugar Snap Peas

{ m e a t }

T his is a lovely and sophisticated dish of tender veal cutlets with a luscious sauce of dried shiitake or porcini mushrooms simmered in stock and flavored with shallots. The veal is enhanced with delicate sugar snap peas. This entree is great for Succot or for a festive summertime dinner. If you prepare it for Passover or other meals in spring, use asparagus instead of sugar snap peas and substitute matzo meal for the flour used to coat the veal. Steamed New Potatoes with Parsley Oil (page 50) make a good accompaniment.

To get a head start on the preparation, make the mushroom sauce and keep it in the refrigerator. You can also remove the ends from the sugar snap peas. Just before serving, cook the peas, sauté the veal, and finish the sauce.

1 ½ ounces dried shiitake or other mushrooms
2 medium shallots, minced
½ teaspoon dried thyme
1 ½ cups beef or chicken broth
1 pound veal scallops, ¼ inch thick, patted dry
¼ cup all-purpose flour
Salt and freshly ground black pepper

2 tablespoons vegetable oil
¼ cup dry sherry or white wine
1 ½ teaspoons potato starch, dissolved in 1 tablespoon dry sherry or white wine
1 pound sugar snap peas, trimmed
1 tablespoon chopped parsley (optional)

Soak the mushrooms in hot water to cover for 20 minutes. Remove the mushrooms from the soaking water and rinse. Cut into ½-inch pieces; if using shiitake mushrooms, discard their stems. Put the mushrooms in a medium saucepan with the shallots, thyme, and 1 cup broth. Bring to a boil. Simmer uncovered 10 minutes. Reserve in pan.

Pat the veal pieces dry. Spread the flour on a large plate. Sprinkle the veal with salt and pepper on both sides. Heat the vegetable oil in a large, heavy nonstick skillet over medium-high heat. Lightly coat 2 pieces of veal with flour on both sides. Tap and shake to remove excess flour. Add coated veal pieces to skillet. Sauté veal about 1 minute per side or until lightly browned and just tender. Transfer to a heatproof platter in 1 layer, cover, and keep warm in a low (250° F.) oven. Continue with remaining veal pieces.

Add the sherry and ½ cup broth to the pan and bring to a boil, stirring and scraping to dissolve any brown bits. Strain into mushroom sauce. Bring the sauce to a simmer over medium heat. Whisk potato starch mixture to blend, then gradually whisk the starch mixture into the simmering sauce. Return to a boil, whisking, until thickened. Remove from heat. Taste and adjust seasoning.

Meanwhile, add the peas to a large saucepan of boiling salted water and boil uncovered over high heat 3 minutes or until crisp-tender. Drain well.

To serve, spoon the sauce over the veal and sprinkle with the parsley if desired. Serve with the peas.

. . . .

Makes 4 servings

Nutritional information per serving: 326 calories; 10.2 g fat—29.3% calories from fat;
1.8 g saturated fat; 95 mg cholesterol

Kosher Cassoulet

{ m e a t }

Cassoulet, one of the glories of French country cooking, is made of layers of beans and a variety of meats, poultry, and sausages that bake slowly together. It seems to be a take-off on cholent, a classic of kosher cooking. In addition to meat, traditional cassoulet in France often contains confit, which is preserved duck or goose. It is salted with coarse salt before being slow-cooked in fat. Indeed, making confit has a lot in common with the process of koshering.

1 pound dried white beans, such as
  great northern (about 2⅓ cups)
3 medium onions, 1 peeled and
  studded with 2 whole cloves and 2
  chopped
1 medium carrot, peeled
2 bay leaves
1 tablespoon vegetable oil
2 pounds boneless lean lamb
  shoulder, cut into 1-inch cubes
6 garlic cloves, chopped

1 28-ounce can tomatoes, drained
  and chopped
1½ cups water
Salt and freshly ground black pepper
2 thyme sprigs, or ½ teaspoon dried
5 parsley stems, without leaves
1 tablespoon chopped fresh basil, or
  1 teaspoon dried
12 ounces low-fat kosher beef
  frankfurters or sausage, sliced
¼ cup unseasoned bread crumbs

Sort through the beans; discard any broken beans or stones. Soak the beans in cold water to generously cover for 8 hours or up to overnight. Rinse the beans. Drain and put them in a large saucepan. Add enough water to cover them by at least 2 inches. Add the clove-studded onion, carrot, and 1 bay leaf and push them into the beans. Cover and bring to a boil over medium heat. Simmer over low heat for about 1½ hours or until just tender, adding hot water if necessary so beans remain covered. Keep the beans in their cooking liquid.

Meanwhile, heat the vegetable oil in a large, heavy casserole. Add the lamb cubes to the pan in 2 batches and brown them on all sides over medium-high heat; reduce the heat if pan juices become too dark. Remove the lamb, add the chopped onion, and sauté over medium-low heat about 5 minutes or until lightly browned. Add the garlic and cook 30 seconds. Stir in the tomatoes and cook 2 minutes.

Return the lamb to the pan. After the beans have cooked at least 30 minutes, add 1 cup bean liquid to the lamb. Add 1½ cups water and a little salt and pepper. Tie the thyme, remaining bay leaf, and parsley stems together with string or in cheesecloth and add. Sprinkle in thyme if using dried. Bring to a boil. Cover and simmer 1 to 1½ hours or until the lamb is tender. Discard the herb bundle and skim off excess fat. Add the basil, taste the liquid, and adjust seasoning.

Preheat the oven to 400°F. Discard the onion and carrot from the beans. With a slotted spoon, put half the beans in a large gratin dish or shallow baking dish in an even layer. With a slotted spoon, arrange the lamb in the dish and top with frank-furter slices. Spoon the remaining beans on top. Reserve the remaining bean liquid. Ladle enough of the lamb cooking liquid into the gratin dish to come nearly to the top of the beans; if there isn't enough, add a little of reserved bean cooking liquid.

Sprinkle the cassoulet with the bread crumbs and bake for about 30 minutes or until hot and golden brown. Serve from baking dish.

. . . .

Makes about 6 servings
Nutritional information per serving: 808 calories; 18.5 g fat—24.7% calories from fat; 6 g saturated fat; 195 mg cholesterol

Tuscan Lamb with Peas

{ m e a t }

*B*y combining rich lamb with a liberal quantity of vegetables and with rice, you get a tasty springtime one-dish meal that is also low in fat. Serve a green salad or an asparagus salad as a first course, and fruit or sorbet for dessert.

1½ pounds boneless lamb shoulder
Salt and freshly ground black pepper
2 teaspoons olive oil
2 medium onions, chopped
2 large garlic cloves, chopped
1 tablespoon fresh rosemary leaves, minced, or 1 teaspoon crumbled dried

3 pounds ripe tomatoes, peeled, seeded, and chopped, or 3 28-ounce cans tomatoes, drained and chopped
3½ cups water
1½ cups long-grain rice
3½ pounds fresh peas, shelled, or 3½ cups frozen peas, thawed

Cut the lamb into 1-inch pieces and pat them dry. Season the lamb with salt and pepper to taste. In a heavy casserole, preferably nonstick, heat the olive oil over medium-high heat and brown the lamb in batches, transferring the browned pieces to a plate. Add the onions and sauté over medium heat, stirring, 3 minutes. Add the garlic and rosemary and sauté for ½ minute. Stir in the tomatoes. Return the lamb to the casserole with any juices that have accumulated on the plate and add ½ cup water. Bring to a boil, stirring. Simmer, covered, over low heat, stirring occasionally, for 1½ hours. Simmer, uncovered, for 15 minutes. Skim the fat from the cooking liquid.

Bring the rice and 3 cups water to a full boil in a large saucepan over high heat. Cover and cook over low heat, without stirring, 15 minutes or until just tender.

In a large saucepan of boiling salted water, cook the fresh peas (not frozen) for 3 minutes. Drain the peas in a colander. Add fresh or frozen peas to the casserole and simmer, uncovered, for 15 minutes, or until the meat is very tender when pierced with a sharp knife, the peas are tender, and the sauce thickens slightly. Taste for seasoning. To serve, spoon stew and its sauce over the rice.

· ·

Makes 4 to 6 servings
Nutritional information per serving: 694 calories; 23 g fat—29.5% calories from fat; 8.9 g saturated fat; 65 mg cholesterol

Moroccan Lamb Tajine with Prunes and Onions

{ m e a t }

Like Ashkenazic beef tsimmes, this dish features prunes and honey. But it also contains saffron, which lends a special flavor. It's great for Rosh Hashanah or Succot with couscous, its traditional accompaniment, or with rice. To give color to the plate and vitamins to the meal, serve the lamb with carrots, roasted red peppers, or lightly cooked green beans.

Be sure to buy lean lamb. If there is fat, be conscientious in cutting off as much as possible.

2½ pounds boneless lamb shoulder
2 large onions, minced
Salt (optional) and freshly ground
   black pepper
1½ cups beef or chicken broth or
   water

Large pinch of saffron threads (about
   ⅛ teaspoon)
1 2-inch cinnamon stick
1 teaspoon ground ginger
1¼ cups pitted prunes
2 tablespoons honey

Cut off fat from the lamb. Cut the lamb into 1-inch cubes. Combine the lamb, onions, and pepper in a heavy casserole. Cover and cook over low heat, stirring occasionally, 5 minutes. Add the broth, saffron, cinnamon stick, and ginger; push cinnamon stick into liquid. Bring to a boil. Cover and simmer over low heat, turning pieces occasionally, about 1 hour or until lamb is tender.

Add the prunes to the casserole and cook uncovered over medium heat 15 minutes or until just tender. Add the honey and cook over medium heat, occasionally stirring very gently, 5 minutes. Taste and adjust seasoning, adding salt if needed. Discard the cinnamon stick. Serve hot.

. . . .

Makes 4 to 6 servings

Nutritional information per serving: 667 calories; 17.6 g fat—29.2% calories from fat; 6.9 g saturated fat; 222 mg cholesterol

Mediterranean Lamb Stew
with White Beans

{ m e a t }

*L*amb stew with beans is a frequently prepared family supper in southern France, Greece, Israel, and other countries bordering the Mediterranean. Serve this one with rice or simply with country bread.

1 cup dried great northern or other
    white beans
2 bay leaves
½ teaspoon dried thyme
5 cups water
Salt and freshly ground black pepper
1 tablespoon vegetable oil
2 pounds boneless lamb shoulder,
    excess fat trimmed, cut into 1-inch
    cubes

1 large onion, chopped
3 large garlic cloves, chopped
1 28-ounce can tomatoes, drained
    and chopped
1 small carrot, halved lengthwise
1½ teaspoons chopped fresh
    oregano, or ½ teaspoon dried
Cayenne pepper
2 tablespoons chopped parsley

Sort the beans, discarding any broken ones and any stones. Soak the beans in cold water to cover in a cool place for 8 hours or overnight. Or, for a quicker method, combine the beans and 3 cups water in a large saucepan, bring to a boil, and boil 2 minutes; cover and let stand off heat 1 hour.

Rinse the beans and drain. Combine the beans with 1 bay leaf, ¼ teaspoon thyme, and 4 cups water in a medium saucepan. Bring to a boil, cover, and cook over low heat 1 hour. Add a pinch of salt and cook about ½ hour longer or until just tender. Discard the bay leaf.

Heat the vegetable oil in a heavy, wide casserole. Add the lamb cubes in batches and brown on all sides over medium-high heat. Remove to a plate with a slotted spoon, add the onion to the casserole, and cook over low heat 5 minutes. Add the garlic and cook 30 seconds. Stir in the tomatoes and cook 2 minutes.

Return the lamb to the casserole. Add remaining 1 cup water, the carrot, remaining bay leaf, remaining ¼ teaspoon thyme, and a little pepper. Bring to a boil, cover, and simmer 45 minutes or until lamb is tender. Discard the bay leaf. Skim off any excess fat from stew. Drain the beans, reserving their cooking liquid, and add beans to stew. If the stew is too soupy, cook uncovered 5 minutes more; if too thick, add a few tablespoons bean cooking liquid and simmer over low heat 2 minutes. Add the oregano and cayenne to taste; taste and adjust seasoning. Serve sprinkled with parsley.

. . . .

Makes 4 servings

Nutritional information per serving: 604.5 calories; 16.5 g fat—29.5% calories from fat; 5.8 g saturated fat; 177 mg cholesterol

16
Pasta

Provençal Tomato Pasta with Peppers and Zucchini

Noodles with Asparagus and Exotic Mushrooms

Pasta Shell and Bean Medley with Tomatoes, Garlic, and Basil

Fettuccine with Roman Tuna Sauce

Fusilli with Barbecued Cod and Roasted Peppers

Linguine with Lima Beans and Smoked Turkey

Spaghetti and Broccoli with Easy Turkey Sauce

Vermicelli with Middle Eastern Meat Sauce

Turkey Moussaka with Macaroni

Egg Noodles

Tomato Pasta

Couscous with Dried Apricots and Walnuts

Couscous with Spicy Vegetables

THE BEST KNOWN PASTA DISHES of the kosher kitchen are noodle kugels. These tasty baked casseroles of noodles can be either savory, often flavored with onions, mushrooms, and other vegetables, or sweet, with apples and cinnamon. For dairy meals, they are enriched with cottage cheese or sour cream, both of which can be used in their fat-free forms.

There is good reason for the popularity of kugels. They can be made ahead and reheated easily for Shabbat, unlike many other pasta dishes. Now you can even make noodle kugel for Passover, as kosher noodles have recently become available, in both egg noodle and yolk-free versions.

Noodle kugel was always my favorite dish on Shabbat menus when I was a child. I especially loved the browned bits that sometimes remained in the pan when the kugel was served. As an adult, my fondness for kugels has not diminished. To make them lower in fat, I use just a bit of oil to sauté the onions and to moisten the noodles, and I substitute egg whites for a portion of the eggs.

On holiday menus, noodles often embellish chicken soup. Fine noodles are popular in many homes, as are star-shaped and alphabet noodles, which children love. If you prepare your own fresh noodles (page 261), their good flavor will be highlighted if you serve them in clear homemade chicken soup. Besides, serving pasta in soup is a healthy, low-fat way to enjoy it.

For weekday meals, pasta is versatile. When I need to get food on the table fast, I generally cook spaghetti, linguine, and other pasta with quick-cooking vegetables such as broccoli or zucchini, then toss them with a bit of olive oil and diced fresh tomatoes or tomato sauce. Depending on what you pair with the pasta, it can become a glamorous entree, such as the Noodles with Asparagus and Exotic Mushrooms (page 252.)

Since pasta is pareve, it is good with either meat or dairy ingredients. If you have roast chicken or turkey left over from Shabbat, you can cut it into strips or dice, heat it, and toss it with cooked pasta, fresh or canned tomatoes, and mushrooms or other vegetables. On the other hand, if you wish to prepare a *milchig* meal, you can sprinkle a pasta-vegetable mélange with grated kosher Parmesan or crumbled feta cheese. Use cheeses with a light hand for low-fat cooking.

Other Pasta Dishes

Orzo Pilaf with Parsley and Thyme (page 17) · Noodles with Poppy Seeds (page 77)
Penne with Zucchini, Garlic, and Feta Cheese (page 114)

Provençal Tomato Pasta with Peppers and Zucchini

{ p a r e v e }

This quick, colorful dish combines green and red peppers sautéed with zucchini and garlic. I often demonstrated it in my "Sixty-Minute Mediterranean Menu" classes. The vegetable mélange can be served as a side dish on its own, but it also makes a tasty topping for pasta. Serve this pasta as a side dish with turkey or veal or as a vegetarian main course.

2 tablespoons plus 2 teaspoons
   extra-virgin olive oil
1 medium red bell pepper, cored,
   seeded, and cut into thin strips
1 medium green bell pepper, cored,
   seeded, and cut into thin strips

Salt and freshly ground black pepper
½ teaspoon dried thyme
3 small zucchini, cut into thin strips
3 large garlic cloves, minced
½ pound Tomato Pasta (page 263)
   or fettuccine

Heat the olive oil in a large, heavy skillet. Add the bell peppers, salt, pepper, and thyme. Cook over medium heat, stirring often, until peppers are softened but still slightly crisp, about 5 minutes. Add the zucchini and garlic and cook until crisp-tender, about 3 minutes.

Add the pasta to a large pan of boiling salted water. Cook uncovered over high heat 2 to 5 minutes for fresh, 7 to 9 for dried, or until just tender but still al dente, or slightly firm to the bite; check by tasting.

Drain the pasta thoroughly and transfer to a bowl. Add the vegetable mixture and toss until well combined. Taste for seasoning. Serve immediately.

. . . .

Makes 2 or 3 main-course or 4 side-dish servings

Nutritional information per serving: 318 calories; 10.1 g fat—28.6% calories from fat;
1.2 g saturated fat; 0 mg cholesterol

Noodles with Asparagus and Exotic Mushrooms

{ d a i r y   o r   p a r e v e }

This is a most elegant pasta dish, ideal for spring. Use any fresh exotic mushroom you can find at your market, such as portobello, shiitake, or chanterelles. For a simpler but still delicious dish, use white or brown button mushrooms.

1 pound asparagus

12 ounces fresh wild mushrooms, such as portobello, shiitake, chanterelles, oyster, or porcini

2 tablespoons vegetable oil

2 tablespoons butter or margarine

Salt and freshly ground black pepper

2 tablespoons minced shallots

1 ½ teaspoons chopped fresh thyme, or ½ teaspoon crumbled dried

1 pound egg noodles

2 tablespoons chopped parsley

Peel the asparagus if over ¼ inch thick. Cut the asparagus tips from the stems. Cut the stems in 2 or 3 pieces, discarding tough ends (about ½ inch from end). Put all of the asparagus in a medium saucepan containing enough salted water to cover it generously. Boil uncovered until asparagus is just tender when pierced with a small sharp knife, 2 or 3 minutes. Drain, rinse with cold running water until cool, and drain.

Gently rinse the mushrooms and dry them on paper towels. Cut them lengthwise into pieces about ½ inch wide if they are large. Discard any tough stems.

In a large skillet, heat the vegetable oil and butter over medium heat. Add the mushrooms and salt and pepper to taste and sauté about 3 minutes. Add the shallots and thyme and sauté over medium-high heat, tossing often, about 3 more minutes or until the mushrooms are browned and tender and any liquid that may have escaped from the mushrooms has evaporated. Add the asparagus. Season to taste with salt and pepper.

Cook the noodles uncovered in a large pot of boiling salted water over high heat, separating strands occasionally with fork, 5 to 7 minutes for dried or until tender but firm to the bite. Meanwhile, reheat the mushrooms and asparagus, uncovered.

Drain the pasta well and transfer to a heated serving dish. Add the mushroom mixture and toss. Taste and adjust seasoning. Add parsley, toss again, and serve.

. . . .

Makes 4 servings

Nutritional information per serving: 480 calories; 14.4 g fat—26.5% calories from fat; 4.4 g saturated fat; 99 mg cholesterol

Pasta Shell and Bean Medley with Tomatoes, Garlic, and Basil

{ p a r e v e }

A colorful mixture of green and yellow snap beans and lima beans is great with pasta, whether you wish to serve it hot as a side dish or cold as a pasta salad. If you shop at farmers' markets or ethnic markets, occasionally you'll find fresh lima beans, which make a tasty contribution to this dish.

1 ½ pounds fresh lima beans, shelled, or 1 ½ cups frozen (about 8 ounces)

6 ounces green beans, ends removed, broken into 2 or 3 pieces

6 ounces wax beans or additional green beans, ends removed, broken into 2 or 3 pieces

8 ounces medium pasta shells (about 3 cups)

2 to 3 tablespoons extra-virgin olive oil

¼ cup chopped green onions (scallions)

8 ounces ripe tomatoes, cut into small dice

2 tablespoons chopped fresh basil leaves, or 2 teaspoons dried

2 tablespoons chopped parsley (if using dried basil)

Salt and freshly ground black pepper

1 tablespoon tarragon vinegar or lemon juice (optional)

Put the lima beans in a large saucepan of enough boiling salted water to cover them generously and cook uncovered over medium-high heat until just tender, 15 to 20 minutes for fresh beans or about 10 minutes for frozen. Add the green beans and wax beans for the last 5 minutes of cooking. Drain well.

Meanwhile, cook the pasta uncovered in a large pot of boiling water over high heat, stirring occasionally, 5 to 8 minutes or until tender but firm to the bite. Drain well. Transfer to a large bowl and toss with the olive oil. Add the green onions, tomatoes, basil, parsley, and salt and pepper to taste. Serve hot, cold, or room temperature. If serving cold, add vinegar or lemon juice if desired.

. . . .

Makes 3 or 4 main-course or 6 to 8 side-dish servings

Nutritional information per serving: 193 calories; 4.2 g fat—19% calories from fat; 0.5 g saturated fat; 0 mg cholesterol

Fettuccine with Roman Tuna Sauce

{ d a i r y   o r   p a r e v e }

*I*talians turn humble canned tuna into a tasty pasta sauce by combining it with fresh tomatoes and a generous amount of garlic. Lightly cooked broccoli or broccoli rabe makes a tasty accompaniment.

2 tablespoons olive oil

6 ounces mushrooms, cut into thin slices

Salt and freshly ground black pepper

6 large garlic cloves, minced

1 pound ripe tomatoes, peeled, seeded, and coarsely chopped, or 1 28-ounce can tomatoes, drained and chopped

12 ounces fettuccine

2 tablespoons butter or margarine, softened

1 6½-ounce can water-packed tuna, drained

3 tablespoons chopped parsley

Heat 1 tablespoon of the olive oil in a large skillet over medium heat. Add the mushrooms and pinch of salt and sauté about 5 minutes or until tender. Add about half the garlic and sauté 30 seconds. Transfer to a plate.

Add the remaining tablespoon oil to the skillet and heat over medium heat. Stir in the remaining garlic, followed by the tomatoes and salt and pepper to taste and cook 12 to 15 minutes or until mixture is thick.

Bring a large pot of water to a boil; add salt, then the pasta. Cook uncovered over high heat, separating the strands occasionally with a fork, following package directions or until tender but firm to the bite. Drain, reserving a little pasta water. Transfer the pasta to a large bowl. Add butter and toss.

Reheat the tomato sauce over low heat. Stir in the tuna and mushrooms. Season with freshly ground pepper. If sauce is dry, add 1 to 3 tablespoons pasta water, 1 tablespoon at a time. Spoon over pasta. Serve sprinkled with parsley.

. . . .

Makes 4 or 5 main-course servings

Nutritional information per serving: 422 calories; 11.9 g fat—25.2% calories from fat; 3.9 g saturated fat; 23 mg cholesterol

Fusilli with Barbecued Cod
and Roasted Peppers

{ p a r e v e }

Barbecued cod is usually found in the smoked fish section of the market. Like lox, it's a popular item for brunch, but it is also a great partner for pasta. For a quick Sunday supper, it's hard to beat this combination, and you can substitute any smoked fish you like. If you don't have roasted peppers, cut a fresh red pepper into strips and add it to the pot of pasta for the last three minutes of cooking. I like to use green onions and fresh tarragon or basil in this dish, but you can substitute any herbs you happen to have.

2 grilled red or green bell peppers
    (page 157)
6 ounces smoked or barbecued cod,
    bones and skin removed
2 tablespoons vegetable or olive oil
8 ounces fusilli

2 tablespoons chopped green onion
    (scallions)
4 teaspoons chopped fresh tarragon,
    or ¼ cup thin strips of basil leaves
Salt and freshly ground black pepper

Cut the peppers into ¼-inch strips. Cut the cod into about ½ × ½ × ¼-inch dice.

In a small skillet, heat the oil and cod gently over very low heat, just until heated through.

Meanwhile, cook the pasta uncovered in a large pot of boiling salted water over high heat about 7 minutes or until tender but firm to the bite. Drain well and transfer to a heated bowl. Add the cod mixture and toss. Add the pepper strips, green onions, tarragon, and salt and pepper to taste. Taste, adjust seasoning, and serve.

· ·

Makes 2 or 3 main-course servings

Nutritional information per serving: 441 calories; 12.9 g fat—26.5% calories from fat; 1.8 g saturated fat; 13 mg cholesterol

Linguine with Lima Beans and Smoked Turkey

{ m e a t }

For this fast, colorful, and satisfying main dish, the pasta, lima beans, and turkey are tossed with an uncooked tomato sauce. The dish gains zip from chopped green onions and fresh cilantro. It makes an easy lunch or supper dish. You might like to serve it a day or two after Shabbat, using 1 or 2 cups of diced chicken left from the Shabbat meal instead of the smoked turkey.

1 10-ounce package frozen lima
    beans, cooked and drained
8 ripe plum tomatoes, diced small
3 tablespoons olive oil
¼ cup chopped cilantro
Salt and freshly ground black pepper

12 ounces linguine
4 ounces sliced lean smoked turkey,
    cut into 2 × ⅜-inch strips
¼ cup chopped green onions
    (scallions)

Combine the lima beans, tomatoes, olive oil, 2 tablespoons cilantro, and salt and pepper to taste in a large bowl.

Cook the pasta in a large pot of boiling salted water uncovered over high heat, stirring occasionally, 7 to 9 minutes or until tender but firm to the bite. Drain well and add to the tomato mixture. Add the turkey and green onions and toss with pasta. Taste and adjust seasoning. Sprinkle the remaining cilantro on top and serve.

Makes 4 main-course servings

Nutritional information per serving: 607 calories; 14.6 g fat—21.5% calories from fat; 2.3 g saturated fat; 19 mg cholesterol

Spaghetti and Broccoli with Easy Turkey Sauce

{ m e a t }

For extra nutrients and a quick, easy entree, I try to always add a vegetable to the water when I am cooking pasta. Broccoli florets are an especially good addition, as they cook quickly, make the dish colorful, and, as a cruciferous vegetable, are full of nutritional benefits.

2 tablespoons olive oil

2 medium onions, chopped

1 pound ground turkey

1 teaspoon ground coriander

1 teaspoon dried rosemary

1 cup (8 ounces) tomato sauce,
   homemade or canned

¾ cup water

Salt and freshly ground black pepper

1 pound spaghetti

1 ½ pounds broccoli, divided into
   small florets

In a large skillet or wide casserole, heat the olive oil, add the onions, and sauté over medium heat about 7 minutes or until softened. Add the turkey and sauté, stirring, until it changes color. Add the coriander, rosemary, tomato sauce, and water. Bring to a boil, stirring, and cook uncovered over low heat 5 to 7 minutes or until sauce is thickened to your taste. Taste and adjust seasoning.

Cook the spaghetti in a large pot of boiling salted water about 7 minutes or according to package instructions, adding broccoli for the last 5 minutes of the spaghetti's cooking time. Drain the spaghetti with the broccoli and transfer to a heated shallow bowl. Serve turkey sauce over spaghetti.

Makes 4 or 5 servings

Nutritional information per serving: 585 calories; 15 g fat—22.9% calories from fat; 3.1 g saturated fat; 72 mg cholesterol

Vermicelli with Middle Eastern Meat Sauce

{ m e a t }

When seasoned with allspice and fresh mint and topped with toasted pine nuts, the standard spaghetti with meat sauce becomes quite exotic. Be sure to use the leanest ground beef or substitute ground turkey breast.

3 tablespoons pine nuts

1 tablespoon vegetable oil

1 medium onion, minced

¾ pound extra-lean ground beef

4 large garlic cloves, minced

¼ teaspoon ground allspice

1 pound ripe tomatoes, peeled, seeded, and chopped, or 1 28-ounce can plum tomatoes, drained and chopped

Salt and freshly ground black pepper

¼ teaspoon hot red pepper flakes

3 tablespoons tomato paste

1 pound vermicelli

¼ cup chopped fresh mint or parsley

Preheat the oven or toaster oven to 350°F. Toast the pine nuts in the oven 3 minutes or until lightly browned, but watch to make sure they don't burn. Remove to a plate.

Heat the vegetable oil in medium skillet over medium heat. Add the onion and sauté about 5 minutes. Add the beef, garlic, and allspice and sauté, stirring often, about 7 minutes or until meat changes color. Add the tomatoes, salt and pepper to taste, and red pepper flakes. Cover and cook 10 minutes. Add the tomato paste, stir until blended, and cook uncovered 5 minutes or until sauce is thick.

Cook the pasta in a large pot of boiling salted water over high heat, separating the strands occasionally with a fork, 6 or 7 minutes or until tender but firm to the bite. Add the mint to the sauce. Taste and adjust seasoning.

Drain the pasta well and transfer to a heated serving bowl. Add about half the sauce and toss. Taste and adjust seasoning. Spoon the remaining sauce in a wide ribbon across the top center of the pasta. Sprinkle with pine nuts and serve.

Makes 4 servings

Nutritional information per serving: 723 calories; 22.9 g fat—28.2% calories from fat; 6.9 g saturated fat; 59 mg cholesterol

Turkey Moussaka with Macaroni

{ m e a t }

Classic moussaka combines a meat filling and a béchamel sauce topping. To make it kosher, many Sephardic Jews simply prepare a velouté sauce without dairy products. This makes it lower in fat as well. To further reduce the fat, I broil the eggplant instead of frying it, use ground turkey instead of beef or lamb, and layer the filling and the eggplant slices with pasta. The result is delectable as well as healthful.

2 tablespoons plus 1 to 2 teaspoons
    olive oil
1 large onion
1 pound ground turkey
2 28-ounce cans diced tomatoes,
    drained
Salt and freshly ground black pepper
1½ pounds eggplant
½ cup chopped parsley

4 large garlic cloves, minced
1 pound macaroni

VELOUTÉ SAUCE
2 tablespoons pareve margarine
3½ tablespoons all-purpose flour
2 cups chicken broth
Salt and freshly ground black pepper
Paprika

Heat 1 tablespoon of the olive oil in a large, deep skillet or sauté pan over medium-low heat. Add the onion and sauté about 10 minutes or until tender. Add the turkey and cook over medium heat, crumbling with a fork, until it changes color, about 7 minutes. Add the tomatoes and salt and pepper to taste and cook over medium heat about 35 minutes or until mixture is quite dry.

Meanwhile, preheat the broiler. Cut the eggplant into slices ¼ inch thick. Arrange the eggplant on a foil-lined broiler pan. Brush lightly with oil, using a total of 4 to 6 teaspoons, and sprinkle with salt and pepper. Broil about 8 minutes. Turn over and broil about 7 minutes or until tender.

Add the parsley and garlic to the meat sauce. Transfer to a large bowl.

Cook the pasta in a large pot of boiling salted water over high heat, stirring occasionally, about 6 minutes or until nearly tender but firmer than usual, since it will be baked. Drain, rinse with cold water, and drain well. Add to the meat mixture and toss. Taste and adjust seasoning.

To make velouté sauce, melt the margarine in a heavy medium saucepan over low heat. Whisk in the flour and cook, whisking, 2 minutes or until foaming but not browned. Remove from heat. Whisk in broth. Cook over medium-high heat, whisking constantly, until the sauce thickens and comes to a boil. Simmer the sauce over low heat, whisking often, 10 minutes. Season to taste with salt and pepper.

Preheat the oven to 350°F. Oil a 13 × 9 × 2-inch baking dish. Put enough eggplant slices in the dish to make 1 layer. Cover with about half the pasta-meat mixture. Cover with another layer of eggplant. Spread the remaining meat mixture on top. Cover with a layer of remaining eggplant.

Reheat the velouté sauce until flowing before using, if it has been allowed to cool. Pour the sauce over the top layer and spread evenly with a spatula. Sprinkle with paprika. Bake the moussaka about 40 minutes or until heated through and top browns lightly. Let stand about 10 minutes before serving. Serve from baking dish.

· ·

Makes 6 to 8 servings

Nutritional information per serving: 456 calories; 13.7 g fat—26.9% calories from fat; 2.7 g saturated fat; 45 mg cholesterol

Egg Noodles

{ p a r e v e }

There's nothing like the fine flavor of homemade noodles, whether you are serving them in comforting golden chicken soup or tossing them with such delicacies as wild mushrooms, asparagus, or smoked salmon. The dough is quick and easy to make with the aid of a food processor. Roll it out using a simple, hand-crank pasta machine.

¾ cup all-purpose flour, preferably
   unbleached
¾ cup fine semolina flour or
   additional all-purpose flour
2 large eggs

¼ teaspoon salt
1 teaspoon vegetable or olive oil
   (optional)
1 to 5 teaspoons water (optional)
A little flour (optional)

Combine the flours, eggs, salt, and oil in a food processor fitted with the metal blade. Process about 10 seconds, until ingredients are blended and dough holds together in sticky crumbs that can be easily pressed together. If crumbs are dry, sprinkle enough water, 1 teaspoon at a time, processing briefly after each addition, until they are moist. Press the dough together to a ball. Knead a few seconds on a work surface, flouring lightly if dough sticks, until it is a fairly smooth ball.

Wrap the dough in plastic wrap, or set it on a plate and cover with an inverted bowl. Let stand 30 minutes. (Dough can be kept up to 4 hours in refrigerator; let stand about 30 minutes to come back to room temperature before using.)

Prepare a pasta rack or generously flour 2 or 3 baking sheets. Turn smooth rollers of a pasta machine to the widest setting. Cut the dough in 4 pieces; leave 3 pieces wrapped or covered. Flatten 1 piece of dough to a 4-inch square and lightly flour it. Run through rollers of machine at the widest setting. Fold in thirds so ends just meet in center, press seams together, and flatten slightly. Run dough through rollers again. Repeat folding and rolling, lightly flouring only when necessary to prevent sticking, until dough is smooth, about 7 more times. Turn the dial of the pasta machine 1 notch to adjust to next narrower setting. Without folding the piece of dough, run it through machine. Continue to feed the dough through the rollers without folding, turning the dial 1 notch each time; dust with flour as necessary and cut dough in half crosswise if it gets too long to handle. Stop when dough is ¹⁄₁₆ inch thick (usually this is on next to narrowest setting of machine).

Hang the dough sheet to dry on a pasta rack or on the back of a towel-lined chair. Repeat with the remaining pieces of dough. Dry the dough sheets about 10 minutes or until they are firmer and have a leathery texture but not until they are brittle; if brittle, they will fall apart when cut.

Cut the pasta dough as desired (see below). Let the noodles dry on the pasta rack or on floured baking sheet. Dry pasta at least 10 minutes, if using immediately, or up to several hours. If the noodles are on the baking sheet, gently toss them occasionally to prevent sticking. (Pasta can be refrigerated, covered loosely, on tray; or it can be gently put in plastic bags. It will keep up to 5 days in refrigerator; it can also be frozen.)

- -

Makes 9 or 10 ounces fresh pasta or about 3 or 4 servings
Nutritional information per serving: 235 calories; 3.1 g fat—12% calories from fat;
0.9 g saturated fat; 106 mg cholesterol

Medium Noodles or Fettuccine: Move the handle of the pasta machine to the
wide noodle setting. Put a sheet of pasta through the machine, holding it with one hand and catching pasta with the other hand. If the strands stick together while being cut, the dough is too wet; dry the remaining dough sheets a bit longer before cutting them. Separate the strands.

Thin Noodles or Tagliarini: Move the handle of the pasta machine to the nar-
row noodle setting. Proceed as for medium noodles.

Tomato Pasta

{ p a r e v e }

This variation of fresh pasta makes use of tomato puree instead of part of the eggs. The puree makes the noodles not only colorful and tasty but also lower in cholesterol. Serve these noodles with Mediterranean-style dishes such as ratatouille (page 302) or Veal Chops with Piperade (page 237), or toss them with sautéed eggplant or zucchini.

1 ½ cups all-purpose flour, preferably
   unbleached
1 large egg
⅓ cup tomato paste
¼ teaspoon salt

1 teaspoon vegetable or olive oil
   (optional)
1 to 5 teaspoons water (optional)
A little flour (optional)

Combine the flour, egg, tomato paste, salt, and oil if desired in a food processor fitted with the metal blade. Process about 10 seconds, until the ingredients are blended and the dough holds together in sticky crumbs that can be easily pressed together. If the crumbs are dry, sprinkle enough water, 1 teaspoon at a time, processing briefly after each addition, until they are moist. Press the dough together to a ball. Knead a few seconds on a work surface, flouring lightly if dough sticks, until it is a fairly smooth ball.

Wrap the dough in plastic wrap or set it on a plate and cover with an inverted bowl. Let stand 30 minutes. (Dough can be kept up to 4 hours in refrigerator; let stand about 30 minutes to come back to room temperature before using.)

Roll as for Egg Noodles (see page 261). When rolling the dough and cutting the noodles, flour generously because tomato dough tends to be sticky.

. . . .

Makes 9 or 10 ounces fresh pasta or about 3 or 4 servings
Nutritional information per serving: 208 calories; 1.9 g fat—8.3% calories from fat;
0.5 g saturated fat; 53 mg cholesterol

Couscous with Dried Apricots and Walnuts

{ m e a t   o r   p a r e v e }

Couscous looks like a grain, but like spaghetti, it is made from durum wheat semolina and is actually a tiny pasta. This couscous recipe is easy and delicious. You can vary the dried fruits and nuts to your taste and according to what you have in your pantry. Serve it with roasted or grilled chicken or with lamb chops.

¼ cup diced walnuts

1¾ cups chicken or vegetable broth

½ cup water

1 10-ounce package couscous
 (1⅔ cups)

¼ cup diced dried apricots

Preheat the toaster oven or oven to 350° F. Toast the walnuts in the oven about 5 minutes or until lightly browned; watch that they don't burn. Transfer to a plate.

Bring the broth and water to a boil in a small saucepan. Stir in the couscous and apricots. Cover the pan, remove from the heat, and let stand 5 minutes. Taste and adjust seasoning. Serve sprinkled with walnuts.

· ·

Makes 4 servings

Nutritional information per serving: 393 calories; 6.1 g fat—14% calories from fat; 0.7 g saturated fat; 1 mg cholesterol

Couscous with Spicy Vegetables

{ p a r e v e }

Couscous with vegetables is often served as a side dish, but it's so substantial that it can be a meal in itself.

When I studied cooking in Paris, I found that couscous was a favorite among students. Many couscous restaurants in the city are kosher, and quite a few are moderately priced. Besides, second and third helpings of couscous with a vegetable sauce were usually free!

You can vary the vegetables in this dish according to the season. Use as many or as few as you like; sometimes this couscous is made in North Africa with only one vegetable.

⅔ cup dried chickpeas, or 1½ cups canned chickpeas, drained and rinsed

2 tablespoons olive or vegetable oil

2 large onions, sliced

1 teaspoon ground cumin

4 large garlic cloves, chopped

Salt and freshly ground black pepper

2 large carrots, peeled and sliced

2 small tomatoes, cored and quartered

½ pound zucchini, cut into thick slices

2 teaspoons tomato paste

Cayenne pepper or hot sauce

QUICK COUSCOUS

1 10-ounce package couscous (1⅔ cups)

1 tablespoon olive or vegetable oil (optional)

½ teaspoon salt

Pinch of black pepper

Pinch of nutmeg

Pinch of ground cloves

To prepare dried chickpeas, see page 72. Reserve cooking liquid.

Heat the oil in a very large skillet or sauté pan and add the onions. Cook over low heat, stirring, until soft but not browned. Add the cumin and garlic and sauté 30 seconds. Add 5 cups chickpea liquid if using freshly cooked chickpeas or water if using canned chickpeas. Add salt and pepper to taste and bring to a boil. Cover and simmer 15 minutes. Add the carrots and simmer 15 minutes. Add the tomatoes, zucchini, and chickpeas. Return to a boil, cover, and simmer 15 minutes. Uncover and simmer 5 minutes.

Remove the vegetables with a slotted spoon and reserve. Reserve 2¼ cups vegetable broth for cooking the couscous and keep it warm. Boil the remaining vegetable broth, stirring often, for about 5 minutes to concentrate its flavor. Whisk in the tomato paste and add cayenne pepper to taste. Taste and adjust seasoning.

To make the quick couscous, bring the reserved 2¼ cups vegetable broth to a boil in a medium saucepan. Stir in the couscous and reduce the heat to low. Add the oil, salt, pepper, nutmeg, and cloves. Cover the pan and heat 1 minute. Remove from the heat and let stand 5 minutes. Taste and adjust seasoning. Fluff gently with a fork.

To serve, pile the couscous in a cone shape on a large platter. Spoon some of the vegetables around the sides. Serve the remaining vegetables and tomato broth in a bowl or tureen. Serve couscous in shallow bowls.

- -

Makes 4 servings

Nutritional information per serving: 537 calories; 13.3 g fat—22% calories from fat; 1.5 g saturated fat; 0 mg cholesterol

17

Grains

Israeli Rice and Lentil Stew with Cumin and Garlic

Saffron Rice with Zucchini and Tomatoes

Basic Rice Pilaf

Yellow Rice with Almonds and Raisins

Rice Salad with Green Beans, Dried Cranberries, and Walnuts

Brown Rice with Asparagus and Herbs

Cabbage and Brown Rice Pilaf with Tomatoes and Curry Spices

Bulgur Wheat Pilaf with Fresh and Sun-Dried Tomatoes

Tabbouli

Wild Rice with Leeks and Carrots

Kasha with Browned Onions and Bow Tie Pasta

WHEAT AND BARLEY are mentioned in the Torah as the grains that flourish in the land of Israel. They also fare well in kosher pots, especially for Shabbat. Different recipes for the Shabbat cholent call for adding whole wheat berries, barley, kasha (buckwheat), or rice. The grains absorb the flavors of the meat, onions, and spices and acquire a delicious taste.

Grains are the classic partner for braised and stewed meats and poultry in kosher cooking. Rice, whether steamed or cooked as pilaf, tastes great with all types of meats and fish—grilled, roasted, or served in sauce. Basmati rice, with its incomparable aroma, is the favorite rice in my house for special occasions. Wild rice too lends a festive air to our holiday menus.

Nutritious brown rice makes savory side dishes or can be mixed with beans or vegetables for vegetarian main courses. Bulgur wheat, a quick-cooking form of wheat, is used like rice in the Middle East as an accompaniment for meats. It is also loved in salads such as tabbouli, in which the bulgur wheat is mixed with tomatoes, green onions, and plenty of parsley.

Nutritionists recommend that we eat more generous portions of grains and smaller amounts of meat. To meet this goal, you should consider the grain as the main course. Serve a liberal mound of rice on the plate and accompany it with vegetables and modest portions of fish or meat. This is a different way of thinking of your menus, but it's a healthful one and is a painless way to make your menus low in fat.

Other Grains Dishes

Bulgur Wheat Pilaf with Peas and Pecans (page 73)
Spinach and Rice Gratin (page 182)

Israeli Rice and Lentil Stew
with Cumin and Garlic

{ p a r e v e }

Rice and lentil stew is so popular in Israel that it is even available in instant versions. Serve it as a side dish with poultry, meat, or fish or as a vegetarian main course. Traditionally it is flavored with onions fried in a lot of oil until deep brown, but you can instead brown the onions by starting to sauté them in very little oil and continuing to brown them while adding spoonfuls of water when the pan is dry.

Generally the lentils and rice are cooked in water, but if you use vegetable broth, the stew will taste even better. A good accompaniment for this dish is Cucumber-Tomato Salad with Yogurt (page 144).

1 cup lentils

2 cups water or vegetable broth

3 tablespoons vegetable oil

2 large onions, chopped

3 large garlic cloves, chopped

1 teaspoon ground cumin

1 ½ cups long-grain white rice

Salt and freshly ground black pepper

2 tablespoons chopped parsley (optional)

Sort the lentils carefully, discarding any stones. Rinse lentils, then combine with the water in a large saucepan. Bring to a boil, cover, and cook over medium heat about 20 minutes or until the lentils are just tender. Drain the liquid into a measuring cup, leaving the lentils in the pan, and add enough water to make 3 cups.

In a heavy skillet, heat the vegetable oil over medium heat. Add the onions and sauté, stirring occasionally, until they are well browned, about 15 minutes. Add the garlic and cumin and sauté 30 seconds; reserve.

Add reserved lentil cooking liquid to pan of lentils and bring to a boil. Add salt and rice and return to a boil. Add the onion mixture. Cover, reduce the heat to low, and cook, without stirring, until the rice is tender, about 20 minutes. Fluff gently with a fork. Season to taste with salt and pepper and lightly stir in the parsley if desired. Serve hot.

. . . .

Makes 5 or 6 servings

Nutritional information per serving: 304.5 calories; 7.3 g fat—21.2% calories from fat;
0.1 g saturated fat; 0 mg cholesterol

Saffron Rice with Zucchini and Tomatoes

{ p a r e v e }

Saffron gives this colorful rice dish a lovely aroma and a golden hue. The rice is delicious with grilled salmon, roast chicken, or broiled lamb chops.

2 cups boiling water

¼ teaspoon crushed saffron threads
   (2 pinches)

1½ tablespoons vegetable oil

1 medium onion, minced

1½ cups long-grain rice

Salt and freshly ground black pepper

2 medium zucchini

1½ tablespoons olive oil

2 medium tomatoes, fresh or canned,
   cut into small dice

2 teaspoons minced cilantro or
   Italian parsley

Combine the boiling water and saffron in a small saucepan. Cover and let stand while sautéing onion.

Heat the vegetable oil in a large saucepan. Add the onion and cook over low heat, stirring occasionally, about 7 minutes or until soft but not brown. Add the rice and sauté 2 minutes, stirring. Add the saffron water and salt and pepper. Bring to a boil, stir once with a fork, and cover. Cook over low heat, without stirring, 18 to 20 minutes or until the rice is tender and the liquid is absorbed. Remove from the heat and let stand, covered, for 10 minutes.

Cut the zucchini into 3 chunks, each about 1½ inches long. Cut each chunk in lengthwise slices about ¼ inch thick and each slice in lengthwise strips about ¼ inch thick. Heat the olive oil in a medium skillet over medium heat. Add the zucchini, salt, and pepper and sauté until barely tender, about 2 minutes. Transfer the zucchini pieces with their oil to a plate.

When the rice is cooked, scatter the tomatoes on top. Cover and let stand 10 minutes. Use a fork to fluff the rice and gently stir in the tomatoes. Add the cilantro and sautéed zucchini and stir in gently. Taste and adjust seasoning.

. . . .

Makes 4 servings

Nutritional information per serving: 373 calories; 11 g fat—26.6% calories from fat;
1.4 g saturated fat; 0 mg cholesterol

Basic Rice Pilaf

{ m e a t   o r   p a r e v e }

Rice pilaf is one of the most useful recipes for low-fat cooking. It has a richer flavor than boiled or steamed rice and is the preferred way to cook rice in much of the Middle East, including Israel, because the grains stay separate rather than sticking together. It's also popular in France, where it is flavored with bay leaves and thyme. French gastronomic historians say the dish originated in Turkey and was brought to western Europe during the time of the Crusades. Others argue that the dish comes from Iran.

To make pilaf, the rice is first sautéed, usually with an onion, then cooked in liquid in a covered pan over very low heat. It is a versatile recipe for kosher meals and tastes different depending on the liquid you use: chicken or meat broth for meat meals and vegetable broth for dairy meals. If you're serving the rice with fish, you'll find the pilaf gains a delicious flavor if you cook it in homemade fish broth. Water can also be used as the liquid, for the most delicate-tasting, lightest-colored rice. To sauté the rice, choose vegetable oil, olive oil, or margarine. Occasionally you might want to use butter for dairy meals or chicken fat for meat meals, but for healthful cooking unsaturated oil is better than these saturated fats.

You can prepare the rice up to two or three days ahead and reheat it in the microwave or in a low oven.

1 ½ tablespoons vegetable oil
1 medium onion, finely chopped
1 ½ cups long-grain white rice
3 cups hot chicken broth, vegetable
  broth, or water

Salt and freshly ground black pepper
1 bay leaf
1 ½ teaspoons chopped fresh thyme,
  or ½ teaspoon dried

Heat the vegetable oil in a large sauté pan or wide casserole. Add the onion and cook over low heat, stirring, about 7 minutes or until soft but not brown. Add the rice and sauté, stirring, about 2 minutes or until the grains turn milky white.

Add the broth, salt, pepper, bay leaf, and thyme. Stir once with a fork and cover. Cook over low heat, without stirring, for 20 minutes. Taste the rice; if not yet tender, simmer 2 more minutes. Discard the bay leaf. Add more salt and pepper if needed. Cover and let stand for 10 minutes. Gently fluff with a fork. Serve hot.

. . . .

Makes 4 servings

*Nutritional information per serving: 336 calories; 6.7 g fat—18.3% calories from fat;
1 g saturated fat; 0 mg cholesterol*

Yellow Rice with Almonds and Raisins

{ m e a t   o r   p a r e v e }

Rice garnished with almonds and raisins is a favorite in many Sephardic homes for holidays and other celebrations. It makes an especially tasty accompaniment for chicken or turkey. In classic cooking, yellow rice is made with saffron. Since this spice is expensive, many people use turmeric instead, but the flavor will be different.

1 ½ tablespoons vegetable oil

1 medium onion, minced

1 ½ cups long-grain rice

3 cups hot chicken or vegetable broth or water

¼ teaspoon saffron threads, or ¾ teaspoon turmeric

Salt and freshly ground black pepper

¼ cup raisins

¼ cup sliced or slivered almonds, lightly toasted

Heat the vegetable oil in a large saucepan. Add the onion and cook over low heat, stirring occasionally, about 7 minutes or until soft but not brown. Add the rice and sauté 2 minutes, stirring. Add the broth, saffron, salt, and pepper. Bring to a boil, stir once with a fork, add the raisins, and cover. Cook over low heat, without stirring, 18 to 20 minutes or until the rice is tender and liquid is absorbed. Remove from the heat and let stand, covered, for 10 minutes. Taste and adjust seasoning. Fluff it with a fork just before serving. Serve hot, garnished with toasted almonds.

· ·

Makes 4 to 6 servings

Nutritional information per serving: 250 calories; 8 g fat—28.4% calories from fat; 1.1 g saturated fat; 1 mg cholesterol

Rice Salad with Green Beans,
Dried Cranberries, and Walnuts

{ p a r e v e }

Dried cranberries give this quick and easy salad a beautiful color, but you can replace them with raisins or currants. The mint-scented salad makes a lovely accompaniment for cold chicken or turkey.

1 ½ cups white rice
Salt and freshly ground black pepper
1 ½ cups finely diced carrots
2 cups cut green beans (in 1-inch
   pieces)
1 to 1 ½ tablespoons herb or white
   wine vinegar

3 tablespoons vegetable oil
¼ cup minced green onions
   (scallions) or sweet white onion
¼ cup dried cranberries
¼ cup walnuts
¼ cup chopped fresh mint

In a large saucepan, bring about 2 quarts water to a boil and add a pinch of salt. Add the rice and boil uncovered about 12 to 14 minutes or until tender; check by tasting. Drain, rinse with cold water, and drain well.

In a medium saucepan, put the carrots and enough water to generously cover them. Bring to a boil and add the green beans. Boil uncovered over high heat 5 minutes or until vegetables are crisp-tender. Drain in a colander, rinse with cold water, and drain well.

Whisk 1 tablespoon vinegar with 3 tablespoons vegetable oil, salt, and pepper. Mix with the rice. Add the carrots, green beans, green onions, cranberries, and walnuts and mix gently. Add the mint. Taste and adjust seasoning; add more oil and vinegar if needed.

. . . .

Makes 6 servings

Nutritional information per serving: 341 calories; 11 g fat—28.7% calories from fat;
1.1 g saturated fat; 0 mg cholesterol

Brown Rice with Asparagus and Herbs

{ d a i r y   o r   p a r e v e }

This delicate dish makes a terrific accompaniment for baked salmon or sea bass. You might like to serve it to celebrate Shavuot, and to follow it with a low-fat cheese cake. It's also great with ratatouille for a vegetarian meal.

1 ½ tablespoons vegetable oil
1 medium onion, finely chopped
1 ½ cups long-grain brown rice
3 cups hot vegetable broth or water
Salt and freshly ground black pepper
1 bay leaf
Pinch of thyme

12 ounces asparagus, peeled if over
 ¼ inch thick
1 tablespoon butter or margarine
2 tablespoons chopped parsley
2 teaspoons chopped fresh tarragon
 (optional)

Heat the vegetable oil in a large sauté pan or wide casserole. Add the onion and cook over low heat, stirring, about 7 minutes or until soft but not brown. Add the rice and sauté, stirring, about 2 minutes.

Add the broth, salt, pepper, bay leaf, and thyme. Stir once with a fork and cover. Cook over low heat, without stirring, for 40 minutes. Taste rice; if not yet tender, simmer 2 more minutes. Discard the bay leaf and add more salt and pepper if needed. Cover and let stand for 10 minutes.

Cut the asparagus tips from the stems. Cut the stems into 2 or 3 pieces, discarding the tough ends (about ½ inch from end). Put all of the asparagus in a medium saucepan containing enough boiling salted water to cover it generously. Boil uncovered until the asparagus is just tender when pierced with a small sharp knife, 2 or 3 minutes. Drain, rinse with cold running water until cool, and drain thoroughly.

Just before serving, melt the butter in a medium skillet over medium heat. Add the asparagus, salt, and pepper and sauté about 1 minute.

Gently fluff the rice with a fork. Stir in the parsley and tarragon if desired. Taste and adjust the seasoning. Gently stir in two-thirds of the asparagus. Serve hot, garnished with the remaining asparagus.

. . . .

Makes 4 servings

Nutritional information per serving: 479 calories; 13 g fat—24.1% calories from fat; 3.5 g saturated fat; 10 mg cholesterol

Cabbage and Brown Rice Pilaf with Tomatoes and Curry Spices

{ p a r e v e }

This savory dish is a hearty, healthy accompaniment for fish, chicken, or meat. You can also make it the center of a dairy meal by serving it with Cucumber Salad with Yogurt Dill Dressing (page 31) or with a small amount of feta cheese or low-fat cheese.

2 tablespoons vegetable oil

2 medium onions, sliced

1 small head cabbage (1 to 1¼ pounds), shredded, or 8 to 10 cups packaged shredded cabbage

6 large garlic cloves, chopped

1 teaspoon ground coriander

2 teaspoons ground cumin

½ teaspoon turmeric

Pinch of ground cloves

2 cups brown rice

4 cups vegetable broth or water

Salt and freshly ground black pepper

1 14½-ounce can diced tomatoes, drained

Heat the vegetable oil in a large casserole or Dutch oven. Add the onions and sauté over medium heat 5 minutes until softened. Add the cabbage, cover, and cook over low heat, stirring often, 5 minutes. Add the garlic, coriander, cumin, turmeric, cloves, and rice and mix well. Sauté, stirring, about 1 minute. Add the broth, salt, and pepper, then stir and bring to a boil. Cover and cook over low heat 30 minutes. Sprinkle the tomatoes over the rice, cover, and cook 5 to 10 minutes or until the rice is tender. Taste and adjust seasoning. Serve hot.

. . . .

Makes 4 main-course or 6 to 8 side-dish servings

Nutritional information per serving: 321 calories; 7 g fat—19.4% calories from fat; 1.1 g saturated fat; 1 mg cholesterol

Bulgur Wheat Pilaf with Fresh and Sun-Dried Tomatoes

A grain that deserves more attention from us is bulgur wheat, which has a rich, nutty taste. Basically bulgur is wheat that has been steamed, dried, and cracked into small pieces. This process makes the wheat fast and easy to cook at home, in contrast to whole wheat kernels, which require soaking and lengthy cooking. Bulgur was one of the world's first fast foods—it has been a staple in the Middle East since ancient times and is the main ingredient in tabbouli.

Since grains are an important part of a healthful menu, using bulgur wheat gives us more variety in our side dishes. Like rice, it can be prepared as a pilaf by being lightly sautéed before the liquid is added.

1 ½ tablespoons vegetable or olive oil

1 medium onion, chopped

1 ¼ cups bulgur wheat

2 ½ cups chicken or vegetable broth or water

¼ cup dry-pack sun-dried tomatoes, cut into bite-size pieces

Salt and freshly ground black pepper

½ teaspoon dried oregano

2 green onions (scallions), thinly sliced

4 plum tomatoes, diced

Heat the oil in a medium saucepan, add the onion, and sauté over medium heat about 5 minutes. Add the bulgur and sauté 2 minutes. Add the broth, sun-dried tomatoes, salt, pepper, and oregano and bring to a boil. Cover and cook over low heat for 15 minutes or until the wheat is tender and the liquid is absorbed. Stir in the green onions and plum tomatoes. Taste and adjust seasoning.

· ·

Makes 4 servings

Nutritional information per serving: 285.5 calories; 7.3 g fat—21.4% calories from fat; 1.1 g saturated fat; 0 mg cholesterol

Tabbouli

{ p a r e v e }

The famous Lebanese salad of bulgur wheat and parsley with fresh mint and tomatoes is a perfect party dish. It is colorful, tangy, and healthy. Classic versions are lavishly moistened with olive oil, but I have lightened the dish considerably while keeping its essential flavors. A yellow bell pepper is not a traditional element of the salad, but I find it's a welcome addition. Serve tabbouli for a vegetarian buffet along with salsa-topped eggplant slices (page 125) or accompany it with low-fat smoked turkey or other lean cold cuts.

5 cups hot water

1½ cups fine or medium bulgur wheat

6 plum tomatoes

½ long (European) cucumber

1 medium yellow bell pepper, cored, seeded, and finely diced (optional)

1 cup chopped parsley, preferably Italian

⅔ cup chopped fresh mint

4 green onions (scallions), cut into thin slices

2 tablespoons fresh lemon juice, or to taste

2 or 3 tablespoons extra-virgin olive oil

Salt and freshly ground black pepper

Pour the hot water over the bulgur wheat in a large bowl and let soak until it is completely cool. Transfer to a colander and drain off excess water. Squeeze the wheat dry and transfer to a large bowl.

Dice the tomatoes and cucumber very small. Mix the diced vegetables, including the bell pepper if using, with the parsley, mint, green onions, and bulgur wheat. Add the lemon juice and olive oil to taste; salad should be fairly tart. Season to taste with salt and pepper. Serve cold or at room temperature.

. . . .

Makes about 8 appetizer or 4 to 6 main-course servings

Nutritional information per serving: 212 calories; 4.9 g fat—18.8% calories from fat;
0.7 g saturated fat, 0 mg cholesterol

Wild Rice with Leeks and Carrots

{ d a i r y   o r   p a r e v e }

Serve this elegant dish for Shabbat, Succot, Thanksgiving, or any other festive meal. When I serve it with roast chicken or turkey, I use oil to sauté the vegetables. The wild rice is also delicious with grilled sea bass and asparagus; for a fish dinner, I like to sauté the vegetables in a bit of butter.

5 cups water
Salt and freshly ground black pepper
1 cup wild rice, rinsed and drained
3 large carrots, peeled
3 large leeks, white and light green
    parts only

2 tablespoons vegetable oil or butter
½ teaspoon dried thyme
1 tablespoon chopped cilantro or
    parsley

Bring the water to a boil in a large saucepan and add a pinch of salt. Add the rice, return to a boil, cover, and cook over low heat 50 to 60 minutes or until the kernels begin to puff open.

Cut the carrots into pieces about 1½ inches long. Slice the pieces lengthwise, then stack the slices and cut in thin lengthwise strips.

Slit the leeks twice lengthwise, from the bottom of the white part upward. Rinse well. Cut the leeks into pieces about 1½ inches long. Flatten each piece and cut into thin strips, using a sharp, heavy knife. Put the strips in a bowl of cold water to rid them of any remaining sand. Remove them from the bowl; sand will sink to bottom.

Heat the vegetable oil in a large sauté pan. Add the carrots, leeks, thyme, and a pinch of salt and pepper. Cover tightly and cook over low heat, stirring often, for 20 to 25 minutes or until the vegetables are tender but not brown; if the pan becomes dry, add a few tablespoons water. If any liquid remains in pan, uncover and cook over medium heat until it evaporates. Remove from the heat; set aside.

Reheat the vegetables if necessary. Drain the rice and add it to the pan of vegetables. Heat together briefly. Taste and adjust the seasoning. Serve hot, sprinkled with cilantro or parsley.

Makes 4 to 6 servings

Nutritional information per serving: 190 calories; 5.1 g fat—23.3% calories from fat; 0.6 g saturated fat; 0 mg cholesterol

Kasha with Browned Onions and Bow Tie Pasta

{ p a r e v e }

The earthy flavor of kasha, or roasted buckwheat, is mellowed in this traditional Russian-Jewish dish by being tossed with pasta. Serve this dish as a hearty vegetarian entree preceded by Red Cabbage Salad with Pears (page 143) or your favorite carrot salad. You can also serve it with chicken or beef, in which case you can use chicken or beef broth as the cooking liquid for the kasha.

2 to 3 tablespoons vegetable oil

2 large onions, sliced

2 cups vegetable broth or water

1 cup medium or large kasha (roasted buckwheat groats, or kernels)

1 large egg, beaten

½ teaspoon dried tarragon

Salt and freshly ground black pepper

8 ounces pasta bow ties or squares

Heat the vegetable oil in a large, heavy skillet. Add the onions and cook over medium-low heat, stirring often, about 15 minutes or until brown; cover the onions if they turn too dark. Transfer to a bowl; cover to keep warm.

In a small saucepan, bring the broth to a boil; cover to keep warm.

Combine the kasha with the beaten egg in a wide bowl and stir with a fork until the grains are thoroughly coated. Add to a heavy skillet and heat it over medium heat about 3 minutes, stirring to keep grains separate. Add the hot broth and stir. Add the tarragon, salt, and pepper. Cover and cook over low heat 15 minutes or until all the water is absorbed. Stir with a fork to fluff. Add the onions, stir lightly, and cover.

Cook the pasta uncovered in a large pot of boiling salted water over high heat, stirring occasionally, 6 to 8 minutes or until tender but firm to the bite. Drain well. Toss with kasha and onions. Taste and adjust seasoning. Serve hot.

. . . .

Makes 4 to 6 servings

Nutritional information per serving: 352 calories; 8.1 g fat—20.3% calories from fat;
1.4 g saturated fat; 36 mg cholesterol

18

Vegetables and Vegetarian Dishes

{ v e g e t a r i a n   m a i n   c o u r s e s }

Pareve Succotash

Indian Vegetable Stew with Ginger and Cilantro

Sephardic Black-Eyed Peas

Eggplant and Rice Casserole with Mushrooms and Garlic

Vegetarian Cholent

Easy Tofu and Mushroom Stew

Beans in a Flash

{ v e g e t a b l e   s i d e   d i s h e s }

Asparagus and New Potatoes with Chives

Pareve Carrot Timbales

Carrots in Dill Sauce

Eggplant with Onion-Tomato Stuffing

Mashed Potatoes for Dairy Meals

Fat-Free Mashed Potatoes for Meat Meals

Roasted Potatoes with Rosemary-Garlic Oil

Butternut Squash with Quick Yogurt Sauce

Summer Green Beans with Tarragon and Tomatoes

Snow Peas with Baby Corn and Chinese Mushrooms

Light Ratatouille with Fresh Herbs

French Stewed Tomatoes

Springtime Vegetable Ragout

Tomatoes Stuffed with Rice, Artichoke, and Mushroom Salad

VEGETABLES ARE HELD in great esteem in the kosher kitchen. They are high-lighted on three major holidays—Passover, Shavuot, and Succot—as all three are related to the agricultural cycle of ancient Israel. These holidays are celebrations of the seasons and produce plays a prominent role in their observance. In addition, some people celebrate Purim with a vegetarian dinner.

We all know how important vegetables are for healthful, low-fat cooking. Their vitamins, minerals, and other nutrients help strengthen our bodies' defenses against disease. Vegetables also add colors and flavors to menus. One roast chicken dinner might resemble another, but the meal will have a different character depending on whether the vegetable accompanying the chicken is asparagus, carrots, or potatoes.

Since all vegetables are kosher, the whole range of items in the produce aisle can go in the pot. When colorful new varieties of winter squash or baby vegetables arrive, try them. Do not forget the other forms of vegetables available to us—frozen, dried, pickled, and canned. All these can help to enrich and vary our menus. Serve vegetables hot or cold, as side dishes or appetizers, with pistou (page 13), with stewed tomatoes (page 304), or with a light sprinkling of vinaigrette. For dairy meals, you might like to top them with nonfat sour cream or yogurt.

Boiling, steaming, and baking are the best techniques to use for low-fat vegetable cooking. If you wish to sauté vegetables such as onions, peppers, eggplant, or zuc-chini, use a nonstick skillet and just a few teaspoons of oil. Begin sautéing the vegeta-bles as usual, but cover them to help create steam and add a few tablespoons of vegetable broth or water if the pan becomes dry before the vegetables are tender.

Other Vegetable and Vegetarian Dishes

Braised Winter Squash with Onion (page 18) · Stewed Leeks (page 19) · Glazed Carrot Coins with Cranberries (page 20) · Mashed Potato Kugel with Onions and Mushrooms (page 33) · Pareve Onion Pizza (page 46) · Zucchini with Corn and Tomatoes (page 47) · Steamed New Potatoes with Parsley Oil (page 50) · Low-Fat Sweet Potato Latkes (page 58) · Aromatic Cauliflower and Potato Casserole (page 71) Spicy Chickpeas in Tomato Sauce (page 72) · Turnips and Carrots Braised with Spinach (page 75) · Matzo and Vegetable Stuffing (page 95) · Broccoli, Carrots, and Potatoes with Lemon Herb Dressing (page 98) · Glazed Carrots with a Touch of Cinnamon (page 99) · Broiled Eggplant Slices with Fresh Tomato Salsa (page 125) Corn with Peppers and Peas (page 128)

Vegetarian Main Courses

. . . .

Pareve Succotash
{ p a r e v e }

Old-fashioned American recipes for succotash usually include dairy products or occasionally meats in addition to corn and beans. This quick and easy version, flavored with red bell peppers and ripe tomatoes, is colorful and light and can be made with no added fat. It makes a beautiful accompaniment for roast or broiled chicken, turkey, or fish. You can also serve it as a vegetarian main course, accompanied by brown rice and, if you like, a small cube of feta cheese or a scoop of low-fat cottage cheese.

If you have grilled peppers on hand (see page 157), cut 1 pepper into strips and add it to the finished succotash instead of adding a fresh pepper.

1 cup vegetable broth or water
1 10-ounce package lima beans
1 10-ounce package frozen corn, or
   2 cups fresh kernels
1 medium red bell pepper, cored,
   seeded, and diced
2 large ripe tomatoes, diced

2 green onions (scallions), chopped
2 tablespoons chopped cilantro or
   parsley (optional)
2 teaspoons extra-virgin olive oil
   (optional)
Salt and freshly ground black pepper
Cayenne pepper (optional)

In a medium saucepan, bring the broth to a boil. Add the lima beans, cover, and return to a boil; cook over medium heat 2 minutes. Add the corn and return to a boil. Add the red pepper, cover and cook, stirring occasionally, 3 minutes or until vegetables are tender. Drain the liquid; you can save it for making soups.

Add the tomatoes, green onions, and cilantro if desired to the vegetables. Add the olive oil if you like. Season to taste with salt, pepper, and cayenne pepper if desired.

. . . .

Makes 4 or 5 side-dish or 3 main-course servings
Nutritional information per serving: 191 calories; 1.8 g fat—7.7% calories from fat;
0.4 g saturated fat; 1 mg cholesterol

Indian Vegetable Stew with Ginger and Cilantro

{ p a r e v e }

These vegetables stew in a tomato sauce boldly flavored with hot peppers, garlic, cumin, and coriander in two forms—the ground seeds and the fresh green leaves, which are also known as cilantro. Serve this tasty stew over basmati rice or brown rice. Pasta is not part of traditional Indian cuisine, and yet the vegetables in their savory sauce are delicious over orzo (rice-shaped pasta), penne, or other pasta shapes.

1 tablespoon plus 2 teaspoons vegetable oil

1 medium onion, chopped

4 teaspoons minced, peeled fresh ginger

4 large garlic cloves, minced

2 to 3 fresh jalapeño peppers, seeded and minced (see Note opposite)

1 tablespoon ground cumin

1 teaspoon ground coriander

1/2 teaspoon turmeric

2 pounds ripe tomatoes, peeled, seeded, and chopped, or 2 28-ounce cans tomatoes, drained

Salt and freshly ground black pepper

3 large carrots, peeled and cut into diagonal slices about 1/2 inch thick

3 cups small cauliflower florets

1 pound fresh peas, shelled, or 1 cup frozen

4 tablespoons chopped cilantro leaves

Heat the vegetable oil in a heavy, medium saucepan over medium-low heat. Add the onion and cook, stirring, 5 minutes. Add the ginger, garlic, and jalapeño peppers and cook 1 minute. Stir in the cumin, coriander, and turmeric. Add the tomatoes and salt and pepper to taste and stir well to combine with spice mixture. Bring to a boil, cover, and cook over low heat, stirring occasionally (and crushing canned tomatoes), about 30 minutes or until the tomatoes are very soft.

Put the carrot slices in a medium saucepan and cover with water. Bring to a boil. Add the cauliflower and cook 3 minutes or until the vegetables soften slightly but are still crisp. Add the peas and cook 30 seconds. Drain the vegetables and add them to the tomato sauce. Cover and cook over low heat about 5 minutes or until just tender.

Stir in 3 tablespoons cilantro. Taste and adjust seasoning. Serve sprinkled with remaining tablespoon cilantro.

. . . .

Makes about 4 servings

Nutritional information per serving: 201 calories; 7.4 g fat—30% calories from fat;
0.9 g saturated fat; 0 mg cholesterol

N O T E : Wear gloves when handling jalapeño peppers. After cutting, wash your hands, cutting board, and utensils with soap and hot water. Remove the seeds and ribs of jalapeño peppers if you like them to be less hot.

Sephardic Black-Eyed Peas

{ p a r e v e }

We in America tend to think of black-eyed peas as a specialty of the American South, but they are loved in Israel as well. They appear on many Sephardic menus for Rosh Hashanah. Black-eyed peas are available dried, frozen, and in a presoaked version that cooks in less than 30 minutes. This dish is flavorful but not fiery, warming and hearty but not heavy. Serve the black-eyed peas as a side dish with any meat or as a vegetarian main course with rice and a green salad.

½ pound dried black-eyed peas, or 3 to 4 cups frozen black-eyed peas, cooked according to package directions
5 cups water
1 tablespoon tomato paste
¾ teaspoon ground coriander
½ teaspoon ground cumin

½ teaspoon paprika
Salt and freshly ground black pepper
Cayenne pepper
1 tablespoon olive oil
1 large onion, chopped
2 tablespoons chopped cilantro or Italian parsley

Pick over the dried peas, discarding pebbles and broken or discolored peas. Soak dried peas 8 hours or overnight in water to cover generously; or quick-soak by putting them in a medium saucepan with 1 quart water, bringing to a boil, and boiling uncovered 2 minutes, then remove from heat, cover, and let stand 1 hour. Drain the peas and rinse. Put in a medium saucepan and add the water. Bring to a simmer, cover, and cook over low heat about 1½ hours or until tender. Reserve ¼ cup cooking liquid.

Drain the peas and put in a medium saucepan. Mix the tomato paste with reserved pea cooking liquid or water and add to pot. Add the coriander, cumin, paprika, salt, pepper, and cayenne pepper to taste. Bring to a simmer. Remove from heat.

In a heavy nonstick skillet, heat the olive oil, add the onion, and sauté over medium heat, stirring often, about 5 minutes; when the onion begins to brown, add about 1 tablespoon water and continue to sauté until deeply browned. Add onion to pot of peas, cover, and heat gently 5 minutes. Add 1 tablespoon cilantro. Taste and adjust seasoning. Serve hot, sprinkled with remaining tablespoon cilantro.

· ·

Makes 4 side-dish or 3 main-course servings

Nutritional information per serving: 235 calories; 4.4 g fat—16.2% calories from fat; 0.6 g saturated fat; 0 mg cholesterol

Eggplant and Rice Casserole with Mushrooms and Garlic

{ p a r e v e }

For making casseroles and other baked dishes, eggplant is traditionally fried. Naturally, it soaks up a lot of oil in the process. Instead, I like to broil the eggplant for this casserole, and I find this not only makes it low in fat, the result is lighter and tastier! This dish is pareve, so you can serve it with meat or turn it into a vegetarian entree and accompany it with yogurt, or with a Cucumber-Tomato Salad with Yogurt (page 144).

1 large eggplant (about 1¼ pounds),
  cut into slices ¼ inch thick
About 2 tablespoons olive oil
Salt and freshly ground black pepper
1 large onion, chopped
6 ounces sliced mushrooms

4 large garlic cloves, chopped
1 teaspoon paprika
2 cups boiled rice
Cayenne pepper
1 large egg
¾ cup water

Preheat the broiler. Arrange the eggplant on a foil-lined baking sheet or broiler pan. Brush lightly with 1 tablespoon of the oil and sprinkle with salt and pepper. Broil about 8 minutes. Turn over and broil about 7 minutes or until tender.

Preheat the oven to 350°F. Heat the remaining tablespoon oil in large, heavy skillet. Add the onion and sauté 5 minutes over medium heat. Add the mushrooms, salt, and pepper and sauté over medium-high heat, stirring, 2 minutes. Add the garlic and ½ teaspoon paprika and sauté a few seconds. Remove from the heat, add the rice, and mix well. Season to taste with salt, pepper, and cayenne pepper.

Lightly oil a 2-quart casserole. Set aside enough eggplant slices to make 2 layers in the casserole. Dice any remaining slices and add to the rice mixture.

Place 1 layer of eggplant in the casserole. Top with all of the rice mixture, then with the remaining eggplant slices. Beat the egg with the remaining paprika and ¼ cup water. Pour egg mixture over the top of the eggplant. Pour the remaining ½ cup water around the edges of the casserole and bake 30 minutes or until top is brown. Serve hot.

· ·

Makes 4 servings

Nutritional information per serving: 271 calories; 8.8 g fat—28.7% calories from fat;
1.5 g saturated fat; 53 mg cholesterol

Vegetarian Cholent

{ p a r e v e }

The secret to obtaining a meatless Shabbat cholent with a deep brown color and a meaty flavor is to borrow two ingredients from Chinese cooking—soy sauce and dried shiitake mushrooms. This dish is very low in fat—barely over 10 percent of its calories come from fat.

Because the beans cook all night, there is no need to soak them. If you wish to cook the dish for other occasions, just simmer it over low heat for about 2½ hours. Serve the cholent with soy sauce and hot sauce. All you need to accompany this hearty entree is a light salad of tomatoes and cucumbers or a green salad, and fruit for dessert.

1 pound dried white beans, such as
  great northern (2¼ to 2½ cups),
  sorted and rinsed
2 ounces dried shiitake mushrooms
  or other dried mushrooms
2 tablespoons vegetable oil
3 large onions, cut into large dice
8 large garlic cloves, coarsely
  chopped
1 tablespoon chopped peeled fresh
  ginger

4 large carrots, peeled and cut into
  1-inch pieces
1 pound large boiling potatoes,
  peeled and quartered
¾ cup pearl barley, sorted and rinsed
3 tablespoons soy sauce
1 teaspoon sugar
Salt and freshly ground black pepper
9 to 10 cups water
4 large eggs in shells (optional),
  rinsed

Soak the dried mushrooms in hot water to cover 10 minutes. Drain well and rinse. If using shiitake mushrooms, discard tough stems. Cut mushrooms into bite-size pieces.

Heat the vegetable oil in a 5-quart casserole. Add the onions and sauté over medium heat, stirring often, 10 minutes or until brown. Add the garlic and ginger and sauté over low heat for 1 minute. Add the beans, carrots, potatoes, barley, soy sauce, sugar, salt, and pepper. Add about 9 cups water or enough to cover the ingredients by about 2 inches. Stir and bring to a boil. Cover and cook over very low heat for 30 minutes. Set the eggs if desired on top and push them gently into the liquid. Return to a simmer. Cover and cook in a very low oven (about 180°–200° F.) overnight. Serve hot.

. . . .

Makes 6 to 8 servings

Nutritional information per serving: 389 calories; 4.9 g fat—11% calories from fat;
0.8 g saturated fat; 0 mg cholesterol

Easy Tofu and Mushroom Stew

{ p a r e v e }

Tofu is suitable for a variety of uses, not just for recipes from the Far East. I like it as a substitute for chicken in a Mediterranean-style sauce such as this, with mushrooms, onions, garlic, tomatoes, and thyme. Serve this tasty tofu stew over brown or white rice or orzo. For a festive vegetarian dinner, you might like to serve it with wild rice and garnish it with fresh thyme sprigs.

Now that kosher low-fat tofu has become available, use it to lower the fat even further.

2 tablespoons olive oil
1 large onion, sliced
3 large garlic cloves, chopped
1 pound medium mushrooms, quartered
Salt and freshly ground black pepper
1 28-ounce can diced tomatoes, drained

¼ teaspoon hot red pepper flakes
1½ teaspoons dried thyme, crumbled
1 14-ounce package regular or firm tofu
2 tablespoons chopped parsley
6 cups hot cooked brown rice, for serving

In a heavy, wide casserole, heat the olive oil. Add the onion and sauté over medium heat 7 minutes. Stir in the garlic, and immediately add the mushrooms, salt, and pepper. Sauté, stirring, about 3 minutes. Add the tomatoes, red pepper flakes, and 1 teaspoon thyme and bring to a boil. Cover and simmer over low heat, stirring often, about 10 minutes.

Thoroughly drain the liquid from the tofu. Cut the tofu into ¾-inch cubes. Add to the casserole, spoon a little of sauce over the tofu cubes, and sprinkle them with salt, pepper, and remaining ½ teaspoon thyme. Cover and heat gently, without stirring, about 3 minutes. Taste and adjust the seasoning. Sprinkle with chopped parsley and serve over brown rice.

. . . .

Makes 4 servings

Nutritional information per serving: 548 calories; 15.1 g fat—24% calories from fat; 2.1 g saturated fat; 0 mg cholesterol

Beans in a Flash

{ p a r e v e }

These savory beans are ready in less than 5 minutes. Serve the beans with low-fat beef or chicken frankfurters for a quick supper, or, if you would like a vegetarian meal, serve them with white or brown rice.

1 15- or 16-ounce can pink or white beans

1 teaspoon olive or vegetable oil

2 large garlic cloves, minced

1 14½-ounce can diced tomatoes, drained

Salt and freshly ground black pepper

Cayenne pepper

Drain the beans. In a medium saucepan, heat the oil over low heat, add the garlic, and sauté 10 seconds. Add the tomatoes and cook 2 minutes. Add the beans and heat through. Season to taste with salt, pepper, and cayenne pepper. Serve hot.

. . . .

Makes 4 servings

Nutritional information per serving: 161 calories; 1.9 g fat—10.1% calories from fat;
0.3 g saturated fat; 0 mg cholesterol

Vegetarian Side Dishes

. . . .

Asparagus and New Potatoes
with Chives

{ p a r e v e }

I love to serve this delicate dish on Passover or for any springtime celebration. It's a lovely accompaniment for salmon or sole. The potatoes are delicious steamed, but you can boil them instead; the cooking time will be the same.

1 pound new potatoes, scrubbed
   well
Salt and freshly ground black pepper

1 pound asparagus
1 tablespoon vegetable oil
1 tablespoon snipped fresh chives

Peel the potatoes if desired. Bring at least 1 inch of water to a boil in the base of a steamer—boiling water should not reach holes in top part of steamer. Set the potatoes in the steamer top and sprinkle with salt. Cover tightly and steam over high heat about 20 minutes or until tender when pierced with a sharp knife. Remove the potatoes, drain briefly on paper towels, slice in half, or quarters if large, and transfer to a serving bowl.

Cut the asparagus tips from the stems. Cut the stems into 2 or 3 pieces, discarding tough ends (about ½ inch from end). Put all of the asparagus in a medium saucepan containing enough boiling salted water to cover it generously. Boil uncovered until the asparagus is just tender when pierced with a small sharp knife, about 3 minutes. Drain well and add to the potatoes. Toss with the vegetable oil, salt, pepper, and 2 teaspoons chives. Serve sprinkled with remaining chives. Serve hot or warm.

. . . .

Makes 4 servings

Nutritional information per serving: 146 calories; 3.8 g fat—21.6% calories from fat;
0.5 g saturated fat; 0 mg cholesterol

Pareve Carrot Timbales

{ p a r e v e }

These bright orange carrot timbales are sophisticated in appearance but simple to prepare. They taste wonderful on their own or as an accompaniment for fish, veal, lamb, beef, chicken, or turkey.

1 ¼ pounds carrots, peeled and cut
  into ¼-inch slices
1 medium russet potato, peeled,
  halved, and sliced
Salt and freshly ground black pepper

2 teaspoons pareve margarine
2 large eggs
2 large egg whites
½ teaspoon sugar, or to taste

Preheat the oven to 400°F. Generously grease five ⅔-cup ramekins, using some margarine. In a saucepan, cover the carrots and potato with water and add a pinch of salt. Bring to a boil, cover, and cook 15 minutes or until very tender. Drain well. Puree in a food processor until smooth.

Melt the margarine in the pan from the carrots. Add the puree and cook over low heat, stirring often, about 1 minute. Remove from the heat.

Whisk the eggs and egg whites in a medium bowl. Gradually whisk in the vegetable puree. Season to taste with salt, pepper, and sugar. Divide the mixture among the ramekins. Tap each to pack down mixture and smooth tops. Set the ramekins in a roasting pan in the oven. Add enough boiling water to the pan to come halfway up the sides of the ramekins. Bake 35 to 40 minutes or until firm; a cake tester inserted into mixture should come out clean. Add water to the pan during baking if most of it evaporates.

Using a metal pancake turner, remove the molds from the water. Cool 3 minutes. Serve hot, in the molds.

· ·

Makes 5 servings

*Nutritional information per serving: 128.5 calories; 4.1 g fat—28.2% calories from fat;
1 g saturated fat; 85 mg cholesterol*

Carrots in Dill Sauce

{ d a i r y }

This is a favorite way to prepare carrots in Romania, Hungary, Poland, and other Eastern and Northern European countries. Other vegetables, such as beets, parsnips, peas, and cauliflower, can benefit as well from being matched with a dill sauce. Serve these carrots with baked or poached fish or with rice and another vegetable dish as a vegetarian meal.

If you wish to prepare this dish for serving with chicken or meat, substitute chicken or vegetable broth for the milk and use nondairy margarine rather than butter.

2 pounds carrots, peeled and sliced
Salt and freshly ground black pepper
2 tablespoons butter or margarine
2½ tablespoons all-purpose flour

1⅓ cups skim milk
Salt and ground white pepper
Cayenne pepper (optional)
2 tablespoons snipped fresh dill

In a medium saucepan, cover the carrots with water and add salt. Bring to a boil, cover, and reduce heat to medium low. Cook 8 to 10 minutes or until the carrots are tender when pierced with a sharp knife. Drain the carrots, reserving ¼ cup cooking liquid. Cover the carrots to keep them warm.

Melt the butter in a small, heavy saucepan over low heat. Whisk in the flour. Cook, whisking constantly, about 3 minutes or until the mixture turns light beige. Remove from the heat. Add the milk, whisking. Bring to a boil over medium-high heat, whisking. Add a pinch of salt and white pepper. Simmer uncovered over medium-low heat, whisking often, for 5 minutes. Taste and adjust seasoning, adding cayenne pepper to taste if desired.

Gently stir the carrots into the sauce and heat briefly. If the sauce is too thick, stir in a little of the reserved carrot cooking liquid. Stir in the dill. Taste and adjust the seasoning. Serve hot.

Makes 5 or 6 servings

Nutritional information per serving: 122 calories; 4.2 g fat—29.5% calories from fat;
2.5 g saturated fat; 11 mg cholesterol

Eggplant with Onion-Tomato Stuffing

{ p a r e v e }

Many old-fashioned recipes call for frying eggplants before stuffing them, but this baked eggplant is easier to prepare, is low in fat, and is delicious. Since it is pareve, you can serve it at any meal, but it's especially appropriate for festive meals, such as for Shabbat, Shavuot, or Succot. If you wish to prepare it for Passover, substitute matzo meal for the bread crumbs.

2 small eggplants (1 pound each)	½ teaspoon dried oregano
Salt and freshly ground black pepper	6 garlic cloves, minced
2 tablespoons olive oil	3½ tablespoons bread crumbs
2 medium onions, sliced	¼ cup parsley
2½ pounds ripe tomatoes, peeled, seeded, and chopped	2 tablespoons tomato paste
	¼ cup water

Preheat the oven to 450°F. Remove the green caps and halve the eggplants lengthwise. With a sharp knife, score the flesh of each half lightly to make a border about ⅜ inch from skin, following around the shape of the eggplant. Score lightly a few times in center of eggplant. Place the eggplants cut side up in a lightly oiled roasting pan or shallow baking dish. Sprinkle them with salt and with 1 tablespoon olive oil. Bake 25 minutes or until the flesh is tender when pierced with a knife.

Meanwhile, in a large nonstick skillet, heat the remaining tablespoon olive oil. Add the onions and sauté over medium heat 3 minutes, stirring. Cover and cook over low heat, stirring often, about 10 minutes. Add 1 or 2 tablespoons water if the pan becomes dry or onions turn too dark. Remove the onions from the skillet. Add the tomatoes, oregano, salt, and pepper. Cook, stirring occasionally, about 25 minutes or until mixture is thick. Remove half the tomato mixture and reserve for sauce.

Let the eggplant cool slightly. Cut gently along border and remove the pulp carefully with a spoon; do not pierce eggplant skin. Drain the pulp 5 minutes in a colander. If the shells are watery, drain them upside down also. Return the eggplant shells to a shallow baking dish.

Chop the eggplant flesh and add to the tomato mixture in the skillet. Add the onions, garlic, bread crumbs, and parsley. Taste and adjust seasoning; filling should be well seasoned with salt and pepper.

Spoon the filling into the eggplant shells. Bake about 15 minutes or until the eggplant is very tender and hot.

Meanwhile, reheat the remaining tomato mixture. Add the tomato paste and water, or enough to thin sauce to desired consistency. Taste and adjust seasoning.

Serve the eggplant hot, warm, or at room temperature accompanied by tomato sauce.

. . . .

Makes 4 servings

Nutritional information per serving: 241.5 calories; 8.9 g fat—30% calories from fat;
1.1 g saturated fat; 0 mg cholesterol

Mashed Potatoes for Dairy Meals

{ d a i r y }

You don't have to give up creamy mashed potatoes when you prepare a healthy meal. You simply mash the potatoes with skim milk and a touch of butter for a dairy meal. Season your potatoes well and they will be delicious.

2 pounds russet potatoes or white
    boiling potatoes, scrubbed
Salt and ground white pepper
2 to 3 tablespoons butter or
    margarine

About ¾ cup skim or low-fat milk
Freshly grated nutmeg

Cut each potato into 2 or 3 pieces. Put in a saucepan and add enough water to just cover and a pinch of salt. Cover, bring to a boil, and simmer over medium heat about 20 minutes or until potatoes are very tender. Drain thoroughly, cool slightly, and peel. Mash with a potato masher in the saucepan or puree the potatoes in a food mill or potato ricer and return to the saucepan.

Add the butter and a little milk to the potatoes and season with salt, pepper, and nutmeg. Heat over low heat, stirring vigorously with a wooden spoon, until the puree is light and smooth. Add the remaining milk gradually, still stirring vigorously over low heat. The potatoes should be soft but not soupy; if the mixture is too stiff, beat in a few tablespoons milk. Taste and add more salt, pepper, and nutmeg if desired. Serve hot.

. . . .

Makes 6 servings

Nutritional information per serving: 164 calories; 4 g fat—21.4% calories from fat;
2.4 g saturated fat; 11 mg cholesterol

Fat-Free Mashed Potatoes
for Meat Meals
{ m e a t }

You might think it's impossible to prepare tasty mashed potatoes without milk and butter, but when you try these you'll change your mind. They are made without added fat and are fla- vored with a hint of fresh garlic and chicken broth. When Yukon Gold potatoes are available, I use them because they have a natural buttery taste.

2 pounds potatoes, preferably Yukon
  Gold
2 large garlic cloves, unpeeled

2 to 2½ cups chicken broth
Salt and freshly ground black pepper

Cut each potato into 3 or 4 pieces. Put in a medium saucepan and add the garlic and 2 cups broth. Cover, bring to a boil, and simmer over medium-low heat about 20 minutes or until the potatoes are very tender. Remove the garlic from the pan and set aside. Remove the potatoes with a slotted spoon, cool slightly, and peel them. Mash with a potato masher in a bowl or put potatoes through a food mill or potato ricer. Return puree to saucepan.

Remove the peel from the garlic and mash with a fork. Add the mashed garlic to the potato in the saucepan. Slowly add ⅔ cup of the potato cooking liquid, stirring with a wooden spoon. If you would like softer mashed potatoes, beat in a little more cooking liquid or broth a tablespoon at a time. Season to taste with salt and pepper. Serve hot.

. . . .

Makes 6 servings
Nutritional information per serving: 147 calories; 1 g fat—6.2% calories from fat; 0.3 g saturated fat; 1 mg cholesterol

Roasted Potatoes with Rosemary-Garlic Oil

{ p a r e v e }

Fresh rosemary sprigs and chopped garlic cloves lend their aroma to the potatoes as they bake. Serve these savory potatoes with roast chicken or turkey or with braised veal chops.

2½ tablespoons vegetable oil

7 fresh rosemary sprigs, or
   1 teaspoon dried

2 pounds baking potatoes, peeled
   and quartered

¾ teaspoon salt

Freshly ground black pepper

4 large garlic cloves, minced

3 tablespoons hot water

Preheat the oven to 325° F. Pour the vegetable oil into a heavy baking dish that can just hold potatoes in 1 layer and add 3 rosemary sprigs. Add the potatoes and toss to coat them with the oil. Sprinkle them evenly with salt, pepper, garlic, and dried rosemary if using and toss again.

Bake the potatoes uncovered for 30 minutes. Turn them over and bake 15 minutes. Add 2 tablespoons of the hot water to the baking dish, cover tightly, and bake 30 minutes. Add the remaining tablespoon water, cover, and bake 10 minutes or until the potatoes are tender. Serve the potatoes garnished with the remaining fresh rosemary sprigs if using.

. . . .

Makes 6 servings

Nutritional information per serving: 173 calories; 5.9 g fat—29.7% calories from fat; 0.7 g saturated fat; 0 mg cholesterol

Butternut Squash with Quick Yogurt Sauce
{ d a i r y }

For an easy way to enjoy winter squash without added fat, serve the hot squash with a cool, refreshing Turkish-style yogurt sauce. Microwave the squash (see Note below) if you want it ready in a flash.

2 butternut squash (2 to 2½ pounds)	Salt
1 cup plain nonfat yogurt	Cayenne pepper
2 teaspoons dried leaf thyme, crumbled	

Preheat the oven to 400°F. Halve the squash lengthwise and remove the seeds and strings. Oil a large nonstick roasting pan, or line pan with foil and oil the foil. Place the squash skin side up in the prepared pan. Cover and bake 40 to 45 minutes or until tender when thickest part of meat is pierced with a fork.

Mix the yogurt, thyme, salt, and cayenne pepper to taste. Serve hot squash with cold sauce.

. . . .

Makes 4 servings

Nutritional information per serving: 161 calories; 0.4 g fat—2.1% calories from fat; 0.2 g saturated fat; 1 mg cholesterol

NOTE: To microwave butternut squash, halve the squash and remove the seeds and strings. Wrap each half in plastic wrap, or put the squash cut side down in a microwave-safe baking dish and cover with waxed paper. Microwave on high until tender; 2 to 2½ pounds of squash take about 15 minutes. Check by piercing meat in its thickest part with a fork.

Summer Green Beans with Tarragon and Tomatoes

{ p a r e v e }

Fresh tarragon and ripe tomatoes contribute flavor and aroma to this dish. When the thin French beans called haricots verts are available, use them. They are superb prepared this way. Otherwise, use green snap beans or yellow wax beans.

If you are cooking green vegetables ahead, here is a way to keep their color bright. After boiling or steaming the vegetable, rinse it with cold water and drain it well. You can later reheat the vegetable by putting it in a pan of hot water or by microwaving it; the vegetable will retain its good color and fresh taste.

1 ½ pounds green beans, ends
   removed, broken into 2 pieces
2 teaspoons olive oil
¾ pound ripe tomatoes, peeled,
   seeded, and diced

Salt and freshly ground black pepper
2 teaspoons chopped fresh tarragon,
   or ½ teaspoon dried

Place the beans in a large saucepan of boiling salted water and boil 5 to 7 minutes or until crisp-tender. Drain in a colander or strainer.

Heat the olive oil in the same saucepan, add the tomatoes, and heat over medium heat. Add the beans, sprinkle with salt and pepper, and toss well over heat. Add the tarragon and toss again. Taste and adjust seasoning. Serve hot.

. . . .

Makes 4 servings

Nutritional information per serving: 92 calories; 2.8 g fat—23.4% calories from fat;
0.4 g saturated fat; 0 mg cholesterol

Snow Peas with Baby Corn
and Chinese Mushrooms
{ p a r e v e }

The flavors of fresh ginger, soy sauce, and sesame oil permeate this colorful Oriental vegetable medley. Cook the mushrooms with vegetable broth or, if you like, use chicken or beef broth if you're serving them to accompany poultry or meat. The vegetables also make a lovely vegetarian entree with jasmine or basmati rice.

20 dried shiitake mushrooms (about 2 ounces)

¾ pound snow peas, rinsed, ends removed

12 ears canned baby corn, halved

4 teaspoons vegetable oil

2 teaspoons minced, peeled fresh ginger

¾ cup vegetable, chicken, or beef broth

2 tablespoons soy sauce

2 tablespoons rice wine or sherry

2 teaspoons sugar

1 teaspoon roasted sesame oil

Rinse the mushrooms, then soak them in hot water for ½ hour. Remove the mushrooms, reserving the liquid. Rinse again and cut off stems.

Place the peas in a large saucepan of boiling salted water and boil uncovered over high heat 1 minute or until crisp-tender. Add the corn and boil a few seconds. Drain both in a colander, rinse with cold water, and drain well.

Heat the vegetable oil in a heavy medium saucepan over medium heat. Add the ginger and stir 15 seconds. Add the mushrooms, broth, soy sauce, wine, and sugar. Bring to a boil, cover, and cook over low heat, stirring occasionally, about 5 minutes or until mushrooms are tender. Add 2 or 3 tablespoons reserved mushroom soaking liquid if pan becomes dry. Add snow peas and corn and heat through. Off the heat, add the sesame oil and toss. Serve hot or cold.

. . . .

Makes 4 servings

Nutritional information per serving: 318 calories; 6.8 g fat—19.5% calories from fat; 1 g saturated fat; 0 mg cholesterol

Light Ratatouille with Fresh Herbs

{ p a r e v e }

Ratatouille is a wonderful accompaniment for meat or fish, but classic recipes often call for large amounts of oil. This version has plenty of onion, garlic, and herbs to keep the aromatic character of the dish, but it is light. You can serve it with brown rice for a terrific warm-weather vegetarian luncheon entree.

If your markets carry slender Japanese or Chinese eggplants, I recommend them for this Mediterranean specialty. They taste rich even when you're using just a small amount of oil, and have fewer seeds than common eggplants.

1 ½ tablespoons olive oil

2 medium onions, halved and thinly sliced

2 medium red bell peppers, seeded and diced

1 medium green bell pepper, seeded and diced

1 pound small zucchini, cut into small dice

Salt and freshly ground black pepper

6 fresh thyme sprigs, or 1 teaspoon dried thyme

1 bay leaf

4 large garlic cloves, chopped

1 pound Japanese eggplant, cut into ½-inch slices, or Italian eggplant, cut into ¾-inch dice

2 pounds ripe tomatoes, peeled, seeded, and chopped

1 tablespoon chopped fresh oregano (optional)

¼ cup slivered fresh basil leaves

Heat 1 tablespoon of the olive oil in a large, heavy, wide casserole. Add the onions and red and green peppers and sauté 3 minutes over medium heat. Add the zucchini, salt, and pepper. Stir, cover, and cook 3 minutes. Transfer vegetables to a bowl.

Tie the fresh thyme sprigs and bay leaf together. Heat the remaining ½ tablespoon olive oil in the casserole. Add the garlic, eggplant, salt, and pepper and sauté over medium heat, stirring, 1 minute. Add the tomatoes, thyme, and bay leaf and bring to a boil over high heat. Cover and cook over medium heat 15 minutes.

Return the zucchini-pepper mixture to the casserole and mix gently. Bring to a boil and add the oregano if using. Cook uncovered over medium-low heat, stirring occasionally, 10 minutes or until the vegetables are very tender. Taste and adjust the seasoning; season generously with pepper. Remove the bay leaf and thyme sprigs. Stir in half the fresh basil. Serve hot or cold, sprinkled with the remaining fresh basil.

· ·

Makes 4 servings

Nutritional information per serving: 172 calories; 6.4 g fat—29.6% calories from fat;
0.9 g saturated fat; 0 mg cholesterol

French Stewed Tomatoes

{ p a r e v e }

Whether you serve this tomate concassée *as a vegetable accompaniment or a chunky sauce, it has numerous uses in low-fat cooking. Spoon it into broiled mushrooms as a stuffing or use it as a topping on baked or broiled eggplant slices. Toss it with cooked pasta or rice, or simply serve several spoonfuls alongside grilled chicken or steak as a bright, flavorful accent.*

1 ½ teaspoons olive or vegetable oil
½ cup minced onion
3 medium garlic cloves, minced
2 pounds ripe tomatoes, peeled, seeded, and finely chopped

1 ½ teaspoons fresh thyme leaves, or
  ½ teaspoon dried
1 bay leaf
Salt and freshly ground black pepper

Heat the oil in a large, heavy nonstick skillet. Add the onion and cook over medium-low heat, stirring, until soft but not browned, about 7 minutes; add 1 tablespoon water during cooking if pan becomes dry. Add the garlic and cook 30 seconds. Add the tomatoes, thyme, bay leaf, and salt and pepper to taste and bring to a boil. Cook, uncovered, over medium heat, stirring often, 10 to 15 minutes or until tomatoes are very soft and mixture is fairly thick; reduce the heat if necessary, as it burns easily. Discard the bay leaf. Taste and adjust seasoning.

. . . .

Makes 4 servings

*Nutritional information per serving: 71 calories; 2.5 g fat—28% calories from fat;
0.3 g saturated fat; 0 mg cholesterol*

Springtime Vegetable Ragout
{ p a r e v e }

When I come home from the farmers' market with bagfuls of fresh vegetables, this is the type of dish I love to make. It is bursting with the goodness and sweet taste of fresh spring vegetables—baby potatoes, small squash, new carrots, and sugar snap peas accented with fresh dill and sweet onions, which melt into the cooking liquid. You can adapt the recipe according to the vegetables and herbs available at your market. Other good additions are asparagus, green beans, and fresh fava beans.

Serve this vegetarian stew as a side dish or as a light main course with yogurt and country bread.

2 teaspoons vegetable oil
2 medium red onions, chopped
1 cup water
1 pound small new potatoes, such as Yukon Gold
1/2 pound medium carrots, cut into diagonal slices 1/2 inch thick
Salt and freshly ground black pepper

1/2 pound pattypan squash, cut into eighths
Pinch of cayenne pepper
1/2 pound sugar snap peas, ends removed (see Note below)
1/4 cup snipped fresh dill

Heat the vegetable oil in a sauté pan over medium heat. Add the onions and sauté 5 minutes. Add the water and bring to a boil. Add the potatoes, carrots, salt, and pepper and return to a boil. Cover and simmer over low heat 15 minutes. Add the squash and sprinkle with cayenne. Cover and simmer 10 minutes. Add the peas; cover and simmer 3 minutes or until crisp-tender. Add the dill, taste, and adjust seasoning. Serve hot.

· ·

Makes 4 side-dish servings
Nutritional information per serving: 187 calories; 2.9 g fat—13.2% calories from fat; 0.4 g saturated fat; 0 mg cholesterol

N O T E : The sugar snap peas will stay bright green if you cook them for a few minutes in a separate pan of boiling water, then add them to the stew, but it's easier to cook them along with the other vegetables.

Tomatoes Stuffed with Rice, Artichoke, and Mushroom Salad

{ p a r e v e }

Tomatoes filled with a colorful rice and vegetable salad accented with red peppers and curry vinaigrette make tasty pareve appetizers. They are great for Shavuot as well as for Shabbat, especially during summer. For brunch or a light lunch, you can serve these tomatoes as a vegetarian entree or as an accompaniment for poached salmon.

6 large, ripe but firm tomatoes

4 artichokes or thawed and trimmed
    frozen artichoke hearts

1 cup long-grain rice

2 tablespoons white wine vinegar

$\frac{1}{2}$ teaspoon curry powder

Salt and freshly ground black pepper

$3\frac{1}{2}$ tablespoons vegetable oil

$1\frac{1}{4}$ cups cooked peas

1 cup sliced mushrooms

$\frac{1}{2}$ red or yellow bell pepper, seeded
    and slivered

2 tablespoons slivered fresh basil

Cut the tomatoes in half horizontally. Remove the interior with a teaspoon, leaving a layer of pulp attached to the skin to form a shell. Turn the tomatoes over on a plate and let drain about 30 minutes. Prepare and cook artichoke hearts according to instructions on page 158. Dice the artichoke hearts.

In a large saucepan, boil about 2 quarts water and add a pinch of salt. Add the rice and boil uncovered 12 to 14 minutes or until just tender but still firm; check by tasting. Drain, rinse with cold water, and drain well.

In a small bowl, stir the vinegar, curry powder, salt, and pepper with a whisk; whisk in the vegetable oil. Taste and adjust seasoning.

In a large bowl, combine the rice with the diced artichokes, peas, mushrooms, half the slivered bell pepper, and half the basil. Mix gently. Add the vinaigrette and mix well. Taste and adjust seasoning. Refrigerate until ready to serve. Just before serving, fill the tomato halves with the rice salad. Garnish with the remaining slivered bell pepper and basil.

. . . .

Makes 6 servings

Nutritional information per serving: 249 calories; 8.7 g fat—29.7% calories from fat;
1 g saturated fat; 0 mg cholesterol

19

Breads and Desserts

Pareve Poppy Seed Muffins

Challah

Round Raisin Challah for Rosh Hashanah

Water Bagels

Low-Fat Strawberries Romanoff

Polish Strawberry Soup with Sour Cream

Fresh Strawberry Sauce

Peach Soup with Mint

Vanilla-Scented Apple Compote

Rice Pudding with Dried Cranberries

Mango Sorbet with Kiwi Slices

Pink Grapefruit Sorbet

Pear Blintzes with Pear Honey Sauce

Almond Meringue Ice Cream Cake

Double Chocolate Ice Cream Cake

Profiteroles with Vanilla Frozen Yogurt and Strawberry Sauce

Nectarine Blackberry Crisp

No-Bake Raspberry Cream Pie

Hawaiian Angel Food Cake à la Mode

IN JEWISH TRADITION, every meal begins with a blessing over bread. Jewish bakeries have a reputation for their excellent bread, and bagels, rye bread, and challah have been popularized by Jewish bakeries throughout the United States.

Baking bread at home is a special treat. If you want to bake a challah but don't have time to make dough, you can purchase shaped challah dough and bake it in your oven. It has that "fresh from the oven" aroma, but it does not compare with the pleasure of making your own. Homemade challah (page 310) is delicious and surprisingly easy to make. You can braid the dough or, for Rosh Hashanah, shape it in the customary spiral form.

Desserts in the kosher kitchen are often pareve, so that they can be eaten after meat or dairy meals. I learned how to adapt dessert recipes to make them pareve from my mother. If a cake recipe is made with buttermilk, she often substitutes orange juice. If it calls for milk, she taught me to use applesauce instead. Butter is easy to replace; you simply use pareve margarine instead. These methods do seem to work; I don't remember their causing major flops, either in my mother's kitchen or in my own!

Fruits play an important part in observing many Jewish holidays. There are apples and honey for Rosh Hashanah, fruit-based haroset for Passover, fruits to decorate the succah. Fruit is also important in making desserts that are both pareve and low in fat. Sorbets, for example, are elegant, pareve, and fat free. Salads of seasonal fruit also make tasty finales to meals and are perfect after hearty main courses.

Other Desserts

Low-Fat Honey Cake with Cocoa and Sweet Spices (page 22) · Pears in Red Wine (page 29) · Cinnamon-Swirled Coffee Cake with Light Sour Cream (page 34) Double Apple Cake with Honey and Cinnamon (page 51) · Hamantaschen with Citrus Prune Filling (page 78) · Chocolate-Dipped Apricots (page 80) · Passover Hazelnut-Almond Cake with Raspberry Sauce (page 102) · Genoa Almond Cake with Poached Fruit (page 104) · Walnut Meringues (page 106) · Low-Fat Lemon Cheesecake (page 117) · Orange Chiffon Cake (page 135)

Pareve Poppy Seed Muffins

{ p a r e v e }

Muffins are part of the American-Jewish culinary repertoire. Like other quick breads, these low-fat, not-too-sweet muffins can play the role of sweet rolls in a meal. The poppy seeds, a popular ingredient in Jewish breads and cakes from Eastern Europe, provide a pleasing accent for these muffins. When blueberries are in season, prepare the variation for a more dessertlike muffin that's great for breakfast, brunch, or a snack.

6 teaspoons poppy seeds

$\frac{1}{3}$ cup plus 1 teaspoon sugar

2 cups all-purpose flour

1 tablespoon baking power

$\frac{1}{4}$ teaspoon baking soda

$\frac{1}{4}$ teaspoon salt

1 large egg

1 cup orange juice

1 teaspoon finely grated lemon rind

3 tablespoons vegetable oil

Preheat the oven to 400°F. Line 12 muffin cups of 2½-inch diameter with cupcake papers or lightly brush the cups with oil.

In a small dish mix 1 teaspoon poppy seeds and 1 teaspoon sugar. Sift flour, baking powder, baking soda, and salt into a large bowl. Stir in remaining 5 teaspoons poppy seeds. In a medium bowl combine egg, orange juice, lemon rind, oil, and remaining $\frac{1}{3}$ cup sugar, whisk to blend. Add orange juice mixture to flour mixture and stir gently with wooden spoon until just blended. Do not beat.

Divide batter among muffin cups, filling each about two-thirds full. Sprinkle muffins lightly with poppy seed–sugar mixture. Bake about 20 minutes or until golden brown. Cool about 5 minutes in pan on a rack before removing. Serve warm or cool.

. . . .

Makes 12 muffins

*Nutritional information per serving: 153 calories; 4.7 g fat—27.8% calories from fat;
0.6 g saturated fat; 18 mg cholesterol*

Blueberry Muffins: Rinse 1½ cups blueberries and pat them dry. Gently stir them into the batter after adding the orange juice mixture.

Challah

{ p a r e v e }

Making challah is a very satisfying experience. You will love the smell of challah baking in your oven and the flavor of your golden brown homemade challah.

2 packages (5½ teaspoons) active
dry yeast

1½ cups warm water (105 to 115° F.)

About 6 cups unbleached all-purpose
flour

4 tablespoons sugar

⅓ cup vegetable oil

4 large eggs, at room temperature

2½ teaspoons salt

1 large egg, beaten with a pinch of
salt, for glaze

4 teaspoons poppy or sesame seeds
(optional)

Sprinkle the yeast over ½ cup of the water in a small bowl. Sprinkle 2 teaspoons sugar over the yeast. Let stand about 10 minutes or until foamy.

Sift 5 cups of flour into a very large bowl (see Note, opposite). Make a large well in center of the flour. Add the yeast mixture, remaining 3 tablespoons plus 1 teaspoon sugar, vegetable oil, eggs, remaining 1 cup water, and salt. Mix ingredients in well with a wooden spoon. Mix in flour, first with a spoon, then by hand, until the ingredients form a soft, sticky dough. Knead the dough vigorously on a work surface about 7 minutes or until very smooth; during kneading, add more flour 1 tablespoon at a time if dough sticks, adding just enough to make dough manageable.

Put the dough in a large oiled bowl and turn over to oil all surfaces. Cover with a warm, slightly damp towel or plastic wrap and let rise in warm, draft-free area about 1¼ hours or until doubled in volume.

Lightly knead the dough again on the work surface. Clean the bowl if necessary. Return the dough to the bowl, cover, and let rise again about 1 hour or until doubled.

Lightly oil 2 baking sheets. Knead the dough lightly, flouring lightly only if the dough sticks. Shape the dough in a rough cylinder. Cut in 6 equal parts to make 2 breads. Knead 1 part briefly and shape into a cylinder. Roll the cylinder back and forth on the work surface, pressing and elongating the cylinder from the center to the edges, to form a smooth rope about 20 inches long and about ¾ inch wide and tapered slightly at the ends. Repeat with 2 more parts.

Put the 3 ropes side by side, with one end of each closer to you. Join the ends far from you, covering the end of the rope on your right side with end of center rope, followed by the end of the left rope. Press to join ends. Bring left rope over center one; bring outer ropes alternately over center one, braiding tightly. Pinch the ends and tuck them underneath. Set the challah carefully on a baking sheet. Shape another challah from remaining pieces of dough.

Cover the breads with a slightly damp towel and let rise about 1 hour or until nearly doubled.

Position a rack in the center of the oven and preheat to 375° F. Brush each challah gently with beaten egg and sprinkle with sesame or poppy seeds if desired. Bake 40 minutes or until the top and bottom of the breads are firm and they sound hollow when tapped on the bottom. Carefully transfer the breads to a rack and let cool. They are best on the day they are made. (Breads can be kept, wrapped, 1 day at room temperature; or they can be frozen.)

. . . .

Makes 2 medium loaves
Nutritional information per serving: 254.5 calories; 7 g fat—24.9% calories from fat;
1.1 g saturated fat; 66 mg cholesterol

N O T E : To use a mixer instead of making dough by hand, sift 5 cups of flour into the bowl of a mixer fitted with a dough hook. Make a large, deep well in the center. Add the yeast mixture, remaining sugar, oil, eggs, remaining water, and salt. Mix at medium-low speed, pushing the flour in often and scraping dough down occasionally, until ingredients form a soft sticky dough that just begins to cling to hook; it will take about 7 minutes. Knead by mixing at medium speed for about 7 minutes or until dough is smooth and almost cleans the sides of the bowl. Pinch the dough quickly; if it sticks to your fingers, beat in more flour 1 tablespoon at a time until dough is no longer very sticky. Dough should be soft and smooth. Let rise as directed.

Round Raisin Challah for Rosh Hashanah

{ p a r e v e }

The traditional challah for Rosh Hashanah is spiral shaped and a bit sweeter than usual. I like to stud it with golden raisins and to flavor it with honey, to symbolize a sweet New Year.

1 cup plus 6 tablespoons warm water
   (105 to 115° F.)
1 tablespoon sugar
2 packages (5½ teaspoons) active
   dry yeast
About 6 cups all-purpose flour
¼ cup honey

⅓ cup vegetable oil
4 large eggs
2 teaspoons salt
1 cup golden raisins
1 large egg, beaten with a pinch of
   salt, for glaze

Combine ½ cup of the water and 2 teaspoons sugar in a small bowl. Sprinkle the yeast over the mixture. Let stand until foamy, about 10 minutes. Oil or grease a large bowl.

Sift 5½ cups of flour into the bowl of a mixer fitted with a dough hook (see Note, opposite). Make a large, deep well in the center. Add the yeast mixture, remaining teaspoon sugar, honey, vegetable oil, eggs, remaining ½ cup plus 6 table-spoons water, and salt. Mix at medium-low speed, pushing flour in often at first and scraping dough down occasionally from bowl and hook, until ingredients come together to a soft, sticky dough. Add ½ cup flour and beat until blended in. Knead by mixing at medium speed, scraping down twice, until dough is smooth and almost cleans the sides of the bowl, about 5 minutes. Pinch the dough quickly; if it sticks to your fingers, beat in more flour 1 tablespoon at a time until the dough is no longer very sticky. If you have added flour, knead the dough again by mixing at medium speed about 2 minutes. Dough should be soft, smooth, and elastic.

Put the dough in the oiled bowl and turn over to oil all surfaces. Cover with a warm, slightly damp towel or plastic wrap and let rise in a warm, draft-free area until nearly doubled in volume, about 1¼ hours.

Knead the dough lightly in a bowl to knock out air. Cover and let rise again until nearly doubled, about 1 hour. Rinse the raisins, drain, and dry on paper towels. Oil 2 baking sheets.

Knead the dough lightly on a floured work surface. Divide in 2 pieces. Pat 1 piece of dough to approximately a 9-inch square on the work surface. Sprinkle evenly with half the raisins; pat them into dough. Roll up tightly from one end to other, as in making a jelly roll; lightly flour the surface if the dough begins to stick.

Roll the dough back and forth on the work surface, pressing with your palms, to form a smooth rope about 28 inches long. Wind the dough around one end in a spiral. Tuck the other end underneath and pinch firmly to attach it to the dough. Press the whole loaf firmly with your hands to give it an even round shape. Carefully set the loaf on the oiled baking sheet. Repeat with the second half of dough and raisins.

Cover the shaped loaves with a warm, slightly damp towel and let rise until nearly doubled in size, about 1 hour. Meanwhile, position a rack in the center of the oven and preheat to 375°F.

Brush the risen loaves gently with egg glaze. Bake 15 minutes. Reduce heat to 350°F. and bake about 30 minutes more or until top and bottom of breads are firm and breads sound hollow when tapped on bottom.

Carefully transfer each challah to a rack and cool.

. . . .

Makes 2 medium loaves

Nutritional information per serving: 285 calories; 6.7 g fat—21% calories from fat;
1.1 g saturated fat; 66 mg cholesterol

NOTE: To make the dough by hand instead of in mixer, after proofing mixture of water, sugar, and yeast for 10 minutes, sift 2¾ cups of flour into a large bowl. Make a large, deep well in the center. Add the yeast mixture, remaining sugar, honey, oil, eggs, remaining water, and salt. Mix the ingredients with a wooden spoon until blended. Mix in flour, first with a spoon, then by hand, until ingredients come together to a dough. Dough should be soft and sticky. Knead in ¼ cup flour. Knead the dough vigorously on the work surface until very smooth and elastic, about 7 minutes; during kneading, add more flour 1 tablespoon at a time if the dough sticks, adding just enough to make the dough manageable. Let dough rise as directed.

Water Bagels

{ p a r e v e }

These bagels do not contain egg and are therefore cholesterol free. Making bagels at home is fun; it's a good project to do with children on a rainy day. Each bagel is made from a ball of dough that you twirl on your finger to make a hole. To give them their characteristic chewy texture, the bagels are then boiled before being baked. They won't come out as even in shape as those you buy, but they'll taste great and will smell wonderful when you remove them from the oven.

4 cups bread flour

1 cup plus 2 tablespoons warm water (105 to 115°F.)

1 package (2¾ teaspoons) active dry yeast

1 teaspoon sugar

⅓ cup vegetable oil

1¾ teaspoons salt

FOR BOILING AND GLAZE

2 quarts water

1½ tablespoons sugar

1 large egg, beaten with 1 tablespoon water and a pinch of salt (optional, for glaze)

Sift the flour into a large bowl. Make a well in the center. Pour in ¼ cup warm water. Sprinkle the yeast on top and add the sugar. Leave for 10 minutes until yeast is foamy.

Into the well in the flour, add the vegetable oil, remaining ¾ cup plus 2 tablespoons water, and salt. Mix with a wooden spoon until the ingredients begin to come together to a dough. Mix in the remaining flour from the well by hand.

Knead the dough vigorously on a work surface until very smooth and no longer sticky, about 10 minutes. Put the dough in a clean oiled bowl, cover with a damp cloth, and let rise in a warm, draft-free place about 1 hour or until puffy but not doubled in volume. (Dough can be made 1 day ahead; after it rises for 30 minutes, punch it down, cover it with a damp cloth, and refrigerate it. Let it come to room temperature before continuing.)

Knead the dough again lightly. Roll it to a thick log, then cut it in 12 pieces with a floured knife. Roll each piece of dough to a very smooth ball on an unfloured surface, rolling it over and over and pressing firmly. Flatten each ball slightly. Flour your index finger and push it through the center of the ball of dough to make a hole. Twirl the piece of dough around your finger to stretch the hole, then insert 2 fingers and continue twirling. Gently pull the edges to give the bagel a more even shape (remember, the hole will close considerably during rising and baking). Cover and let rise on a floured board 15 minutes.

Preheat the oven to 400° F. Bring the water and sugar to a boil in a large saucepan. Add 3 or 4 bagels and boil 1 minute. Turn them over and boil 1 minute. If holes begin to close, force them open the with handle of a wooden spoon. With a slotted spoon, transfer them to a cloth. Repeat with remaining bagels.

Lightly flour 2 baking sheets. Transfer the bagels to the sheets and brush them lightly with egg glaze if desired. Bake about 20 minutes or until browned; if both baking sheets don't fit on the center oven rack, bake one above the other and switch their positions after 10 minutes. Serve the bagels warm, or cool them on a rack and wrap them.

· ·

Makes 12 bagels

*Nutritional information per serving: 229 calories; 6.9 g fat—27.3% calories from fat;
0.8 g saturated fat; 0 mg cholesterol*

Low-Fat Strawberries Romanoff

{ d a i r y }

In the classic version of this popular dessert, you top each portion with whipped cream, but the orange-marinated berries are also delicious with the vanilla-flavored sour cream–yogurt topping. For fleishig meals, the marinated strawberries are good on their own.

1 quart fresh strawberries
3 to 4 tablespoons sugar
¼ cup fresh orange juice
¼ cup Curaçao or other orange
   liqueur

TOPPING (OPTIONAL)
½ cup nonfat sour cream
½ cup plain nonfat yogurt
2 teaspoons sugar
1 teaspoon vanilla extract

Put the berries in a glass bowl and sprinkle with the sugar, orange juice, and liqueur. Toss lightly. Cover and refrigerate 30 minutes. Spoon into wineglasses or dessert dishes.

For the topping, mix the sour cream with the yogurt, sugar, and vanilla. Spoon a dollop of cream on each serving. Serve immediately.

. . . .

Makes 4 servings

Nutritional information per serving: 186 calories; 0.6 g fat—4.1% calories from fat;
0.1 g saturated fat; 1 mg cholesterol

Polish Strawberry Soup
with Sour Cream

{ d a i r y }

*S*trawberry sauce becomes the basis of a rich and refreshing cold dessert soup in this recipe, which combines the flavors of fresh and poached berries. If you wish to serve this dessert for Passover, prepare it with potato starch.

2 cups strawberries, hulled

2 cups water

1 to 1 ¼ cups **Fresh Strawberry Sauce** (page 318)

6 to 7 tablespoons sugar

1 tablespoon cornstarch or potato starch, dissolved in 2 tablespoons cold water

1 ¼ to 1 ½ cups nonfat sour cream or plain yogurt

Slice 1 pretty strawberry into 4 slices and reserve for garnish. In a saucepan, bring the remaining berries and water to a simmer. Cover and simmer about 8 minutes or until the berries are soft and the liquid is red. Remove the berries with a slotted spoon and puree in a food processor or blender until smooth. Mix the puree with the strawberry sauce.

Add the sugar and dissolved cornstarch to the strawberry cooking liquid in the pan and bring to a simmer, stirring. Remove from the heat. Whisk 1 cup sour cream until smooth, then gradually whisk cooking liquid into it. Stir in the strawberry puree mixture. Chill thoroughly.

Ladle the mixture into bowls. Garnish each serving with a dollop of the remaining sour cream, topped with a strawberry slice.

. . . .

Makes 4 servings

Nutritional information per serving: 201 calories; 0.7 g fat—3% calories from fat; 0.1 g saturated fat; 1 mg cholesterol

Fresh Strawberry Sauce

{ p a r e v e }

Use this easy-to-make sauce in the Polish Strawberry Soup with Sour Cream, or on its own to accompany such desserts as frozen yogurt, angel food cake, or cheesecake. It's also delicious mixed with a medley of sliced fruit as a flavorful fruit salad.

4 cups strawberries, hulled (see Note below)

6 tablespoons sugar, or to taste

2 teaspoons lemon or lime juice, or to taste

In a food processor, puree the strawberries with the sugar until smooth. Add lemon juice to taste and more sugar if desired. Refrigerate, covered, until ready to serve.

. . . .

Makes about 2 cups or about 8 servings

Nutritional information per serving: 59 calories; 0.3 g fat—4% calories from fat;
0 g saturated fat; 0 mg cholesterol

N O T E : When ripe fresh strawberries are not available, you can use frozen strawberries.

Peach Soup with Mint

{ p a r e v e }

This soup is inspired by a dessert I learned from Parisian chef Pierre Vedel, when I studied at La Varenne Cooking School. It makes a refreshing finale for summer meals.

Juice of 1 lemon
8 ripe medium peaches (about 2½ pounds)
¼ cup sugar

16 to 20 small mint leaves, plus sprigs for garnish
½ cup dry white wine, such as Chardonnay

Boil enough water to cover the peaches, about 10 cups, and add the lemon juice. Add the peaches, cover, and cook over low heat 5 minutes. Remove the peaches and let cool to lukewarm. Remove the peels. Cut the flesh from 4 peaches and puree in a food processor with the sugar and the mint leaves until smooth. Add the wine and process briefly until blended.

Cut the remaining 4 peaches into thin wedges toward the pit. Add to the soup. Refrigerate 1 or 2 hours. Serve garnished with mint sprigs.

. . . .

Makes 4 servings
Nutritional information per serving: 194 calories; 0.3 g fat—1.4% calories from fat;
0 g saturated fat; 0 mg cholesterol

Vanilla-Scented Apple Compote
{ p a r e v e }

*I*f you like baked apples, you will appreciate this apple compote, which cooks much faster. To finish meals with meat, serve the compote unadorned. On other occasions, you might like to top it with low-fat vanilla ice cream or frozen yogurt.

If any syrup is left over, you can use it to make compote from more fresh or dried fruit or as a light sauce for ice cream. If vanilla beans are not available, or for a different taste, substitute 1 cinnamon stick.

¾ cup sugar
3 cups water
1 vanilla bean
Rind of 1 lemon or 1 orange,
    removed with a vegetable peeler
    (optional)

1 ¼ pounds Golden Delicious or
    Granny Smith apples (4 medium)
1 tablespoon lemon juice

Combine the sugar, water, vanilla bean, and lemon or orange rind if desired in a medium saucepan. Bring to a boil over medium-high heat, stirring gently to dissolve the sugar. Remove from the heat.

Peel the apples, halve, and remove the cores. Cut each half in two. Return the syrup to a boil and add the apple quarters and lemon juice. Reduce the heat to low, then cover with a lid that is a bit too small for saucepan to keep apples submerged. Cook 8 to 12 minutes or until the apples are very tender when pierced with the point of a knife.

If you prefer a thicker syrup, remove the apples with a slotted spoon and simmer the syrup a few minutes or until thickened to taste. (Apples can be kept in their syrup about 4 days in refrigerator.) Let the apples cool in their syrup. Serve warm, at room temperature, or cold.

. . . .

Makes 4 servings

Nutritional information per serving: 230 calories; 0.5 g fat—1.9% calories from fat;
0.1 g saturated fat; 0 mg cholesterol

Rice Pudding with Dried Cranberries

{ d a i r y }

Cooking rice with milk and sugar turns it into a creamy rice pudding, even when you use skim milk. This dessert gains flavor and aroma from freshly grated lemon rind and a vanilla bean and is studded with bright red dried cranberries.

6 cups water

1 cup arborio or other short-grain rice

4 cups skim milk

1 vanilla bean

Pinch of salt

6 tablespoons sugar

Grated rind of 1 lemon

⅓ cup dried cranberries

Cinnamon, for sprinkling (optional)

Choose a large, heavy saucepan so the milk will not boil over and so it will not scorch. Bring the water to a boil in a large, heavy saucepan and add the rice. Boil uncovered 7 minutes; drain well.

Bring the milk and vanilla bean to a boil in the same saucepan over medium-high heat, stirring occasionally. Add the rice and salt. Cook uncovered over medium-low heat, stirring often, 15 to 20 minutes or until the rice is very soft and absorbs most of the milk. The rice should look creamy, not soupy and not dry. When the rice is cooked, stir in the sugar and lemon rind. Cook 1 minute, stirring. Remove from the heat and stir in the cranberries. Serve warm, sprinkled with cinnamon if desired.

. . . .

Makes 5 or 6 servings

Nutritional information per serving: 270 calories; 1.2 g fat—3.9% calories from fat; 0.2 g saturated fat; 3 mg cholesterol

Mango Sorbet with Kiwi Slices

{ p a r e v e }

Sorbet makes a wonderful pareve dessert and is virtually fat free. One of the best and smoothest is made from ripe mangoes. Serve the sorbet garnished with fresh kiwi or mango slices.

¾ sugar

½ cup water

3½ pounds ripe mango (about
   3 large)

1 tablespoon plus 1 teaspoon fresh
   lemon or lime juice

3 ripe kiwifruits

Combine the sugar and water in a small, heavy saucepan. Heat over low heat, stirring gently, until the sugar dissolves. Stop stirring. Bring to a full boil over medium-high heat and boil 30 seconds. Pour into a heatproof bowl and cool completely. Cover and refrigerate 1 hour.

Peel the mango using a paring knife. Cut the flesh from the pit. Puree the mango in a food processor until very smooth. Pour the puree into a large bowl. Add ½ cup plus 1 tablespoon sugar syrup and mix thoroughly. Strain the mixture into a bowl, pressing on the pulp in the strainer. Use a rubber spatula to scrape the mixture from the underside of the strainer. Stir in the lemon juice. Taste, and add more syrup or lemon juice if needed. The mixture should taste slightly too sweet; sweetness of sorbet will be less apparent when it is frozen.

Chill a medium metal bowl and an airtight container in the freezer. Transfer the sorbet mixture to an ice cream machine and process until the mixture has the consistency of soft ice cream; it will not become very firm. Transfer the sorbet as quickly as possible to the chilled bowl; it melts very quickly. Cover tightly and freeze until ready to serve. If keeping sorbet longer than 3 hours, transfer it when firm to an airtight container and cover tightly. (Sorbet is best served on the day it was made but can be kept up to 4 days. If sorbet is frozen solid, soften it very briefly in microwave or in food processor.)

Peel and halve the kiwis and cut into slices. Soften the sorbet slightly before serving. Serve the sorbet in chilled dessert dishes or wineglasses; garnish with kiwi slices.

Makes about 6 servings

*Nutritional information per serving: 293 calories; 0.9 g fat—2.5% calories from fat;
0.2 g saturated fat; 0 mg cholesterol*

Pink Grapefruit Sorbet

{ p a r e v e }

This sorbet makes a refreshing dessert after a hearty meat or chicken dinner. Serve it on its own, with Walnut Meringues (page 106), or as an accompaniment for a winter fruit salad.

1 ½ cups sugar
1 cup water

2 ⅓ cups strained freshly squeezed
pink or red grapefruit juice

Combine the sugar and water in a heavy, medium saucepan. Heat over low heat, stirring gently, until the sugar dissolves completely. Stop stirring. Bring to a full boil over medium-high heat and boil 30 seconds. Pour into a heatproof medium bowl and cool completely. Cover and refrigerate 1 hour or overnight.

Pour the grapefruit juice into a large bowl. Add 1 cup sugar syrup and mix thoroughly. Taste, and add 1 to 3 tablespoons more syrup if needed. The mixture should taste slightly too sweet; sweetness of sorbet will be less apparent when it is frozen.

Chill a medium metal bowl and an airtight container in the freezer. Transfer the sorbet mixture to an ice cream machine and process until the mixture has the consistency of soft ice cream; it will not become very firm. Transfer the sorbet as quickly as possible to the chilled bowl; it melts very quickly. Cover tightly and freeze until ready to serve. If keeping sorbet longer than 3 hours, transfer it when firm to an airtight container and cover tightly. (Sorbet is best served on the day it was made but can be kept up to 4 days. If sorbet is frozen solid, soften it very briefly in microwave or in food processor.)

Soften the sorbet slightly before serving. Serve in thoroughly chilled dessert dishes or wineglasses.

. . . .

Makes 6 servings

*Nutritional information per serving: 231 calories; 0.1 g fat—0.4% calories from fat;
0 g saturated fat; 0 mg cholesterol*

Pear Blintzes with Pear Honey Sauce

{ p a r e v e }

Fruit-filled blintzes make a terrific holiday dessert. These blintzes, topped with a sauce of pear juice and honey, would be ideal for Succot or Hanukkah. Apple filling is very popular, but ripe pears accented with cinnamon also make a delectable filling.

Use the batter in this recipe to prepare dessert, appetizer, or main-course blintzes. If you wish them to be pareve, use water as in this recipe. If you're serving them in a meatless meal, you can substitute skim milk for the water.

BLINTZES
3 large eggs
1 cup plus 3 tablespoons water
¾ cup all-purpose flour
½ teaspoon salt
1½ tablespoons unsalted pareve
   margarine
About 1 teaspoon vegetable oil

FILLING
2 pounds ripe pears
3 tablespoons unsalted pareve
   margarine
4 tablespoons sugar
½ teaspoon ground cinnamon

SAUCE
1 tablespoon cornstarch
2 tablespoons water
2 tablespoons honey
1½ cups pear juice

To make the blintzes, in a blender, combine the eggs, water, flour, and salt. Blend to a smooth batter. Transfer to a bowl, cover, and refrigerate 1 hour.

Melt the margarine in a small saucepan over low heat. Stir the batter and gradually whisk in the melted margarine. Heat an 8-inch nonstick crepe pan or skillet over medium-high heat. Brush the pan lightly with oil, then remove from heat. Working quickly, ladle 3 tablespoons batter into the pan, tilting and swirling the pan until its base is covered with a thin layer of batter. Return the pan to medium-high heat. Loosen the edges of the blintz with a pancake turner, discarding any pieces clinging to the sides. Cook the blintz until its bottom browns lightly, about 2 minutes. Slide the blintz onto a plate. Reheat pan a few seconds, then continue making blintzes, stirring batter occasionally. Brush pan with oil if necessary. Pile the blintzes on a plate as they are done.

To make the filling, peel and halve the pears. Core them, halve them again lengthwise, and cut them into ⅜-inch slices. Melt 1 tablespoon margarine in a large skillet. Add half the pears and sauté over medium-high heat, turning the pieces over from time to time, for 5 to 7 minutes or until pears are tender. Add 2 tablespoons sugar and ¼ teaspoon cinnamon and continue to sauté 1 minute, stirring. Transfer to a bowl. Add 1 tablespoon margarine to the skillet and sauté the remaining pears as above, adding remaining sugar and cinnamon. Mix pears together.

Preheat the oven to 400°F. Spoon about 2 tablespoons filling onto the brown side of each blintz along one edge. Fold over the blintz edges to right and left of filling so that each covers about half the filling; roll up, beginning at edge with filling. Repeat using all the blintzes. Reserve extra filling for garnish. Arrange the blintzes in one layer in a greased shallow baking dish. Dot with small pieces of the remaining tablespoon of margarine. Bake about 20 minutes, or until lightly browned. Meanwhile, dice the pears from the remaining filling.

For the sauce, mix the cornstarch and water in a small cup. In a small saucepan, heat the honey with ¾ cup juice to a boil. Reduce heat to low and gradually whisk in the cornstarch mixture. Simmer 30 seconds to thicken. Remove from heat and gradually stir in the remaining ¾ cup pear juice. Spoon the sauce over the blintzes when serving and garnish with reserved diced pears. Serve hot.

· ·

Makes 6 servings

Nutritional information per serving: 363 calories; 12.5 g fat—29.9% calories from fat;
2.4 g saturated fat; 106 mg cholesterol

Almond Meringue Ice Cream Cake

{ d a i r y }

In Europe, meringues are a favorite partner for ice cream because of their pleasingly crunchy texture and sweet taste. I find that meringues flavored with almonds or other nuts are the best of all. Layer these meringues with your favorite flavors of low-fat ice cream, ice milk, or frozen yogurt to create an elegant dessert. It's perfect for Shavuot or for any dairy meal. If you'd like to make a pareve version, use two sorbets of contrasting colors instead of ice cream.

⅔ cup whole blanched almonds or
   slivered almonds

⅔ cup sugar

1 tablespoon plus 1 teaspoon
   cornstarch

4 large egg whites, at room
   temperature

⅛ teaspoon cream of tartar

1½ pints coffee-flavored frozen
   yogurt

1½ pints low-fat vanilla ice cream

Position a rack in the center of the oven and preheat to 300°F. Lightly grease and flour 2 nonstick baking sheets, tapping each to remove excess flour. Using an 8-inch springform pan rim as guide, trace a circle onto each baking sheet, drawing it around the outside of the springform rim. Fit a ½-inch plain tip in a pastry bag.

Grind the almonds with ½ cup sugar in a food processor until as fine as possible. Transfer to a medium bowl. Sift the cornstarch over the almond mixture. Stir lightly.

Beat the egg whites with the cream of tartar in a large bowl to soft peaks. With mixer at high speed, gradually beat in remaining 2⅔ tablespoons sugar; beat 15 seconds or until whites are just stiff and shiny but not dry.

Sprinkle about one-third of the almond mixture over the whites while folding gently; continue sprinkling and folding as gently and as quickly as possible until just blended.

Immediately transfer the mixture to the pastry bag, using a rubber spatula. Beginning at the center of the circle marked on baking sheet, pipe the meringue evenly in a tight spiral until circle is covered. If there are holes, pipe a small dot of meringue in each one. Pipe another spiral on the second baking sheet. Pipe any remaining meringue in mounds about 1 inch in diameter and ¾ inch high, giving them rounded tops.

Bake the meringues 30 minutes. (If both baking sheets do not fit on central rack, bake them on 2 racks and switch their positions after 15 minutes.) Reduce the oven temperature to 275°F. and continue baking until meringues are light brown, dry, and just firm but not hard, about 10 to 15 minutes; to check, touch center of each meringue very lightly—your finger should not leave impression in mixture. Meringues burn easily if overbaked, but remain sticky if underbaked. They will become firmer as they cool.

Immediately release the meringues gently from the baking sheets, using large metal spatula. If they are sticky on bottom, bake 5 more minutes or until dry. Cool on a rack. (Meringues can be kept up to 5 days in airtight container in dry weather; or they can be frozen.)

Carefully trim the meringue circles, using the point of a sharp paring knife, so that one just fits into an 8-inch springform pan and the second is about ¼ inch smaller than first all around, so there will be a small space between edge of this meringue and the side of the pan.

Set the larger meringue round in the springform pan with sides closed. Soften the frozen yogurt briefly in refrigerator, just until spreadable. Top meringue in pan with the softened frozen yogurt in spoonfuls. Carefully but quickly spread smooth. Set second meringue on top, centering it so that sides do not touch pan. Freeze 10 minutes.

Soften the ice cream in the refrigerator just until spreadable. Spoon enough ice cream around the edge of the top meringue to cover edge generously. Gently push the ice cream between the edge of the meringue and the edge of the pan so it meets the coffee layer. Spoon the remaining ice cream over the top of the meringue. Gently smooth the top. Cover and freeze 8 hours or overnight. (Ice cream cake can be prepared up to 5 days ahead; if kept for longer, meringues soften.)

Set the cake on a platter. Run a thin-bladed flexible knife around the edge. Release the spring and remove the sides of the pan. Serve immediately. Cut carefully with a sharp knife.

. . . .

Makes 8 servings

Nutritional information per serving: 276 calories; 9.6 g fat—30% calories from fat; 2.6 g saturated fat; 11 mg cholesterol

Double Chocolate Ice Cream Cake
{ d a i r y }

Sweet, crunchy cocoa meringues layered with chocolate ice cream—it's hard to believe that such a rich-tasting dessert can be low in fat. For an elegant touch, you might like to garnish each serving with fresh raspberries.

¼ cup unsweetened cocoa powder
¾ cup confectioners' sugar
4 large egg whites
¼ teaspoon cream of tartar

½ cup granulated sugar
2½ pints low-fat chocolate ice cream
    or chocolate frozen yogurt

Preheat the oven to 200°F. Lightly grease the corners of 3 small baking sheets; line with foil. Grease and lightly flour the foil. Using an 8-inch springform pan as a guide, trace an 8-inch circle onto 2 baking sheets. Have ready a rubber spatula for folding and a pastry bag fitted with a ½-inch plain tip. Using a paper clip, close the end of the bag above the tip so mixture will not run out while you fill bag.

Sift the cocoa and confectioners' sugar into a medium bowl. In another large, dry bowl, whip the egg whites with the cream of tartar until stiff. At high speed, gradually beat in the granulated sugar and whip until whites are very shiny. Gently fold in cocoa mixture as quickly as possible.

Immediately spoon the meringue into the pastry bag. Remove the paper clip. Beginning at the center of a circle marked on a baking sheet, pipe the meringue in a tight spiral until circle is completely covered. Repeat with second circle. Pipe the remaining mixture in small kisses, or mounds with pointed tops, about ½ inch in diameter and 1 inch high.

Place the meringue circles in the center of the oven, if space allows, and kisses on shelf underneath. Bake kisses 1½ hours and circles about 2½ hours or until firm and dry. To test meringue kisses, remove one and cool 2 minutes. Break it apart; it should be dry and crumbly and not sticky. Using a large metal spatula, immediately remove the kisses from the foil; cool on a rack. (Reserve kisses for serving with coffee, tea, ice cream, or fruit.)

When the meringue circles are done, gently release from the foil, using a large metal spatula. Peel off any remaining foil. If the circles are sticky on the bottom, return to foil-lined baking sheets; bake 30 minutes longer. Cool on a rack. Put in airtight containers as soon as they are cool.

If necessary, carefully trim the meringue circles with a sharp knife so they fit in an 8-inch springform pan. Set 1 meringue circle in pan. Slightly soften the ice cream in the refrigerator until spreadable. Spread about 3 cups ice cream over the meringue. Spread smooth to side of pan. Freeze 20 minutes, meanwhile returning remaining ice cream to freezer.

Set second meringue on top. Freeze 5 minutes. Spread with the remaining 2 cups ice cream. Freeze at least 6 hours or overnight. (Ice cream cake can be kept 5 days in freezer; if kept longer, meringues soften.)

Set the cake on a platter. Run a thin-bladed knife around the edge of the cake. Release the spring and remove the side of the pan. Serve immediately.

· ·

Makes 10 to 12 servings
Nutritional information per serving: 167 calories; 3.9 g fat—19.6% calories from fat; 2.3 g saturated fat; 3 mg cholesterol

Profiteroles with Vanilla Frozen Yogurt and Fresh Strawberry Sauce

{ d a i r y }

Vary the taste of the filling of these elegant pastries by using low-fat chocolate, chocolate chip, or strawberry ice cream, or by serving them with Raspberry Sauce (page 102). You can turn them into pareve profiteroles by filling them with a low-fat dairy-free ice cream, such as one based on rice or tofu, and by using margarine rather than butter in the cream puff dough.

CREAM PUFF DOUGH
½ cup all-purpose flour
½ cup water
2 tablespoons butter or margarine,
   cut into cubes
¼ teaspoon salt

2 large eggs
About 2 tablespoons confectioners'
   sugar
1 pint vanilla frozen yogurt
Fresh Strawberry Sauce (page 318)

To make the cream puffs, preheat the oven to 425° F. Sift the flour into a small bowl. In a small, heavy saucepan, combine the water, butter, and salt. Heat over low heat, stirring, until the butter melts. Bring to a boil, remove from the heat, and add the flour all at once. Beat vigorously with a wooden spoon until the mixture is smooth. Return to low heat for ½ minute, beating vigorously with wooden spoon. Let cool 2 minutes.

Add 1 egg to dough and beat with wooden spoon until smooth. Using a fork, beat the second egg in a small bowl. Add the beaten egg gradually to the dough, about one-quarter at a time, beating well after each addition. The whole egg may not be needed; add only enough so mixture falls heavily from the spoon when lifted.

Lightly grease a baking sheet. Take 1 tablespoon of dough and, with another tablespoon, push it onto baking sheet. Continue with remaining dough. Bake for 25 minutes or until golden brown and firm; cracks that form during baking should also turn brown. Immediately cut baked puffs in half horizontally with a serrated knife. Let cool.

Before serving, soften yogurt in refrigerator. Spoon enough yogurt into each cream puff to fill it generously. Set on a tray, cover, and keep in freezer until ready to serve, preferably not longer than 24 hours. At serving time, spoon a little Fresh Strawberry Sauce over each puff.

. . . .

Makes about 8 servings

Nutritional information per serving: 170.3 calories; 5.2 g fat—26.6% calories from fat;
1.4 g saturated fat; 56 mg cholesterol

Nectarine Blackberry Crisp

{ d a i r y   o r   p a r e v e }

*F*ruit baked with a crisp oatmeal topping is an irresistible dessert. Its homey simplicity appeals to the cook too, as it is quick and easy to prepare. If you like, serve the crisp with a scoop of low-fat vanilla ice cream.

1 ½ pounds nectarines, pitted and
  sliced

2 cups blackberries

⅔ cup brown sugar

1 tablespoon cornstarch

1 tablespoon lemon juice

1 cup quick-cooking oats (not
  instant)

¼ teaspoon ground cinnamon

3 tablespoons melted butter or
  margarine

Preheat the oven to 350°F. Combine the nectarines and blackberries in a bowl. In a small bowl, mix ⅓ cup brown sugar and the cornstarch. Add to fruit. Add the lemon juice and toss to combine. Spoon into a shallow, square 8- or 9-inch baking dish.

In a bowl, mix the oats, remaining ⅓ cup sugar, the cinnamon, and melted butter. Sprinkle mixture evenly over fruit. Bake about 40 minutes or until the topping is golden brown. Serve warm or cool in bowls.

. . . .

Makes 6 servings

Nutritional information per serving: 249 calories; 7.3 g fat—24.8% calories from fat;
3.7 g saturated fat; 15 mg cholesterol

No-Bake Raspberry Cream Pie

{ d a i r y }

Prepare this quick and easy pie when guests are coming on short notice. With its glazed raspberry topping, it has the attractive look of a tart from a fancy patisserie. And with its creamy vanilla filling, nobody would guess that it's also low in fat.

1 8-ounce package nonfat cream cheese (bar type, not spreading type)

6 tablespoons sugar

¼ cup nonfat sour cream

1 teaspoon vanilla extract

1 9-inch (6-ounce) packaged graham cracker crust

2 cups fresh raspberries

⅓ cup red currant jelly

2 teaspoons water

1 teaspoon kirsch or other fruit brandy (optional)

Cut the cream cheese into a few pieces and let soften slightly. Beat in a mixing bowl until smooth. Beat in the sugar, followed by the sour cream and vanilla. Pour into crust. Refrigerate, uncovered, 10 minutes. Arrange the raspberries on top of the cheese filling, beginning at outer edge of pie.

Melt the jelly with the water in a small saucepan over low heat, stirring often. Off the heat, stir in the kirsch if desired. Cool slightly. Brush or spoon the jelly over the berries; spoon any remaining jelly in the spaces between them. Refrigerate uncovered about 30 minutes or until ready to serve. If there is any leftover pie, refrigerate it uncovered.

. . . .

Makes 6 servings

Nutritional information per serving: 265 calories; 7.6 g fat—28.5% calories from fat; 1.6 g saturated fat; 0 mg cholesterol

Hawaiian Angel Food Cake à la Mode
{ d a i r y }

This is unbeatable when fresh pineapples are available. Use the aromatic poaching syrup to moisten the angel food cake slices and the pineapple pieces to garnish them. Kosher angel food cake is readily available, making this dessert convenient and easy. When fresh blackberries or raspberries are available, use a few as a colorful decoration for each serving.

1 cup sugar
3⅓ cups water
1 vanilla bean
Rind of 1 lemon, removed with a
    vegetable peeler (optional)
1 4-pound pineapple

1 tablespoon lemon juice
8 slices angel food cake
8 scoops low-fat vanilla ice cream
12 to 16 blackberries or raspberries
    (optional)

Combine the sugar, water, vanilla bean, and lemon rind in a medium saucepan. Bring to a boil, stirring gently to dissolve sugar. Remove from heat.

Peel the pineapple and cut crosswise into ½-inch-thick slices. Remove the tough cores with a small cookie cutter. Return the syrup to a boil and add the pineapple slices and lemon juice. Reduce heat to low, then cover with a lid that is a bit too small for saucepan, to keep pineapple submerged. Cook about 8 minutes or until the pineapple slices are tender at the edges. Let the pineapple cool in the syrup. Refrigerate in a covered container.

To serve, cut each pineapple slice in half. Top each slice of cake with a scoop of ice cream, a half-slice of pineapple, and a few berries if desired. Sprinkle with vanilla syrup from poaching the pineapple. Serve remaining pineapple and syrup separately.

. . . .

Makes 8 servings

Nutritional information per serving: 158 calories; 1 g fat—6% calories from fat;
0.1 g saturated fat; 0 mg cholesterol

Glossary of Terms for Kosher Cooking

Ashkenazic — Jews of Eastern and Central European origin. There is a slight difference in the interpretation of certain Passover laws between Ashkenazic and Sephardic rabbis.

Blech or Plata — A hot plate for keeping food warm on Shabbat.

Bsari (Hebrew) — Same as *fleishig*.

Fleishig (Yiddish) — Meats, foods containing meat ingredients, or meals containing meat.

Gelatin — A product used to thicken and gel desserts, dairy products, and other foods. Gelatin is often made from animal bones and cannot be used in kosher dairy products. If gelatin is used in Kosher cooking, the producer must use "kosher gelatin," which is of vegetable origin. For dessert making, kosher gelatin can be purchased in packets.

Glatt Kosher (Yiddish) — Kosher meat examined after slaughter and found completely free of even the slightest imperfection. The term is also used to refer to restaurants with an ultra-strict degree of kashrut.

Halavi (Hebrew) — Same as *milchig*.

Hametz or Chometz — Literally, "leavened"; not kosher for Passover.

K — A label that often appears on foods, meaning kosher.

Kashering — A procedure for making certain utensils used year-round suitable for Passover, and for cleaning the oven, burners, and kitchen sink for Passover.

Kashrut — The principles of keeping kosher, based on the Torah and developed by rabbis in the Talmud and other religious writings.

Kitniyot (Hebrew) — Legumes; a group of foods not eaten by Ashkenazic Jews during Passover, and including beans, peas, corn, rice, and other grains. Some products are labeled "kosher for Passover only for those who eat kitniyot," meaning that Sephardic Jews may eat them during Passover but Ashkenazic Jews may not.

Kosher (adjective) — Suitable for eating according to the Jewish dietary laws.

Kosher (verb) — To salt and soak kosher, properly slaughtered meat or poultry before cooking in order to make it kosher.

Kosher Salt — Coarse salt used to kosher meat or poultry.

Matzo or Matzah — Flat, unleavened, crackerlike bread used for Passover. Classic matzo is made only of flour and water and is used at the Seder. Today there is also egg matzo, whole wheat matzo, and matzo flavored with onion, garlic, and other flavors.

Matzo Farfel — Very small square pieces of matzo, about the size of cornflakes. Farfel is good as breakfast cereal during Passover and is also used to make stuffings, muffins, matzo balls, and other recipes in which small pieces of matzo are needed.

Matzo Cake Meal — A very fine, flourlike form of matzo meal, used for cakes.

Matzo Meal — Finely ground matzo, somewhat coarser than flour. In many recipes, it is used as a substitute for bread crumbs. Matzo meal is used to make matzo balls, cakes, stuffings, and breading, and to bind kugels and other casseroles.

Matzo Shmura or Shmura Matzah — Matzo made from grain that is watched from harvesttime to prevent any contact with water, which could cause it to leaven. Some people use this matzo for the Seder.

Milchig (Yiddish) — Dairy foods, foods containing dairy ingredients, or meals containing dairy foods.

Ⓤ — A label that often appears on foods, meaning kosher according to the Union of Orthodox Jewish Congregations.

ⓊP — Kosher and pareve.

ⓊD — Kosher for dairy meals.

Parve or Pareve — Neutral; food containing neither milk or meat, and kosher for eating with either meat or dairy meals.

Potato Starch — Flour made from potatoes. Unlike wheat flour and cornstarch, it is kosher for Passover and is a popular ingredient in Passover cakes.

Rennet — A product used in making many hard cheeses, which is of animal origin and therefore makes those cheeses nonkosher. Some vegetarian stores sell cheeses with the label "no animal rennet."

Sephardic — Jews of Mediterranean and Middle Eastern origin. *Sepharad* refers to Spain in Hebrew, and the term originally referred to Jews who had lived in Spain and the descendants of those exiled in 1492, who went to Greece, Turkey, and other Mediterranean lands and as far as Holland. However, today the term often refers to all Jews who are not from Eastern and Central Europe, and includes Yemenite and Iraqi Jews, who do not trace their origins back to Spain.

Traif — Not kosher.

Index

About the Author

Faye Levy received her Jewish education at the Hebrew Academy of Washington, D.C., where she recently received the "Eishet Hayil" or Woman of Valor Award; her college education at the Hebrew University in Jerusalem and Tel Aviv University, where she graduated magna cum laude; and her culinary education during six years at Ecole de Cuisine La Varenne in Paris.

Faye Levy's International Jewish Cookbook was published in 1991 to rave reviews. Her *International Vegetable Cookbook* won the James Beard Cookbook Award in 1994 as the best book of the year in the category of fruits, vegetables, and grains. She won cookbook awards from the International Association of Culinary Professionals for her books *Vegetable Creations, Chocolate Sensations,* and *Classic Cooking Techniques.*

Levy is a weekly kosher cooking columnist for the *Jerusalem Post.* She has written articles on Jewish holiday cooking for major newspapers throughout the United States, as well as for *Gourmet* and *Bon Appétit* magazines and for Israel's foremost women's magazine, *At.*

For the last seven years Levy has been a nationally syndicated cooking columnist for the Los Angeles Times Syndicate. In her biweekly column she emphasizes fast, easy, and delicious dishes that are low in fat. This kind of light, fresh food is very popular with her students in the cooking classes Levy teaches at Santa Monica College and at cooking schools in the Los Angeles area. She and her husband/associate, Yakir Levy, enjoy cooking and vegetable gardening in their home in Woodland Hills, California.

Conversion Chart
{Equivalent Imperial and Metric Measurements}

American cooks use standard containers, the 8-ounce cup and a tablespoon that takes exactly 16 level fillings to fill that cup level. Measuring by cup makes it very difficult to give weight equivalents, as a cup of densely packed butter will weigh considerably more than a cup of flour. The easiest way therefore to deal with cup measurements in recipes is to take the amount by volume rather than by weight. Thus the equation reads:

1 cup = 240 ml = 8 fl. oz.   ½ cup = 120 ml = 4 fl. oz.

It is possible to buy a set of American cup measures in major stores around the world.

In the States, butter is often measured in sticks. One stick is the equivalent of 8 tablespoons. One tablespoon of butter is therefore the equivalent to ½ ounce/15 grams.

Liquid Measures

Fluid Ounces	U.S.	Imperial	Milliliters
	1 teaspoon	1 teaspoon	5
¼	2 teaspoons	1 dessertspoon	10
½	1 tablespoon	1 tablespoon	14
1	2 tablespoons	2 tablespoons	28
2	¼ cup	4 tablespoons	56
4	½ cup		110
5		¼ pint or 1 gill	140
6	¾ cup		170
8	1 cup		225
9			250, ¼ liter
10	1¼ cups	½ pint	280
12	1½ cups		340
15		¾ pint	420
16	2 cups		450
18	2¼ cups		500, ½ liter
20	2½ cups	1 pint	560
24	3 cups		675
25		1¼ pints	700
27	3½ cups		750
30	3¾ cups	1½ pints	840
32	4 cups or 1 quart		900
35		1¾ pints	980
36	4½ cups		1000, 1 liter
40	5 cups	2 pints or 1 quart	1120

Solid Measures

U.S. and Imperial Measures		Metric Measures	
Ounces	Pounds	Grams	Kilos
1		28	
2		56	
3½		100	
4	¼	112	
5		140	
6		168	
8	½	225	
9		250	¼
12	¾	340	
16	1	450	
18		500	½
20	1¼	560	
24	1½	675	
27		750	¾
28	1¾	780	
32	2	900	
36	2¼	1000	1
40	2½	1100	
48	3	1350	
54		1500	1½

Oven Temperature Equivalents

Fahrenheit	Celsius	Gas Mark	Description
225	110	¼	Cool
250	130	½	
275	140	1	Very Slow
300	150	2	
325	170	3	Slow
350	180	4	Moderate
375	190	5	
400	200	6	Moderately Hot
425	220	7	Fairly Hot
450	230	8	Hot
475	240	9	Very Hot
500	250	10	Extremely Hot

Any broiling recipes can be used with the grill of the oven, but beware of high-temperature grills.

Equivalents for Ingredients

all-purpose flour—plain flour
coarse salt—kitchen salt
cornstarch—cornflour
eggplant—aubergine

half and half—12% fat milk
heavy cream—double cream
light cream—single cream
lima beans—broad beans

scallion—spring onion
unbleached flour—strong, white flour
zest—rind
zucchini—courgettes or marrow